'HEAVEN-TAUGHT F

'HEAVEN-TAUGHT FERGUSSON'

Robert Burns's Favourite Scottish Poet

❧

Poems and Essays
edited by Robert Crawford

TUCKWELL PRESS

First published in Great Britain in 2003 by
Tuckwell Press Ltd
The Mill House
Phantassie
East Linton
East Lothian, Scotland

ISBN 1 86232 201 5

The poems in this book were commissioned by the University of
St Andrews, with financial support from the Scottish Arts Council

The publishers acknowledge subsidy from the Scottish Arts Council
towards the publication of this volume

Typeset by Hewer Text Ltd, Edinburgh
Printed and bound by Bell & Bain Ltd, Glasgow

in memory of
Matthew P. McDiarmid

Contents

Acknowledgements and Note on Texts

Many people and institutions helped with this book and the events which led to it. The University of St Andrews through its St Andrews Scottish Studies Institute commissioned the poems with the generous support of the Scottish Arts Council. StAnza, Scotland's Poetry Festival, hosted several events as part of its programme in St Andrews in 2000. The Edinburgh International Book Festival invited a number of the contributors to read their poems at the 2000 Festival's Robert Fergusson Supper, and the Writers' Museum in Edinburgh displayed some of the poems as part of its 2000 Fergusson and Stevenson exhibition. BBC Radio 3 commissioned the editor to make five programmes based around the contents of this book. Among many personal debts of gratitude incurred are those to Struther and Greta Arnott, Tony Ashe, Dave Batchelor, Gavin Bowd, Neil Corcoran, Lilias Fraser, Jill Gamble, Christine Gascoigne, Shonagh Irvine, Brian Johnstone, Faith Liddell, Scott Lyall, Christopher MacLachlan, the late Colin Matthew, Frances Mullan, James Robertson, Alastair Work, and to the members of the Robert Fergusson Society. The Fergusson celebrations involved, it sometimes seemed, a cast of thousands. All should be thanked, but a special word of gratitude is due both to this book's contributors and publisher for keeping faith with the project over several years. Thanks also to Hamish Whyte for compiling the index.

My wife, Alice, and children, Lewis and Blyth, lived through all this exuberance and slog with surprising equanimity. Their love and support were essential and are treasured.

Though I met this book's dedicatee only once, I know that all who work on Fergusson's poetry and biography are in his debt. That he should have produced his magisterial edition around the same time as he was tutoring Seamus Heaney is all the more remarkable. The text of Fergusson's poems used here throughout is that of Matthew McDiarmid, and it has been mined by all the contributors, not least the author of the introduction. McDiarmid's two-volume *The Poems of Robert Fergusson* (Edinburgh: Blackwood for the Scottish Text Society, 1954–6) remains the standard edition. Though it is out of print, thanks to the generosity of the electronic publisher Chadwyck Healey the basic text of the poems from this edition is electronically available free of charge on the Robert Fergusson website set up by the St Andrews Scottish Studies Institute at http://www.st-andrews.ac.uk/institutes/sassi/ This website also contains other information about the poet and is linked to the website of the Robert Fergusson Society. Readers who want a readily accessible modern paperback edition of a glossed selection of Fergusson's poems with a lively introduction can turn to the *Selected Poems* edited by James Robertson for Birlinn in 2000, while a further annotated selection of Fergusson and other Scottish poets, *Before Burns*, has been edited for the Canongate Classics series by my St Andrews colleague, Christopher MacLachlan. With some exceptions, most notably David Daiches and Fred Freeman in their book-length studies of the poet, relatively few critics have devoted sustained attention to Fergusson over the last century. It is good to work on him at a time when interest in his poetry is again growing. I hope this book contributes to that increase.

R.C.
St Andrews

Notes on the Contributors

Meg Bateman's *Aotromachd agus dàin eile / Lightness and other Poems* was published by Polygon in 1997 and won a Scottish Arts Council Book Award. She is a co-editor of the anthology *Scottish Religious Poetry* (St Andrew Press, 2000) and lectures at Sabhal Mòr Ostaig, Skye.

John Burnside's collections of poetry include *Swimming in the Flood* (Cape, 1995), *A Normal Skin* (Cape, 1997), and *The Asylum Dance* (Cape, 2000). His novels include *The Dumb House* (Cape, 1997) and *The Mercy Boys* (Cape, 1999). He also writes short stories and screenplays. He lives in Fife and is Lecturer in English at the University of St Andrews.

Robert Crawford's collections of poems include *A Scottish Assembly* (Chatto, 1990), *Masculinity* (Cape, 1996) and *Spirit Machines* (Cape, 1999); with Mick Imlah he edited *The New Penguin Book of Scottish Verse* (2000). His critical books include *Devolving English Literature* (Second Edition, EUP, 2000) and *The Modern Poet* (OUP, 2001). He is Professor of Modern Scottish Literature at the University of St Andrews.

Ian Duncan is author of *Modern Romance and Transformations of the Novel: The Gothic, Scott, Dickens* (CUP, 1992) and is writing a book for Princeton University Press on Walter Scott the novel in Edinburgh during the Romantic period. He has produced editions of works by John Buchan, Walter Scott, and Arthur Conan Doyle for OUP's World's Classics series. He is Professor of English at the University of California, Berkeley.

Douglas Dunn's collections of poetry include *Elegies* (Faber, 1985), *The Donkey's Ears* (Faber, 2000) and *The Year's Afternoon* (Faber, 2000). He edited *The Faber Book of Twentieth-Century Scottish Poetry* (1992) and *The Oxford Book of Scottish Short Stories* (1995). Author of two collections of short stories, he is Professor of English at the University of St Andrews.

W. N. Herbert has taught at the universities of Durham, Newcastle, and Lancaster. His collections of poetry include *Forked Tongue* (Bloodaxe, 1994), *Cabaret McGonagall* (Bloodaxe, 1996), and *The Laurelude* (Bloodaxe, 1998). His critical works include *To Circumjack MacDiarmid: The Poetry and Prose of Hugh MacDiarmid* (Clarendon Press, 1992). With Matthew Hollis he edited the anthology of poets' writing about poetry, *Strong Words* (Bloodaxe, 2000).

Tracey Herd's first collection of poems, *No Hiding Place*, was published by Bloodaxe in 1996. Originally from East Kilbride, she has lived and worked in Dundee for the last decade and was recently Writer in Residence at the University of Dundee. She has won an Eric Gregory Award and a Scottish Arts Council Writer's Bursary.

Kathleen Jamie's collections of poetry include *The Way We Live* (Bloodaxe, 1997), *The Queen of Sheba* (Bloodaxe, 1994) and *Jizzen* (Picador, 1999). She has been awarded the Hawthornden Prize, the Geoffrey Faber Memorial Prize, a Paul Hamlyn Award, and several other major literary prizes. She lives in Fife and is Lecturer in English at the University of St Andrews.

Andrew Macintosh is a graduate of St Andrews University where he wrote a dissertation on Norman MacCaig as well as a postgraduate thesis on Robert Garioch and Scottish poetic tradition. Like Robert Fergusson he was schooled in Dundee and takes an enthusiastic interest in music.

Carol McGuirk is Professor of English at Florida Atlantic University. Her books include an edition of Burns's *Selected Poems* for Penguin (1993) as well as *Robert Burns and the Sentimental Era* (Georgia UP, 1985; reprinted by Tuckwell Press in 1996) and the edited collection, *Critical Essays on Robert Burns* (G. K. Hall, 1998). She has taught in Scotland as well as in the USA.

Susan Manning holds the Grierson Chair in the Department of English Literature at the University of Edinburgh. She is author of *The Puritan-Provincial Vision: Scottish and American Literature in the Nineteenth Century* (CUP, 1990), and of *Fragments of Union: Making Connections in Scottish and American Writing* (Palgrave, 2002). She has also edited Henry Mackenzie's *Julia de Roubigné* (Tuckwell Press, 1999).

Edwin Morgan's *Collected Poems* appeared from Carcanet in 1990, and his *Collected Translations* from the same publisher in 1996. Formerly a Professor of English Literature at the University of Glasgow, Morgan is one of Scotland's most distinguished poets, has worked in both Scots and English, and has written on Robert Fergusson's poetry.

Les Murray's *Collected Poems* was published by Carcanet in 1991. Among his other works is the remarkable verse novel *Fredy Neptune* (Carcanet, 1998). His collections of essays include *The Paperbark Tree: Selected Prose* (Carcanet, 1992). Australia's most celebrated poet, Murray has long-standing connections with Scotland, and visits regularly.

Don Paterson's *Nil Nil* (Faber, 1993) won the Forward Prize for the best first book of poems. His second collection, *God's Gift to Women* (Faber, 1997), won the T. S. Eliot Prize, and his most recent collection of poems is *The Eyes* (Faber, 1999). He works as Poetry Editor for Picador and has edited a selection of Burns's poetry for Faber (2001); he also holds a Lectureship in English at the University of St Andrews.

Matthew Simpson studied English Literature at Oxford and Scottish Literature at St Andrews, where he wrote a postgraduate dissertation on Robert Fergusson. He has recently completed his St Andrews doctorate on student literary culture in the eighteenth-century university.

Janet Sorensen is Associate Professor of English at Indiana University, Bloomington. Her book, *The Grammar of Empire: Language and Cultural Identity in Eighteenth-Century Britain*, was published by Cambridge University Press in 2001. She has published several articles on eighteenth-century literature, including a piece on Fergusson's flyting with Samuel Johnson.

Matthew Wickman is Assistant Professor of English at Brigham Young University, Utah. He has published on eighteenth-century poetry in *ELH*, and on eighteenth-century Scottish literature in *PMLA*. He is completing a study of Ossian, evidence, and eighteenth-century Scottish culture.

Introduction

ROBERT CRAWFORD

'Heaven-taught Fergusson', wrote Robert Burns in stylish admiration.[1] This tribute was only one of many bonds between Scotland's national poet and the poetic master whom he most loved, but never met. The Edinburgh man of letters Henry Mackenzie had termed Burns a 'heaven-taught ploughman'.[2] The label stuck. In contrast, the late Robert Fergusson had been no farmboy and had spent almost half his short life in formal education. Yet in calling him 'heaven-taught', Burns pays tribute to a fellow poet's genius. He wishes to link himself to a writer whose example both terrified and inspired him. Later Scottish poets have admired Fergusson in similarly strong terms. The poems in this book continue a tradition of homage while sounding their own contemporary notes. Sometimes gleeful, sometimes solemn, '*Heaven-Taught Fergusson*' both winks at and scrutinises a poet who was in several ways strikingly different from Burns. Poets and critics from three continents come together in this volume. In various ways their soundings suggest just what it is about Fergusson that makes him still seem 'heaven-taught'.

Right at the start it should be acknowledged that in his afterlives as in his life Robert Fergusson's fate has been to languish as well as to shine. 'God will damn Robert Ferguson eternally', scribbled an eighteenth-century reader at St Andrews University. After these words someone else, perhaps Fergusson himself, added: 'Judge not lest ye be judged'.[3] Posterity has damned Fergusson in several ways. Crudely, it has often forgotten him. To affirm that, one needs to think not of an audience of eager Burnsians or Scottish literature specialists, but of poetry's wider international readership. Until very recently, Fergusson's poetry had been out of print for several years. Though there have been occasional studies of his work, this is the first volume of essays about Fergusson for half a century. Its contributors demonstrate that Fergusson matters to the wider community of poetry as well as to the more specialised halls of English-speaking academia. Indeed, as this book demonstrates, he was a product both of that wider community and of university education. In such a combination lies something of his peculiar modernity. Over the past three centuries many poets have had to come to terms with the

1

academic study of vernacular literature, negotiating with the university milieu even as they made their verse. Fergusson is the first such modern poet.[4] In this way, too, he was a pioneer.

Precursor of Burns, herald of the modern poet, lively, sophisticated, and alluring, Fergusson has a secure place in recent anthologies of Scottish verse. Yet despite some local success in his own short lifetime, this poet was in danger of descending into oblivion even in the decade after his death. Most of the republishing of his work and the memorialising of him took place only after Burns's celebrated complaint to the Bailies of the Canongate that 'the remains of Robert Ferguson the so justly celebrated Poet, a man whose talents for ages to come will do honor, to our Caledonian name, lie in your church yard among the ignoble Dead unnoticed and unknown'.[5] To press his case, Burns calls Fergusson 'so justly celebrated', yet the point of his letter is that Fergusson is actually ignored. Burns's praise is an exercise in confident wishful thinking. His paeans to this precursor are bound up with his own aspirations as a poet. Those words, 'a man whose talents for ages to come will do honor, to our Caledonian name', are phrases for Burns suppers.

Here, as elsewhere, Burns is mapping himself on to Fergusson in order to project their linked destinies. Fergusson, that 'Brother in the muse', terrified Burns by his example of 'misfortune', yet also provided vital sustenance for the younger man's own poetic trajectory.[6] God did damn Robert Fergusson, perhaps – by making him Robert Burns's favourite Scottish poet. So too often Fergusson has been remembered only as Burns's John the Baptist, his role forever a supporting one, his voice valued merely for sounding rather like that of the master. Yet we are right to recall Fergusson in the context of Burns; to have been the favourite native fellow-bard of the greatest poet of Scotland is tremendous. At the same time, remembering Fergusson through Burns may too easily become another way of forgetting him. Fergusson does not deserve the perdition of neglect, albeit oblivion with a medal attached.

'Heaven-Taught Fergusson' examines several aspects of this remarkable poet's work in detail, in addition to looking at his links with Burns. After reading the volume, readers will be alert to something of Fergusson's importance for his own time and for ours. Still, it would be naive to assume that everyone will begin by knowing a great deal about this Scottish poet or his work. The rest of the present introduction is designed to supply a short biographical account of Fergusson, alongside some remarks on the enduring distinction of his verse. Fergusson's life was so short that we may too easily notice only its brevity. I want to call attention to some details of its content, and relate them to how and what this 'vera brither' wrote.

Robert Fergusson was born on 5 September 1750 in the Cap-and-Feather Close (now demolished), off the High Street, Edinburgh. He was the fourth of the five children of William Fergusson (1714–1767), a clerk from Tarland in Aberdeenshire, and his wife Elizabeth Forbes (b. 1714), daughter of John Forbes of Templeton in the parish of Kildrummie, also in Aberdeenshire. While his father was working as clerk to Walter Fergusson, Writer to the Signet in Edinburgh, the sickly seven-year-old Robert was sent for six months to Mr Philp's private school in Niddry's Wynd. From 1758 for four years he went to Edinburgh's High School, getting a good grounding in Latin, before moving to Dundee's Grammar School. There in 1762 he was awarded the David Fergusson mortification, a scholarship for those with his surname. Having spent the summer of 1764 with his mother on his uncle John Forbes's farm at Roundlichnot, near Old Meldrum, Aberdeenshire, the sometimes ailing Robert progressed on the same scholarship to St Andrews University.

Fergusson's upbringing, then, situates him rather differently from Burns, who was nine years his junior. The elder Robert's life was predominantly urban. He may have had rural ancestry, and spent a few (reportedly uneasy) months on his uncle's farm, but he was a city boy. His only extended period of residence outside a substantial urban centre was as a St Andrews student. That experience, too, separates him from Burns, who attended no university, and whose being hailed as 'Heaven-taught ploughman' draws attention to that fact among several others. For Burns in turn to call Fergusson 'Heaven-taught' is a form of bonding, and of homage, but also in some ways misleading. Fergusson *was* 'Heaven-taught'; but he was also tutored by professors.

The St Andrews Arts curriculum of the period let Fergusson study Greek and Latin throughout his course, along with Mathematics and Logic in the second year, Mathematics and Moral Philosophy in the third year, and Natural Philosophy in the fourth. Fergusson was a highly educated man; later he was recalled discussing Greek verse in an Edinburgh drawing-room. His own poetry shows a deeply imbibed classical education, but the literature studied in St Andrews during the 1760s was not only that of the ancients. An unusual aspect of St Andrews at this time was the teaching of Rhetoric by Robert Watson, Professor of Logic, Rhetoric, and Metaphysics, whose lectures dealt with the study of English literary texts, emphasising the importance of Anglocentric politeness, while ignoring the Scottish vernacular. Of late Watson's work has been the subject of considerable scholarly attention which has viewed it in terms of the so-called 'Scottish invention of English literature', that is the development of the university subject of 'English'; Watson's project has also been linked to the growth of a British imperial ideology, and the suppression of such markers of Scottish cultural difference as Scots language and Scotticisms.[7] Yet Watson's teaching did encourage students to treat English-language literary writings – in poetry, the drama, and in prose fiction – with a new professional seriousness that was part of the Scottish Enlightenment's drive towards 'improvement'. It was for this reason, surely, that Watson was selected to converse with Dr Johnson when he visited St Andrews with Boswell in 1773 and dined at Watson's house along with James Craig, 'the ingenious architect of the new town of Edinburgh'.[8] Johnson seemed a little impatient with Robert Watson's professorially studied carefulness in composition, but Watson was part of an interest in this improving topic at eighteenth-century St Andrews that is now well documented.

What all this means is that Robert Fergusson was perhaps the first significant poet to read English literary texts at a university as part of his course. Fergusson therefore becomes emblematic of that familiar modern figure: the poet who studies literary texts at university in order both to learn from them and to react against his teaching, even his teachers. In his absorbing of an officially mediated tradition conveyed through the institutional channels of higher education, and in his determined evolution of a style in reaction to this, Fergusson is far closer to most of today's poets than is Burns. Fergusson's university training was something new in the history of English-language poetry, and his reaction to it is particularly striking. That reaction should not be seen simply in terms of rejection or assimilation, but as a complex modification of, celebration of, and attack on the materials and forms offered by his education.

Considered the best singer at St Andrews, Fergusson was often asked to officiate as clerk at morning and evening prayers. His abilities were not confined, though, to literature or to song. An excellent student mathematician, he became the favoured pupil of the poet and scholar William Wilkie, Professor of Mathematics. Wilkie, as would Fergusson to some extent, brought together the worlds of farm and classroom; given Fergusson's awareness of Wilkie's interest in agricultural improvement, it may be that this city boy learned more about the world of agriculture from his professor than from his farmer uncle. Again, like Fergusson, Wilkie was bilingual in his writing; he was attempting some sort of creative accommodation that would include writing in English as well as writing in Scots. In this regard, though most of his loyalties lay with English, Wilkie represents a substantially different and more generous attitude to native language than that held by his colleague, Watson. Anecdotes recall Wilkie as eccentric (he was notorious for liking to sleep in dirty bedlinen, and would complain if a hostess offered him clean sheets). Nonetheless, he was a significant Scottish Enlightenment literary figure. Best known, and now embalmed, as 'the Scottish Homer' for his English-language *Epigoniad*, he also wrote in Scots during Fergusson's student days. Fergusson's later memorial 'Eclogue' praised his teacher's ability to inspire 'Scholars and bards'.[9] Employed for two summers to make a fair copy of Wilkie's lectures, Fergusson knew Wilkie well, and his coupling of the words 'Scholars and bards' hints at something which characterises his own work – a sophisticatedly-worn learning fused to a deep engagement with the culture of his people. Again, this combination makes Fergusson exemplary, not just in eighteenth-century terms, but with regard to modern poetic practice. If we now take it for granted that poets should be both local and cosmopolitan, wild and sophisticated, learned and vernacular, then this reinforces the extent to which Robert Fergusson might be called the first modern poet.

A poetic combination of roles of bard and scholar is clearly present in Fergusson's celebrations of other St Andrews University figures. Matthew Simpson's essay examines these in meticulous detail. Fergusson's seriocomic 'Elegy' on the death of the mathematician David Gregory is remarkable for its presentation of Euclidean geometry in Scots verse, relishing such expressions as ' surd roots'. This is surely the first time that phrase had been used in any variety of English poetry. Its deployment signals a glee in developing capacious language which can delight in vernacularity, but also in scientific expression. Suspended between professorial knowledge and vernacular spoofing, this virtuoso poem, which may be the earliest of Fergusson's works to survive, is absolutely remarkable in the way it plays both sides of the field, fusing the outlandishly mathematical with pacy local registers. It is comical and beautiful, cerebral, felt and punchy at once. Effortlessly, it says,

He could, by *Euclid*, prove lang sine
A ganging *point* compos'd a line;[10]

That expression, 'lang sine', slips past almost unnoticed, though it has become the most famous of all Scots phrases. It existed before Burns, and was perhaps first used in a poem once attributed to Sir Robert Ayton, but in Fergusson's poem it is hard not to suspect the ghost of a translingual pun on the mathematical 'sine' of sines and cosines; more attractive, maybe, is the absolutely easy way in which the familiar vernacular expression sits alongside the learned name of Euclid, and how that word 'compos'd' in the next line links mathematics to music and poetry. Not just the surface but also the subcutaneous life of language here – Scots and English informing one another – is being used to the full. In some ways Fergusson matters most as a poet able to combine with superb energy kinds of vocabulary – scientific, vernacular, bookish, plain, pacy – rather than simply as a writer who happens to use Scots as well as English. Certainly this ability to elasticate and mix kinds of language was something Fergusson discovered in his St Andrews poems.

Some years later, in 1773, he wrote another elegy in the 'Standard Habbie' Scots verse form on John Hogg, the University Porter, and in his address 'To the Principal and Professors of the University of St Andrews, on their superb treat to Dr Samuel Johnson' Fergusson attacked his alma mater for its sycophantic reception of Johnson on his visit, and for failing to champion Scottish vernacular culture. I have looked more closely at that poem in the book *Robert Burns and Cultural Authority*, attending to its easy, parodic mixture of lecture-room terms, allusions to Johnson's *Dictionary*, and delighted deployment of distinctively Scottish terminology.[11] 'To the Principal and Professors' is again exemplary in its bringing together these different sorts of diction, drawing on several areas of language to enrich and energise the poem. It is in some ways Fergusson's strongest and most mature reaction to the Anglocentric, Rhetoric and Belles-Lettres literary training given him by his university, and it is rightly becoming a standard anthology piece, one central to discussions of eighteenth-century Scottish literary culture. The poem is also characteristically gleeful, and, even as it deploys with ease its academic terminology, it reinforces the idea that the most important thing a university training may offer a poet is something to react against. It would be wrong, though, to suggest that St Andrews at this time was naively Anglocentric, just as it would be daft to forget how many of the finest Scottish poets from Dunbar and Gavin Douglas through George Buchanan, William Fowler and Robert Ayton had been educated there. Certainly, his time at St Andrews would seem to have developed in Fergusson a marked commitment to Scottish culture. As the accounts of their visit by Boswell and Johnson testify, it was as hard in Fergusson's day as it is in our own to be in St Andrews without becoming aware of the contested nature of cultural power in Scotland. Towards the end of his time as a student, Fergusson, who appears to have held anti-Union and Jacobite sympathies, is said to have begun work on a tragedy dealing with the death of William Wallace.

Fergusson at St Andrews was not just a writer, he was a rioter. The poet was involved in a St Andrews student 'riot' in 1768 and offered up a mock-prayer for one of his friends in front of the assembled professors, an act which almost led to his expulsion. The intervention of William Wilkie apparently saved him from this fate. Yet such actions did not make Fergusson universally popular with his fellow students. He seems to have been seen by some at least as a brilliant but wild and dangerous figure. Among surviving St Andrews marginalia several predict Fergusson's damnation. In addition to the comment about looming damnation, there is also, in a different hand, the more colourful attack which tells us

> The wonderful Wonder of wonders, Robert Ferguson is a damned eternal Puppy a stinking fairy [several words inked out] a reptile of the serpent kind a snake in human form stain'd with infamy and wickedness sprung however from a dunghill. This serpent Robert Ferguson spews a filthy froth of pustulent matter which if it happens to light on the skin will corrupt to a wound and spread a leprosy or the [?French] pox.
> O Filthy Brat Rob. Ferguson amend before you end[12]

Here in these spirited comments, which would appear to be written by an anonymous fellow student, we sense already formed the dangerous libertinism which seems to have accompanied Fergusson's brilliance, making him seem a proto-Romantic harbinger not just of Burns but also of Byron, not yet mad but certainly bad and dangerous to know.

Fergusson left St Andrews in May 1768, without graduating (an omission common at the time), but would not settle to a profession. Early in 1769 he spent six months on his uncle's farm at Roundlichnot, leaving under a cloud. In September 1769 he took a job as clerk in the Commissary Office, Edinburgh, copying legal documents at the rate of a penny a page. Fergusson's clerkliness (we might remember that his father had worked as a lawyer's clerk) should be recalled alongside the suggested libertinism. Such surviving documents as the presentation copy of his poems given to David Herd suggest a meticulous, scholarly and ambitious nature.[13] In the volume given to Herd someone has carefully tabulated a bibliography of Fergusson's poems published in periodicals since the publication of the book. There is nothing slap-dash about the list or about Fergusson's signed inscription, a fact that again attests to the complex mixture that was Fergusson's personality as a writer.

He became a friend of Edinburgh singers and musicians, including the visiting Italian singer, Giusto Ferdinando Tenducci, who performed some songs by him. That Italian name may usefully remind us that Fergusson was no Wee Scotlander. 'On the Death of Scots Music' laments the erosion of native culture, yet calls to its defence Shakespeare (supplier of the poem's epigraph), while the Macgibbon lamented in the poem is (Matthew McDiarmid's note points out) no Habbie Simson, but a musician who led the Gentlemen's Concert in Edinburgh, and was 'thought to play the music of Corelli, Geminiani, and Handel, with great execution and judgment'.[14] This fact complicates Fergussson's praise of Scotland's native music, examined in the present book by Douglas Dunn and by Matthew Wickman; it sits oddly with his apparent denunciation of 'crabbit queer variety/Of sound fresh sprung frae *Italy,/* A bastard breed!', suggesting that even the culture which Fergusson champions is, as he would have known, a highly sophisticated, even cosmopolitan construction.[15] Such ironies may be awkward, but ultimately they are part of the urbane nature of Fergusson and his poetry.

A friend of several actors, this poet relished Edinburgh's theatre-life. In 1771 *The Weekly Magazine, or Edinburgh Amusement* published three 'Pastorals' by Fergusson, written in the manner of Shenstone. These were followed by other poems in English, and the poet appears to have enjoyed a passionate friendship with a young woman, designated 'Stella' in a series of poems. Though we may think of him as a Scots poet, delighting in his thirty-five poems in Scots, we should remember that the bulk of Fergusson's work was written in English, a language which, especially towards the end of his career, he saw as a vehicle for his deepest feelings. So, as Susan Manning points out in her essay here, Fergusson's example complicates naive assumptions that Scottish poets think in English but feel in Scots.

In 1772 Fergusson published several poems in Scots in *The Weekly Magazine*. Poems such as 'The Death of Scots Music', 'Caller Oysters' and 'To the Tron Kirk Bell' celebrated in racily sophisticated vernacular language the pleasures of Edinburgh. Fergusson was hailed by his actor friend Frederick Guion as 'The LAUREAT' of that city.[16] That title is significant, not least because it marks Fergusson as substantially different from Burns. 'EDINA! *Scotia's* darling seat!' is one of Burns's more risible opening lines, and palls beside the start of Fergusson's 'Auld Reikie'. Burns declaims as an impressed 'Stranger', which he is; Fergusson writes as a delighted native who has spent long enough away from his home town to enjoy it all the more.[17] Only in the twentieth century would the work of such different poets as Norman MacCaig and Robert Garioch challenge Fergusson's claim to the title of Edinburgh's laureate; probably Fergusson still retains his laurels, and Ian Duncan's essay helps explain why this should be so. Fergusson's ability to write an absolutely convincing urban poetry in Scots again makes him exemplary for later writers. His legacy is a meaningful one for poets of my own generation, as several of the poems in this book demonstrate. Not least, it matters to W. N. Herbert, who considers Fergusson's legacy to today's Scots verse. Fergusson was protean. In this, not least, lies his power. He was accomplished as a poet of rural life, as 'The Farmer's Ingle' demonstrates; he had a liking for such sophisticated, classically grounded forms as the pastoral and eclogue; he seems to have been happy to 'breath a while the caller air/ 'Mang herds, an' honest cottar fock,/ That till the farm and feed the flock' ('Hame Content'); he relished excursions to Fife, just as he liked to look across to Edinburgh from the countryside. Urban and rural, he was at home in both these Scotlands, and liked to see them to some degree as interpenetrating one another. So in 'Auld Reikie' we have not only the sense of crowded bustle 'Whan Feet in dirty Gutters plash', but also a sense of wild landscape that forms part of the experience of Edinburgh:

> WHILE dandring Cits delight to stray
> To Castlehill, or Public Way,
> Whare they nae other Purpose mean,
> That that Fool Cause o' being seen;
> Let me to ARTHUR'S SEAT pursue,
> Whare bonny Pastures meet the View;
> And mony a Wild-lorn Scene accrues,
> Befitting WILLIE SHAKESPEARE'S Muse:
> If Fancy there would join the Thrang,
> The desart Rocks and Hills amang,
> To Echoes we should lilt and play,
> And gie to MIRTH the lee-lang Day.

> OR shou'd some canker'd biting Show'r
> The Day and a' her Sweets deflour,
> To Holy-rood-house let me stray,
> And gie to musing a' the Day;
> Lamenting what auld SCOTLAND knew
> Bien Days for ever frae her View:
> O HAMILTON, for shame! the Muse
> Would pay to thee her couthy Vows,
> Gin ye wad tent the humble Strain
> And gie's our Dignity again:
> For O, waes me! the Thistle springs
> In DOMICILE of ancient Kings,
> Without a Patriot to regrete
> Our PALACE, and our ancient STATE.[18]

In these lines we have a hint of the more melancholy aspect of
Fergusson, poised on the edge of 'MIRTH'. In the city's 'Wild-lorn
Scene' he summons up not what he calls elsewhere 'An *Ossian*'s fancy',
but rather the familiarly hailed 'WILLIE SHAKESPEARE'S Muse';
Fergusson's delight in the English poet should not be seen as counter
to his lamenting the lack of a modern Scottish 'Patriot' in the lines that
follow. He was sophisticated enough to see that love of English literature
and of Scottish culture could be interwoven. Yet he articulates a clear
and attractive wish for Scotland to regain that lost 'Dignity' symbolised
by the ruinous state of Holyrood Palace, once seat of independent
Scottish monarchs, but unvisited by any British monarch for over a
hundred years before Fergusson's birth. Fergusson the Shakespeare-
lover and friend of the Italian singer remains a champion of Scottish
culture, alert to 'our ancient STATE'. There is a rapid change of mood
between the two stanzas I have just quoted. At the end of the first
Fergusson imagines how the 'lee-lang Day' might be given over to
'MIRTH'. Yet the next moment it is blasted in a way that suggests sexual
libertinism and disease, even at the very House of the Holy Rood:

> OR shou'd some canker'd biting Show'r
> The Day and a' her Sweets deflour,
> To Holy-rood-house let me stray . . .

That vertiginously abrupt mood swing between the two stanzas is quite
typical of Fergusson; it characterises his oeuvre, which extends from the
'Ode to Horror' to the perkiness of 'Leith Races', from slow pastorals to

the energetically lively (yet also fascinatedly disgusting) mock-heroic piece 'The Bugs' where, invoking the pseudo-Homeric *Batrachomyo-machia*, Fergusson presents those 'BUGS abhorrent, who by instinct steal/ Thro' the diseased and corrosive pores', invading 'Edina's mansions'.[19] The pendulum-swings within Fergusson's work, and even within individual poems, as well as what we know of his career, may help explain why he features in Kay Redfield Jamison's study of manic depression and the artistic temperament.[20] At the same time, such a swing from mirth to the cankered is not just some personal indulgence; it is a purposive and striking artistic effect, one which might have appealed to a modernist sensibility, and which also happens to be true to Edinburgh's weather patterns. Fergusson was absolutely at home there, as few other poets have been. Part of Burns was always beyond Edinburgh; Fergusson can become thoroughly immersed in that city. Burns learned from Fergusson how to make pell-mell rapidity an ally in poetry, and how to deploy not just set pieces but sudden switches of emotional state, as he does in 'Tam o' Shanter'. The difference is that Fergusson does all this brilliantly in an urban context, which Burns cannot, or at least does not. For all his sense of literary nature, Fergusson, more than Thomson or Burns or Macpherson or any other eighteenth-century Scottish poet, takes in Scotland's city as well as its rural life, and, in much of his finest work, is quintessentially urban. This makes him unusual among Scottish poets, setting him beside John Davidson and Edwin Morgan. Along with Fergusson's position as perhaps the first significant poet to study English literary texts at university, this urban sensibility may be the most important factor which will contribute to our developing sense of his modernity. Scots for Fergusson was not a rural language; nor, though it could be triumphantly funny, was it a language for the simply comical. Janet Sorensen's essay suggests ways in which Fergusson's deployment of Scots was prescient as well as sparky.

From our viewpoint, it is tempting to relate Fergusson to his near and more distant successors. In his own day another commentator praised him for reviving the tradition of his predecessor Allan Ramsay.[21] It would be completely wrong to suggest that the Scots of Ramsay was unsophisticated, yet there are ways in which, in *The Gentle Shepherd*, for instance, it seems to be consigning itself too readily to the tea-table. Ramsay's pastoralisation of Scots may have charmed Hugh Blair, but Fergusson knew it was far more important to listen to the bustle of modern urban streets. This appeals to us, but, again, we should recall that such projects as 'Auld Reikie' were being developed by a very young man who also had other, clearly learned designs. By the end of 1772 he was planning the publication of his poems in book form, and was reported as hoping to follow in the footsteps of the great Scots translator Gavin Douglas by translating Virgil's *Eclogues* and *Georgics*. Walter Ruddiman, editor of the *Weekly Magazine*, encouraged the impover-ished Fergusson, and gifted to him two suits of clothes. It is also appropriate that Fergusson's major patron should have been this nephew of Thomas Ruddiman, the celebrated Latin Grammarian, Scots glosser, and publisher of Gavin Douglas. Fergusson's was an empower-ingly highbrow as well as an energisingly vernacular milieu. He is again emblematic for associating with workers and with *literati* without apparently being patronised by either. Unlike Burns, he belonged fully to both worlds. Looking at Fergusson alongside Burns, Carol McGuirk's essay in this book highlights differences as well as the more frequently remarked similarities.

In early January 1773 Fergusson's volume of *Poems* was published in Edinburgh under the imprint of Walter and Thomas Ruddiman. Fergusson is known to have inscribed copies to James Boswell, to the Earl of Glencairn (later a patron of Burns), to the ballad collector David Herd, and to several others. Soon after, in 1773, he published *Auld Reikie, A Poem* which, though it attracted little immediate notice, ranks as the supreme vernacular Scots celebration of Edinburgh's bustling streetlife and convivial delights,

> On stair wi' TUB, or PAT in hand,
> The barefoot HOUSEMAIDS looe to stand,
> That antrin Fock may ken how SNELL
> Auld Reekie will at MORNING SMELL.[22]

As I have pointed out, though, there are also darker moments in 'Auld Reikie', without which it would be true neither to its subject matter nor to its poet's temperament. A poem by 'Philanthropus' in the *Weekly Magazine* in December 1772 presented Fergusson as charming Edin-burgh society with his 'quick and lively fancy', as singing lustily, but also as a slovenly youth who 'Wears dirty shirts, nor combs his hair' and who needs to behave more prudently.[23] This liking for 'dirty shirts' might recall Wilkie; the uncombed hair also propels Fergusson forward towards the later cult of the Romantic bohemian which would attract R L Stevenson. Fergusson's friend and early biographer Thomas Som-mers recalled him as 'about five feet, six inches high, and well shaped.

His complexion fair, but rather pale. His eyes full, black, and piercing. His nose long, his lips thin, his teeth well set and white'. Narrow-shouldered and long-limbed, Fergusson had a voice, Sommers remembered, 'strong, clear, and melodious . . . when speaking, he was quick, forcible, and complaisant. In walking, he appeared smart, erect, and unaffected'.[24] That unaffectedness is a crucial part of Fergusson's literary appeal, yet it should never be confused with a lack of nourishing complexity.

In October 1772 Fergusson joined the Cape Club, which met in several Edinburgh taverns 'to pass the evening socially'.[25] The Cape and its doings are a vital part of 'Auld Reikie', welded to Fergusson's vision of the poet as a carouser teetering at times on the edge of a dismal 'last Adieu'. Though it is there in Ramsay, this poet's pub-world of Edinburgh is more insistently present in our picture of Fergusson. Bound up with quasi-masonic, essentially homosocial rituals of clubs such as the Cape (where Fergusson took on the nickname 'Sir Precenter' – as a result of his St Andrews exploits) and hymned the members' acts, a trope developed in Scottish culture of the poet as drunk man. Fergusson, invoking Ramsay, enjoyed this. In 'A Drink Eclogue' he has Whisky proclaim, 'Troth I ha'e been 'ere now the poet's flame,/ And heez'd his sangs to mony blythsome theme'. Burns's poems and his career with the Crochallan Fencibles developed this trope further. It was seized on by Hugh MacDiarmid in his best known work. Romanticised and relentlessly gendered, it persisted in my childhood as the mythology surrounding Rose Street pubs, Norman MacCaig, Goodsir Smith, and their acolytes. This is the mythology that survives in the well-intentioned, in its way splendid depiction of a group of modern Scottish poets by Alexander Moffat in his 1980 painting *Poets' Pub*. It was kept alive, albeit in a disrupted form, in Richard Avedon's 1995 *New Yorker* photograph of a group of Scottish writers in a Glasgow howff, where the pregnant Kathleen Jamie and the teetotal A. L. Kennedy complicate older assumptions about the semiotics of the poets' pub.[26] On the whole, this trope has now become a trap, a journalistic commodity, and an imaginative limitation. Sociability is crucial to Fergusson's muse, but if we think that he learned his poetic trade in the pub, we are wrong.

Fergusson's undoubted love of the Cape Club was bound up with his unaffectedness and his relish of urban pleasures. A drawing of him survives in the Club's Minute Book (in the National Library of Scotland). At the Cape he mixed with ordinary tradesmen as well as with artistic figures such as David Herd and Alexander Runciman, who painted Fergusson's portrait – perhaps the one now in the Scottish National Portrait Gallery – and to whom Fergusson addressed verses. Runciman is said to have used Fergusson as the model for a depiction of the Prodigal Son, hardly the most comical of figures, though one whose career vertiginously balances despair and joviality. That mixture, at the heart of Fergusson's oeuvre and central to his life, tilts decisively in 1773. The change can be heard with horrifying clarity in the magnificent opening and closing lines of 'Job, Chap. III. Paraphrased' which begins 'Perish the fatal DAY when I was born' and closes with the couplets,

> Wild visag'd fear, with sorrow-mingled eye,
> And wan destruction piteous star'd me nigh;
> For though nor rest nor safety blest my soul,
> New trouble came, new darkness, new controul.[27]

Though sections of the poem may seem too close to the barely readable strains of Blair's *The Grave* and Young's *Night Thoughts*, its conclusion possesses a horrific vitality, a terrible sense of endlessness even at the end of the poem; that final word 'controul' brings with it to the modern ear a menace all the more powerful for sounding both authoritative and undefined. Brought up in a Protestant milieu, Fergusson knew the Bible well, but appears to have had difficulties accepting some of the tenets of Christianity, including the doctrine of the Fall. Again, this may have a bearing on a poet whose own work so often veers between the jovial or Edenic and the totally downcast.

In October 1773 Fergusson published *A Poem to the Memory of John Cunningham*, a highly artificial English-language work preoccupied with 'MISFORTUNE' and elegising a poet who had died in Newcastle's madhouse. The same month he wrote to a friend, complaining how 'that fancy which has so often afforded me pleasure, almost denies to operate but on the gloomiest subjects;' in November, he signed a letter 'Yours, in the horrors'.[28] At the end of the year Fergusson had to give up his work at the Commissary Office, and was seriously ill; possibly he had contracted syphilis. His last poems, in English, include that paraphrase of part of the Book of Job, and his 'Ode to Horror'. Severely depressed, Fergusson sought quiet in the village of Restalrig, near Edinburgh, but soon returned to the city, burning many of his poems, and constantly reading the Bible. One recollection has him telling a friend near the North Bridge, Edinburgh, that he had just spotted one of the men who crucified Christ. On 2 July 1774 the Cape Club took up a collection to aid Fergusson who, after showing some signs of recovery, fell downstairs, became delirious and was committed to a cell in Edinburgh's Bedlam where he lay weeping fully clothed on a bed of straw. He died on 17 October 1774, and was buried on 19 October in the Canongate Kirkyard in his unmarked grave.

In 1779 Walter and Thomas Ruddiman issued a further volume by Fergusson, *Poems on Various Subjects*; in 1782 and 1785 fuller, collected editions of Fergusson's work appeared from the same publisher, but only after Burns's efforts did a stream of other memoirs and tributes emerge. Though they never met, Burns and Fergusson had friends in common. When Burns was awaiting the publication of the Edinburgh edition of his own work in 1787 he complained about the lack of a headstone at Fergusson's grave; eventually he paid for and composed the inscription for such a memorial. He also addressed three poems to Fergusson, more than he addressed to any other poet. Outside Scotland, Fergusson was read, but his impact was at best fugitive. One of his last poets was an 'Ode to Disappointment'.

On 21 April 1802, after listening to Coleridge reading his 'Dejection' ode, Dorothy Wordsworth, 'in miserable spirits', went to bed in the afternoon and 'Read Ferguson's life and a poem or two'.[29] By early May Dorothy's Scotophile brother was at work on 'Resolution and Independence', that poem so alert to how 'As high as we have mounted in delight/ In our dejection do we sink as low'. The word 'dejection' comes, no doubt, from Coleridge. Yet Fergusson lives also in the lines which conclude the poem's most celebrated stanza:

> I thought of Chatterton, the marvellous Boy,
> The sleepless Soul that perished in his pride;
> Of Him who walked in glory and in joy
> Following his plough, along the mountain-side:
> By our own spirits are we deified;
> We Poets in our youth begin in gladness;
> But thereof come in the end despondency and madness.[30]

In this poem Wordsworth's leech-gathering Scottish protagonist symbolises endurance. The work celebrates a northern voice. The first two lines of the stanza deal with Chatterton, the following two lines with Burns; the conclusion, surely, draws on Burns's admired 'brother'. Fergusson was for the Wordsworths a well-known modern instance of a poet whose career not only mixed gladness and despondency but also ended spectacularly in madness. These great Romantic lines suggest another way in which Fergusson's example underlies the figuration of the modern poet. Yet Fergusson's presence in Wordsworth's stanza is almost invisibly submerged; only in Scotland, and largely among Scottish poets, has his reputation been fully cherished.

In the nineteenth century Robert Louis Stevenson regarded him as 'so clever a boy, so wild . . . so like myself' and planned to add words to his tombstone 'as the gift of one Edinburgh lad to another'.[31] In the twentieth century Sydney Goodsir Smith edited *Robert Fergusson, 1750–1774, Essays by Various Hands* (1952) in which Hugh MacDiarmid, Robert Garioch and other Scottish poets paid tribute to the eighteenth-century poet and bonded his work to their own. It is a tribute to Fergusson's versatility and tonal range that all of these substantially different poets were able to see in his work something with which their own might be identified. However, as Andrew Macintosh's essay in the present volume shows, Garioch was rather wary of being packaged as a sort of Robert Fergusson *redivivus;* over-simplified versions of Fergusson may have contributed to that view which confines Garioch to the role of pawky laureate of Edinburgh, rather than giving him full credit for those darkly superb poems 'The Muir' and 'The Wire'. MacDiarmid saw in Fergusson a mastery of a poetry of declarative statement, though Fergusson's ludic swoop far outdistances MacDiarmid's. The protean nature of Fergusson's work, its range of vocabulary and intellect, and its pace, laughter, darkness, and rapid tonal shifts should never be forgotten; however awkward many modern readers may be about the Scots language of his finest work, these features will preserve his vitality.

This book has its origins in a year-long celebration of Robert Fergusson held throughout 2000 at the University of St Andrews to mark the 250th anniversary of the poet's birth. At the heart of the celebrations was the commissioning of ten poems paying tribute (directly or obliquely) to Fergusson. This commission, supported by the Scottish Arts Council, came from St Andrews University, through its Scottish Studies Institute, and is thought to be the most ambitious single act of poetic commissioning ever carried out by an academic institution. Scottish universities should do more to encourage contemporary poets, and the Fergusson commissions are a way of linking the long, some-times prickly and glorious history of St Andrews' relations with Scottish poets to its support for contemporary poetry, a commitment reflected in the fact that five of the commissioned poets now work at Fergusson's old university. It was fitting that all the poems were read by the poets at a unique event in St Andrews as part of the StAnza 2000 poetry festival which also marked the launch of *The New Penguin Book of Scottish Verse*. The time has come both locally and internationally to reassess that 'damned eternal Puppy' who wrote of St Andrews with both affection and resentment. There are certainly ironies in his *alma mater* celebrating the poet who so cheeked its Principal and Professors, but, as one of the commissioned poets remarked recently, 'How could anyone not like Fergusson?' The contributors to this book would all agree, and would question his damnation.

Notes

1. Robert Burns, *Poems and Songs*, ed. James Kinsley (Oxford: Oxford University Press, 1969), 258.
2. Henry Mackenzie, unsigned essay in *The Lounger* 97 (9 December, 1786), repr. in Donald A. Low, ed., *Robert Burns: The Critical Heritage* (London: Routledge and Kegan Paul, 1974), 70.
3. Reproduced as Plate II in Robert Crawford, ed., *Launch-site for English Studies: Three Centuries of Literary Studies at the University of St Andrews* (St Andrews: Verse, 1997).
4. So I argue in my book *The Modern Poet* (Oxford: Oxford University Press, 2001).
5. *The Letters of Robert Burns*, ed. J. De Lancey Ferguson, 2nd edn ed. G. Ross Roy, 2 vols. (Oxford: Clarendon Press, 1985), I, 90.
6. Burns, *Poems and Songs*, ed. Kinsley, 258.
7. See Robert Crawford, ed., *The Scottish Invention of English Literature* (Cambridge: Cambridge University Press, 1998), especially the introduction and the chapter by Neil Rhodes.
8. See *Johnson's Journey to the Western Islands of Scotland and Boswell's Journal of a Tour to the Hebrides*, ed. R. W. Chapman (London: Oxford University Press, 1970), 202 (Boswell, 19 August 1773).
9. Matthew P. McDiarmid, ed., *The Poems of Robert Fergusson* (Edinburgh: Blackwood for the Scottish Text Society, 1954–6), 2 vols., II, 85. Hereafter this work is cited as 'McDiarmid'.
10. *Ibid.*, II, 1.
11. Robert Crawford, 'Robert Fergusson's Robert Burns' in Robert Crawford, ed., *Robert Burns and Cultural Authority* (Edinburgh: Edinburgh University Press, 1997), 1–22.
12. Reproduced as Plate III in Crawford, ed., *Launch-site for English Studies*.
13. This is now in St Andrews University Library.
14. McDiarmid, II, 257.
15. *Ibid.*, II, 39.
16. *Ibid.*, I, 32.
17. Burns, *Poems and Songs*, ed. Kinsley, 249–50.

18. McDiarmid, II, 117.
19. *Ibid.*, II, 146–7.
20. Kay Redfield Jamison, *Touched with Fire: Manic Depression and the Artistic Temperament* (New York: Free Press, 1993).
21. McDiarmid, I, 33.
22. *Ibid.*, II, 110.
23. *Ibid.*, I, 46–7.
24. *Ibid.*, I, 59.
25. *Ibid.*, I, 50.
26. *The New Yorker*, December 25, 1995 and January 1, 1996, 98–99.
27. McDiarmid, II, 230.
28. *Ibid.*, I, 67–8.
29. Dorothy Wordsworth, *Journals*, 2nd edition, ed. Mary Moorman (London: Oxford University Press, 1971), 113–4.
30. William Wordsworth, *Poetical Works*, ed. Thomas Hutchinson, revised by Ernest de Selincourt (London: Oxford University Press, 1969), 155–6.
31. *The Letters of Robert Louis Stevenson*, ed. Bradford A. Booth and Ernest Mehew (New Haven: Yale University Press, 1994–5), 8 vols., VIII, 290–1.

ROBERT FERGUSSON NIGHT

St Andrews University A.D. 2000

All the Fergussons are black
I've heard said in the Outback.
Sub rosa, the Scots empire ranged wide.
I hope Scotland proportions her pride
now to the faith her lads kept with
all the subject folks they slept with.
I know for you this wasn't an issue.
Madness made a white man of you

disastrously young. You stayed alive
just long enough to revive
from Scottish models and kings
such mediaeval things
as documentary verse-television
and writing in Scots for the brain.
In that, you set the great precedent
for every vernacular and variant

the world-reach of English would present.
Now you're two hundred and fifty
and gin some power the giftie
gied ye of a writership-in-revenance
you'd find a death-cult called Romance
both selling and preserving a scrubbed Reekie
and the now-posh Highlands. Very freaky.
You might outdo Dr Johnson in polite

St Andrews now, that Reformation bombsite.
I fear you mightn't outdraw golf there:
golf keeps from the door the wolf there –
but nobody does what you showed aversion
to already in your time, poetical inversion.
Metrics too, now, are Triassic pent amateur
and 'Rhyme is for Negroes', I heard in Berlin:
the speaker was a literary Finn.

19

Such talk, now at last, is a sin
in place of much that wasn't. Madness
for instance. The Bedlams yielded to medicine:
even madness has, a little. Madness:
would you rise from the grave back through madness?
It took you and left us Burns
of the Night. Many jubilant returns:
this at last is Robert Fergusson Night.

Les Murray

Robert Fergusson and
St Andrews Student Culture

MATTHEW SIMPSON

On 13 April 1765, during Robert Fergusson's first year at St Andrews University, the professors of the United College noted in their weekly minutes the death of one of their number, David Gregory.[1] No doubt they would have been pleased that a student was writing an elegy for him, had they known. It is not difficult to imagine the sort of composition they might have expected, because when another member of the Gregory dynasty died a few years later, just such a fitting poem was published in Edinburgh's *Weekly Magazine*. It was written at Balliol College, Oxford, by a Scot called Andrew Greenfield, an exact contemporary of Robert Fergusson, and was entitled 'Verses occasioned by the Death of Dr John Gregory, late Professor of Physic in the University of Edinburgh'.[2] A few stanzas of Greenfield's poem will help to recall the conventions of respectable obituary verse, as to style and attitude, and also to identify a particular concept of the university to which I shall return later on:

> Far from the gay, to seek the lonely shade,
> With heaving breast the muse dejected turns,
> Sighs to the wave that murmers in the glade,
> And Isis echoes what Edina mourns.
>
> O thou so greatly lov'd, so quickly lost!
> The tear that oe'r thy grave unbidden flows,
> Prints on the living turf a fairer boast,
> Than all the fame that sculptur'd pride bestows.
>
> Science on thee, her early fav'rite, smil'd,
> Lur'd from the mazes of her dark retreat,
> And led thee swiftly thro' the boundless wild,
> To those blest bow'rs where wisdom fix'd her seat . . .
>
> Yet the kind father and the common friend,
> Thine heirs must weep, whom every grace adorns;
> Yet with their sighs the public sorrows blend,
> And Isis echo[e]s what Edina mourns.[3]

Such an obituary the professors at St Andrews might reasonably have hoped for on behalf of their own former colleague. Indeed, Greenfield's poem illustrated many of the rhetorical devices which were being identified for St Andrews students in the lectures of Fergusson's Rhetoric professor, Robert Watson (which is not to say that Watson, a judicious critic, would have overrated its merits).[4]

But the elegy which Robert Fergusson did write for David Gregory began (and continued) in a very different style:

> Now mourn, ye college masters a'!
> And frae your ein a tear lat fa',
> Fam'd *Gregory* death has taen awa'
>   Without remeid;
> The skaith ye've met wi's nae that sma',
>   Sin Gregory's dead.[5]

Fergusson's poem, then, makes a daring departure from the prevailing convention. True, there existed in Scots verse a tradition of more high-spirited elegies, as much send-offs as obituaries, a tradition to which Fergusson's poem is extensively indebted in tone and phraseology. But that sort of elegy was for merely local people – pipers and innkeepers and the like – not for university professors, whose supra-local importance is specifically acknowledged in the fourth lines of Greenfield's first and last stanzas (his 'Isis' being the Thames at Oxford).[6] It was a daring joke to cross conventions in this way, and a joke not likely to appeal to anyone in authority. This establishes an essential point about the elegy on David Gregory: despite its first-line vocative, it must have been written strictly for the students. So much is indeed made clear later on in the poem, when Fergusson is touching on one aspect of the bereavement peculiar to them:

> Sae weel's he'd fley the students a',
> Whan they war skelpin at the ba',
> They took leg bail and ran awa',
>   Wi' pith and speid;
> We winna get a sport sae braw
>   Sin Gregory's dead.

This 'We', the poet and his audience, is a gathering of students: no-one else is going to be feeling the loss of that sport.

It is true that in the last stanza of the elegy, having spoken separately of the particular sorrows of professors and students, Fergusson seems to draw together the whole institution in the proposed regret:

> Great 'casion hae we a' to weep,
> An' cleed our skins in mourning deep . . .

But in fact this turns out to be only a mischievous device for committing the respectable part of the University to the vulgar image in which Gregory is left to await the resurrection:

> For Gregory *death* will fairly keep
> To take his nap;
> He'll till the resurrection sleep
> As sound's a tap.

And that image may be even more vulgar than immediately appears. It seems likely that in the short lines here – 'To take his nap' and 'As sound's a tap' – Fergusson is remembering Allan Ramsay's 'Elegy on Maggie Johnston', another poem in the Scottish tradition of low-style obituary. The relevant stanza in Ramsay's poem, indicating the sort of company that Fergusson's Gregory is made to keep, goes as follows:

> Ae Simmer Night I was sae fou,
> Amang the Riggs I geed to spew;
> Syne down on a green Bawk, I trow
> I took a nap,
> And soucht a' Nicht Balillilow
> As sound's a tap.[7]

The sound sleep imaged by Ramsay, and recalled by Fergusson for Gregory, is the sort that comes after drinking plentifully and throwing up. This foisting of a low image on to a polite company is part of that larger subversive joke which I have already mentioned, a joke prepared for in the respectful (and perhaps deliberately English) title, from which this image and all the rest of the text is to be an extended come-down: 'Elegy, On the Death of Mr David Gregory, late Professor of Mathematics in the University of St Andrews'.

No doubt that is a popular type of joke in the lower parts of any hierarchical institution, but it had particular significance at St Andrews in Fergusson's time, when students and teachers were becoming in important respects more distant from each other. A critical stage in this development had been reached in 1747, the year in which the University had made a substantial economy by combining its two undergraduate colleges, St Leonard's and St Salvator's, to form the United College, with one set of buildings (the former St Salvator's) and with one professoriate. As part of the same reform, a fundamental change in teaching style, which had in fact been under way for some years, was formally completed: all teachers were to specialise as professors of particular subjects, and the old office of regent, or general teacher, was to be disused.

This reform of 1747 permitted an ascent both social and professional for the St Andrews University staff. The social ascent I shall consider a little later. Professionally, these men were better positioned to do research and to publish – and so to make a figure in the larger academic community evoked in Greenfield's poem. This was true of all Scottish academics, for all the Scottish universities had been making the change-over from regenting to fixed professorships, and it largely explains, no doubt, their extraordinary eminence in the latter part of the eighteenth century.[8] By the end of the century, the Scottish universities had indeed the character, in English minds at least, of research institutes rather than seminaries.[9]

However, the end of regenting was not a wholly beneficial event. The regent had been much more than a teacher, and he took with him into oblivion a wide range of pastoral attentions:

> Regents supervised the residence halls, handled the students' funds, and in other ways assumed some of the responsibilities of parents for their often very young charges. They catechized their pupils, went to church with them, quizzed them on the sermons they heard, tutored them, and saw to it that their homework was done. They were also responsible for their boys' moral behaviour.[10]

Much later, in the 1820s, a Royal Commission appointed to investigate the Scottish universities expressed concern at this lost array of pastoralities, and recommended some revival of the regent's office. Even at the time, the change was not approved by all academics and others interested in education.[11] But the doffing of pedagogic chores undoubtedly assisted the professors to escape from that unsatisfactory 'middle rank between parish ministers and country schoolmasters' in which they had hitherto, according to William Thom, a critical observer of their profession, been languishing.[12]

That was the social ascent which I have mentioned. One may not accept William Thom's satirical portrait of an aloof and snobbish professoriate, but it is clear that the old collegiate habit of life was becoming incongruous and unappealing to professors who had polite ideals, improving financial prospects, and families to focus these in the home.[13] At St Andrews, these men became increasingly reluctant to play the pastor in college, especially if that meant lodging there even for occasional tours of duty. Permanent residence on the part of professors was now rare. In these circumstances, residence of students in college came to seem problematic, something best discouraged (and by 1820 it had ceased altogether).[14] Of course, while some students did remain there, collegiate order had to be maintained, and professorial supervision, both formal and casual, did continue; Fergusson's university poems recall some varieties of it.[15] Even so, when John Wesley made a brief tour of the University's buildings in the summer of 1776, he saw what seemed to be evidence of pedagogic neglect. St Salvator's, he noted in his journal,

> has a tolerable Square; but all the windows are broke, like those of a brothel. We were informed, the students do this before they leave the College. Where are their blessed Governors in the mean time? Are they all fast asleep?

Wesley goes on to make an unfavourable comparison between this neglect and the thoroughgoing supervision of students at Oxford (where he had formerly been a tutor).[16]

To some extent, the St Andrews professors reconstructed the college by having students to lodge in their own houses. In this way, they were replacing the communal, monastic model of student life (and Fergusson's poetry shows that he prized such fraternities) with the model of the family, in which Fergusson showed no great interest.[17] It is emblematic of this ideological change that part of the abandoned St Leonard's College was subsequently bought as a family house by Professor Watson, who did indeed take in student-boarders there. But Fergusson, as a bursar, was expected to live in college.[18] Therefore he did not participate in this disbandment, and it was the collegiate form of university life that interested him in all his university poems.

That a distinctive student consciousness persisted in the college is suggested by Wesley's phrase 'the students do this . . .' Here, it seems, is a communal and customary action – the practice of a culture, rather than a stray impulse. But this student culture, in so far as it did survive the decline of a collective college community, had also to resist divisive stresses within the student body itself. One such stress is indicated by the

Gregory poem in that surprising recollection of the 'Fam'd' professor, the '*hector*' of geometry, chasing after delinquent ball-players, a comic image which prompts the question: was this a university campus or a school playground? The answer to that depends, evidently, on the age of the students using it. Fergusson began his studies at St Andrews in a group whose ages ranged from 12 to 21.[19] The situation is rather poignantly reflected in the marginalia which were appearing as a notable medium of student expression in the University's library books at about this time. There, laborious imitations of type-letters and transliterations of professors' names into the newly acquired Greek alphabet – things which one might well find engrossing at the age of twelve – appear alongside more mature delinquencies such as scurrilous attacks on other students' girlfriends, or speculations about the librarians' sex lives.[20] During Fergusson's time, St Andrews was in fact – at least as we would now see it – a university for some people and a school for others.

There were also conspicuous socio-economic disunities among the students. Although communal eating in college did continue, at least for the midday meal, the fare itself was not communal. Bursars like Fergusson received plainer food than the unsubsidised 'boarders'. Even the tablecloths and crockery, it seems, were differential. After these meals, it was the custom for a bursar acting as precentor to lead the singing of a psalm, and Fergusson must often have risen to perform that office on his daily (and probably by no means inadequate) fuel of boiled meat and barley broth, for the benefit of a company some of whom had been enjoying roast beef or roast pork. The inequality in diet was nothing new, but from 1765 the new Chancellor, Lord Kinnoull, was making a definite policy of encouraging genteel and noble families to patronise the University. Principal Tullideph (the fearsome '*Pauly Tam*' of Fergusson's 'Elegy on John Hogg') likewise seems to have favoured the better-born students; he would invite 'all the students of distinguished families' to his house each session, but of 'plebeians by birth' only those who 'distinguished themselves eminently by proficiency in their studies' (which, by all accounts, would not have included Fergusson).[21] Some evidence of social tensions in the University may be found, again, in the marginalia of the period: for instance, at the front of the University Library's copy of Henry Ellis's *Voyage to Hudson Bay* (1748), a student hand has altered the list of titled subscribers so that the Right Honourables become 'Left' Honourables, and His Grace the Duke of Montague becomes His 'Arse' the Duke of Montague.[22] We should not, perhaps, interpret this adolescent humour very earnestly (but another student has commented alongside, 'whoever wrote this should be hanged'). My point is that the mere existence of a body of students does not make a student culture: there must also be a distinctive and consciously shared way of life – a sort of life which, the evidence suggests, was only just surviving at St Andrews in Fergusson's time.

Such, then, was the student body – the 'We' – which Robert Fergusson convoked in his Gregory poem:

> We winna get a sport sae braw
> Sin Gregory's dead.

Now, the 'sport' spoken of in these two lines is not the sport of 'skelpin at the ba' '. Fergusson remembers that game only as the prelude to the more exhilarating business of baiting the professor:

> Sae weel's he'd fley the students a',
> Whan they war skelpin at the ba',
> They took leg bail and ran awa',
>   Wi' pith and speid . . .

If, as seems likely, the game proper was not football (as we might first suppose) but 'caich' – a game played by striking a ball against a wall with the hand – then it may be that the wall in this case was one behind which David Gregory was trying to work.[23] At any rate, the 'sport sae braw' is peculiarly the product of local circumstances, an authentic piece of St Andrews University student culture. And indeed Fergusson was apparently not drawing on merely personal experience for this stanza: it was 'They' not 'We' who 'took leg bail and ran awa' '. In fact, he can have had little direct experience of Gregory's discipline to share with his fellows, for the professor's involvement in university affairs had ceased during February of 1765, only two months or so after Fergusson's arrival.[24]

The same is true of the Maths teaching which Fergusson recalls for his audience. He begins with Gregory's handling of one of the elementary definitions in geometry:

> He could, by *Euclid*, prove lang sine
> A ganging *point* compos'd a line . . .

Formulae of this sort (and the other Maths terms which follow) no doubt acquired considerable resonance in student minds. 'Quid significat punctum?' asks a marginalium in the Library's seventh volume of Rapin's *History of England* (1729). 'Punctum', a point, was also the nickname of the University Librarian in Fergusson's time, and the textbook answer adduced by this scribe is amended accordingly: 'a piece fat with neither parts nor magnitude'.[25] But Fergusson himself would not be beginning his Maths studies at St Andrews until his second year, some months after Gregory's death.[26] So when his poem celebrates the next step in this series of geometrical propositions, the definition of a line ('A ganging *point*'), he is making an appeal to local tradition – what has gone on 'lang sine' – rather than airing his personal knowledge. And so again it is not 'we' but 'They' who will 'hip the maist fek o' their lear, / Sin Gregory's dead.'

Fergusson was deriving his material for the poem, then, from a student heritage, rather than from his own experience. Something of this heritage survives also, for comparison, in the memoirs of the English poet Percival Stockdale, who was at St Andrews a few years before Fergusson. Stockdale remembers Gregory as the good teacher implied in the poem, but he also recalls characteristics which may have made Gregory an appropriate object for a student rag. In half-successful pursuit, perhaps, of that professorial gentility which I have mentioned above, Gregory 'spoke a language which was neither scotch nor english'. He was 'a proud and magisterial gentleman . . . of an intolerant spirit, both in matters of government and religion'. In this character, he had given information which secured the execution of a young man who had been 'out' in 1745.[27]

If all that was true, then no wonder this professor could, as Fergusson says, 'fley the students a' ', and no wonder the solemnities of Fergusson's obituary – the tears and mourning clothes – are somewhat adulterated with signs of good cheer. We may also understand better the likely comic significance, for the students, of the poetical survey of Gregory's Maths: here is not just the implicit macaronic fun of putting into the vernacular the ideas which Gregory himself, 'Whan he did read', had delivered in Latin, but also the impertinence of attributing that sprightly vernacular to one who had, so Stockdale says, noticeably been avoiding it. But the question here is not really whether all this about Gregory was true or fair, but whether it was current legend among the students, as Stockdale's memories suggest that it was (he could not, for instance, have known first-hand about the Jacobite business). As such, Fergusson inherited it. So although the verse form of Fergusson's poem, and much of its poetic manner, come from literary sources, its matter and sentiment are expressions of the local, unwritten lore, the oral tradition, of the students.

The elegy on David Gregory is a poem, then, which plays back to the students their own culture. It is the only one of Fergusson's poems which certainly survives from his St Andrews days, and to us it seems a freakish *tour de force* for a boy of fourteen, but when Fergusson's friend and biographer Thomas Sommers recalls Fergusson's student poetry, he says 'Every day produced something new, the offspring of his fertile pen, which was frequently employed in satyrising the foibles of his professors, and of his fellow students'.[28] So, allowing for some exaggeration in Sommers's memory, the elegy on David Gregory must have been one of many such poems airing the common life of the students for their own delectation. Even as a boy, it seems, Fergusson had a talent for identifying distinctive elements in his social setting, and for inducing his fellows to know and relish them. In so far as the student culture was a faltering one, as I have suggested that it was, his was a talent for rallying and rescuing it. In this respect, what we find in the Gregory poem is a forerunner of Fergusson's more mature poetry in Scots, written for an Edinburgh audience which was experiencing equivalent fracturings. By then, however, he was finding more in his student experience than the larks of a sub-culture. In order to see how Fergusson came to remember and use that experience in his few later years, I will turn to the three poems written in that period which look back to St Andrews University.[29]

In the poem 'Elegy on John Hogg, late Porter to the University of St Andrews' (*Poems*, ii. 191–4), Fergusson recalls his college days in some affectionate detail. Picturing the evenings spent in the porter's lodge, he writes,

> On einings cauld wi' glee we'd trudge
> To heat our shins in Johnny's lodge;
> The de'il ane thought his bum to budge
>   Wi' siller on us:
> To claw *het pints* we'd never grudge
>   O' MOLATIONIS.

> Say ye, *red gowns!* that aften here
> Hae toasted bakes to *Kattie*'s beer,
> Gin 'ere thir days hae had their peer,
>   Sae blyth, sae daft;
> You'll ne'er again in life's career
>   Sit ha'f sae saft.

29

Since this poem is about the college porter, it necessarily pictures the below-stairs region of college life. Its humour is partly made out of the truculent persistence there of Hogg's unpolished Scottish culture – especially his wholly ungentrified presbyterianism, with its Biblical tags and interest in what he calls 'hell's flame'. From this theological position, Hogg naturally lumps together professors and students as apostates:

> I hae nae meikle skill, quo' he,
> In what you ca' philosophy;
> It tells that baith the earth and sea
> > Rin round about;
> Either the Bible tells a lie,
> > Or you're a' out.

But, as I have suggested, college life, particularly as experienced by the bursars, was becoming more of a below-stairs experience in general (*vide* John Wesley's question, 'Where are their blessed Governors?'). In this poem, for instance, Fergusson remembers being roused in the mornings by Hogg the porter, not by the hebdomadar whose office it had formerly been to do the reveille.[30] So it would be understandable if Fergusson himself did not endorse quite the 'I' and 'you' grouping which he puts into Hogg's mind.

In fact, he very noticeably does not endorse it. In the two stanzas of this poem which I quoted first, he is recalling the student experience in its ideal form – the form which will be emblematic of 'thir days' for all 'red gowns' throughout their 'life's career' – and he situates it in the porter's lodge. But it is not only Hogg himself who marks the social significance of the scene there. As so often in Fergusson's poetry, the community is essentially characterised by its eating and drinking, and this conviviality in the lodge conforms to what we discover elsewhere to be Fergusson's ideology of the table. Principally, there are no ambitious or genteel palates among these consumers. In his poem 'The Farmer's Ingle' Fergusson calls such palates 'gentler gabs', and advises their owners to take up farm labour and a plainer diet:

> . . . lat gentler gabs a lesson lear;
> > Wad they to labouring lend an eidant hand,
> They'd rax fell strang upo' the simplest fare,
> > Nor find their stamacks ever at a stand.
> > > (*Poems*, ii. 137)

There were 'gentler gabs' at official college meals in the character of the boarders, but none, apparently, in the porter's lodge: necessarily not, because the lodge's menu is not just egalitarian; it is altogether *table d'hôte*. The fare is what Hogg's wife bakes and brews, and we are told that for as long as they can afford it the students go on consuming that: no question of the 'fav'rite dishes, fav'rite wine' for which discontented eaters 'girn, and whinge, and pine' in the poem 'Hame Content' (*Poems*, ii. 158). Such fussiness of taste, so Fergusson argues in that poem, is what promotes the economic and personal restlessness, the trade and the travel, which threaten Scotland's self-respect and self-sufficiency. In 'The Farmer's Ingle', likewise, Fergusson bases Scotland's proud history and continuing integrity as a nation (in so far as that was continuing) on the home-grown diet, the national *table d'hôte*. So, on that unofficial fringe of St Andrews University life, it seems that the students, who were called, perhaps, but not yet raised by their education or careers out of the demotic Scottish life for which Hogg is the representative, ate and drank as the whole nation should. Fergusson was able to find in his student days, in this memory of relatively unstratified conviviality, a model for the social and economic self-sufficiency whose national value he promoted throughout his Scots verse.

Fergusson did not, then, poetically recall St Andrews student life in order to glorify a merely alternative or subversive culture. In fact, the incompleteness and dependency of that culture were an important part of what he remembered and used when he made his university experience into a model for his critique of Scottish society as a whole. That becomes clear in another retrospective St Andrews poem, the one called 'To the Principal and Professors of the University of St Andrews, on their superb Treat to Dr Samuel Johnson' (*Poems*, ii. 182–5). This poem, which begins with a pompous dinner and ends in a call for a round of drinks, is again concerned with the sociology of food. Its occasion is the visit to the University made by Dr Johnson in 1773. Fergusson, at a censorious distance in Edinburgh, pictures the University preparing an ambitious hospitality:

> I'se warrant now frae France an' Spain,
> Baith COOKS and SCULLIONS mony ane
> Wad gar the pats an' kettles tingle
> Around the college kitchen ingle.

In reality, what James Boswell does indeed remember as a 'very good dinner' seems to have been enjoyed at a hotel.[31] Fergusson may well have known as much, and the scene he invents in the kitchen may be intended as a hilarious unlikelihood, calculated to appeal at least to ex-bursars of St Andrews (and perhaps to all who have spent any of their hungriest years in residential institutions). One such ex-bursar was Percival Stockdale, who remembers this same kitchen as the scene of a drink-inspired practical criticism:

> From the inn, we sallied to the college kitchen; where we found Tommy Band, the under-cook, defenceless and alone. He was cleaning the utensils of the kitchen; or rather, wiping off *old* dirt and substituting *new*. I had long owed this man a grudge, for the slow poisons which he had (though without malice prepense) adminis-tered to me. I immediately proposed, that we should bury him alive beneath a heap of coals. The proposal was accepted with exultation; and Bacchus bowed his approbation of the sentence. We were determined to avenge our passed disgusts, and surfeits, with *coals*; on which our dinners had often been by *him* most dreadfully *carbonaded*. The poor creature was almost an ideot [sic]; but if his remonstrances, and supplications, had been enforced with the eloquence of Cicero, they would have been vain. In short, the black deed was committed; and the entrance of Thomas Miffin, the upper-cook, saved him from something like suffocation.[32]

Stockdale's narrative shows the college kitchen to have had – like the flight from Gregory or the end-of-session windows seen by Wesley – a collective, symbolic power derived from a common student experience ('our dinners'), and it is this cultural significance which Fergusson goes on to exploit in his poem.

When Fergusson comes to devise the menu which he thinks Johnson ought to have been offered, he announces that it will consist in more homely foods:

> Tak tent, ye REGENTS! then, an' hear
> My list o' gudely hamel gear . . .

This proves to be 'hamel gear' not in the sense of Miffin-Band cuisine, but in the larger sense of national fare, featuring especially the staple-food oats, about which Dr Johnson had made the famous anti-Scottish joke in his Dictionary. The revised menu – haggis, sheep's head, and other fiercely Scottish dishes – is used to punish Johnson by shoving Scotland down his throat: accordingly, the respected 'Dr Samuel Johnson' of the poem's English title is softened up for his ordeal as

'SAM, the lying loun' in the text. But the menu is primarily meant to instruct the professors, and they too have their identities recast: the 'Principal and Professors' of the title, who welcomed Johnson and Boswell in that respectable capacity and did their best (as their guests later recorded) to live up to it, become 'Regents, my winsome billy boys!' Here is the same collapsing device used in the Gregory poem, but it is something more than parochial fun here. The term 'Regents' recalls the professors to their traditional, pastoral relation to the students – the students who are implicitly present, both as a defined fraternity and as a dependent class, in the phrase 'college kitchen' and all that phrase evokes (helpfully exaggerated in Stockdale's narrative). It recalls the professors also to a larger pastoral obligation, for Fergusson uses this student appeal to speak not only for the students – the University's dependent class – but also for 'our cottar childer', the agricultural dependant class whose livelihood would depend on loyalty to 'hamel gear' among their prosperous betters: and, beyond the cottars again, the student voice speaks for the whole social and political economy of Scotland, threatened by the defections of its elite:

> Ah! willawins for Scotland now,
> Whan she maun stap ilk birky's mow
> Wi' eistacks grown as 'tware in pet
> In foreign land, or green-house het,
> When cog o' brose an' cutty spoon
> Is a' our cottar childer's boon,
> Wha thro' the week, till Sunday's speal,
> Toil for pease-clods an' gude lang kail.
> Devall then, Sirs, and never send
> For daintiths to regale a friend,
> Or, like a torch at baith ends burning,
> Your house'll soon grow mirk and mourning.

At this point, the poet abruptly becomes involved in a personal altercation about the merits of Fife, from which it appears that the whole foregoing (and vigorously oral) address has been delivered from a tavern, the emblem of conviviality.[33] If the Hogg elegy constructed, out of Fergusson's university experience, a model for national conviviality, this poem, addressed to the professoriate, makes of the University a site for the diagnosis and deploring of conviviality's failure – a public house being the natural place to conceive of and mount such a reproof, as indeed the story of Stockdale's revenge suggests.

The third of Fergusson's poetical recollections of St Andrews has the familiar full-dress title – 'An Eclogue, To the Memory of Dr William Wilkie, late Professor of Natural Philosophy in the University of St Andrews' (*Poems*, ii. 82–5) – but there is no abrupt descent into student demotic: the Scots text which follows is sober and dignified. Nor are there in it any of the cartoons of university life which enrich the other St Andrews poems. Wilkie himself had argued that such 'particular manners' should not appear in 'the higher kinds of poetical composition', and this poem, a pastoral elegy, is indeed a serious and ambitious composition.[34] But if the student voice as Fergusson has elsewhere used it – hilarious, critical, 'particular' – is missing here, the student experience remains fundamental to a poem which is, after all, the earnest tribute of a student to an admired professor.[35]

That much, indeed – Wilkie's identity as an admired professor – is plainly particularised in the title, before the pastoral representation begins. We are therefore prepared to read the pastoralisms which follow as allegorical, if only in the informal and unemphatic manner which was characteristic of Fergusson's general model, the Virgilian eclogue. So Geordie and Davie, the two fellow-shepherds who mourn '*Willy*', are also his former students (Geordie, preparing his music in the first lines, is surely at that point Fergusson himself). As students, they proudly recall Wilkie's Baconian science with its 'Reasons' and 'principles' derived from exploration of nature's 'mystic *ferlies*', and they wistfully refuse to recall ('Be daffin an' ilk idle play forgot') the sort of student humours and recreations which frankly characterise Fergusson's other two elegies. For in this poem it is not student culture separately but a type of the university collectivity which is being evoked. So it is significant that the loss of Wilkie is made poignant by imagery of just that sort of community in food and shelter which seems to have been Fergusson's strongest and most searching memory when he looked back at St Andrews: 'Our *rucks* fu' thick', says Davie,

> are stackit i' the yard,
> For the *Yule-feast* a sautit mart's prepar'd;
> The ingle-nook supplies the simmer fields,
> An' aft as mony gleefu' maments yields.

No doubt Fergusson felt, as he created this prospect of a humanised winter, that October, the month of Wilkie's death and of the poem's composition, brought also the new university session. When Geordie sadly dismisses Davie's untimely promises of comfort, he also relinquishes the prospect of such a university as Wilkie's style of professor-ship implied.

As in the poem 'To the Principal and Professors', the student-professor relation is then enlarged: not, as there, to provide the pattern for, and to plead for, a wider national sociability, but to show that such a wider sociability was actually achieved in Wilkie's life and career. For Willy, Geordie, and Davie are only in part allegorical. Like Allan Ramsay's 'Richy and Sandy' (the pastoral elegy for Joseph Addison which was Fergusson's immediate model), 'An Eclogue' uses the pastoral conventions in a boldly realistic way. The scene is not Arcadia but 'the Fifan plain'. In Ramsay's case, that Scottish realism entailed a second phase of pastoral translation, from Addison once-countrified with 'Shepherd's Crook' to a Scottish revision of him as '*Edie* . . . lean'd out o'er a' Kent'.[36] But in Fergusson's poem, the Scottish attributes tend to draw the pastoral fiction steadily nearer to the literal truth. 'Ye saw yoursell how weel his *mailin* thrave', says Geordie (as if straining to get beyond a merely literary authority for the country lore with which, conventionally as a literary shepherd, he credits Wilkie),

> Ay better faugh'd an' snodit than the lave;
> Lang had the *thristles* an' the *dockans* been
> In use to wag their taps upo' the green,
> Whare now his bonny riggs delight the view,
> An' thrivin hedges drink the caller dew.

And at this point the pastoral convention merges into literal truth, as Fergusson intervenes with a matter-of-fact footnote: 'Dr Wilkie had a farm near St Andrews, at which he made remarkable improvements'.[37]

By this witty management of the pastoral genre, Fergusson makes the poem's subject, rather than the poet, the author of the pastoral translation. It is Wilkie himself who has converted the titular Professor of Natural Philosophy into the model farmer, and made his scientific accomplishments 'remarkable' to Geordie and Davie, not only as allegorised students, but also literally as Scots-speaking rustics. Or rather, Wilkie has made the parties to the conversion – professor and farmer, students and countrymen – compatible and concurrent. That, of course, was something about Wilkie that all reminiscences of him have preserved: he stubbornly resisted the social and cultural separations which might have followed academic distinction. Although he became the friend and colleague of leading churchmen and literati in the Scottish establishment, he remained a conspicuously ungentrified man. He kept his Scots vocabulary and accent at a time when many fellow-Scots were doing their best to shed theirs; he even wrote some verse in Scots. And he did indeed farm scientifically and make his lore in that matter available to his fellow-ruralists: 'The people in the neighbourhood of St Andrews were astonished to find a professor who could talk to them in their own language, and teach them how to raise excellent crops of turnips and potatoes'.[38]

Out of his student memories of this man, then, Fergusson conjectured an ideal university, one defined by country rather than profession, engaging the attention and serving the interest of the whole nation. Stated like that, it may seem a rather nebulously tonic conception, though the ideal of a Scottish professoriate 'organically connected with Scottish society, and independent of metropolitan, Oxbridge values' has been given various and substantial expression since Fergusson's time.[39] Fergusson's own version of the ideal is easier to appreciate alongside the poem with which this chapter began, Andrew Greenfield's obituary for Dr John Gregory. In its tone, and in many of its elegiac properties, the 'Eclogue' has much more in common with Greenfield's poem than it does with Fergusson's own Gregory poem, but it is precisely not on Greenfield's Isis-Edina axis, as one station of an international, intellectual elite, that Fergusson's university is situated. That idea of the university, glanced at in the below-stairs Scottish community of the Hogg elegy and in the comic demotion of David Gregory into the demotic, is expressly caricatured in the Dr Johnson poem, when Fergusson shows his professors using their elevation in order to speak above the nation's head to others like themselves. In its place, Fergusson proposes what he offered for a joke when he wrote as a student, and what he now sees imaged and lost in William Wilkie: a university in a more literal sense, a genuine 'we a' '.

Notes

1. Minutes of the United College, 1751–1765 (St Andrews University Library MS UC400/1), 379.
2. For Andrew Greenfield, see *Alumni Oxonienses, 1715–1886* (4 vols; Oxford: James Parker, 1891), ii. 558.
3. Stanzas 1, 2, 3, and 10 (the last), from *The Weekly Magazine*, March 11, 1773: xix. 352. Greenfield's poem was first published in *The Caledonian Mercury*.
4. See the lecture notes entitled 'A Treatise on Rhetorick' and dated 1758 (St Andrews University Library MS PN173). Watson's lectures are discussed

by several of the contributors to Robert Crawford, ed., *The Scottish Invention of English Literature* (Cambridge: Cambridge University Press, 1998).

5. *The Poems of Robert Fergusson*, ed. Matthew P. McDiarmid (2 vols, London and Edinburgh: Scottish Text Society, 1954–6), ii. 1–2. All quotations from Fergusson are taken from this edition (hereafter cited as *Poems*), except that the titles are given in standard typography.

6. Fergusson's break with tradition is noted by McDiarmid in *Poems*, ii. 248.

7. *The Works of Allan Ramsay*, i, ed. Burns Martin and John W. Oliver (Edinburgh: Scottish Text Society, n.d.), 12.

8. Edinburgh completed the change first, in 1708, and King's College, Aberdeen, last, in 1799.

9. C. J. Wright, 'Academics and their Aims: English and Scottish Approaches to University Education in the Nineteenth Century', *History of Education*, 8/2 (1979), 91–7.

10. Roger L. Emerson, 'Scottish Universities in the Eighteenth Century, 1690–1800', *Studies on Voltaire and the Eighteenth Century*, 167 (1977), 453–74; quotation from p. 459.

11. *Evidence, oral and documentary, taken and received by the Commissioners appointed by his Majesty George IV, July 23rd, 1826; and re-appointed by his Majesty William IV, October 12th, 1830; for visiting the Universities of Scotland*, iii (London: H.M.S.O., 1837), 413–14, and *Report made to His Majesty by a Royal Commission of Inquiry into the State of the Universities of Scotland* (London; House of Commons, 1831), 10. It was respect for regenting as a moral force that delayed adoption of the new system at King's College, Aberdeen: see Paul B. Wood, *The Aberdeen Enlightenment: the Arts Curriculum in the Eighteenth Century* (Aberdeen: Aberdeen University Press, 1993), 68–70. Another critical observer of the change was William Thom, one of whose satirical accounts of the Scottish professoriate's rise in the world is referenced in the next footnote.

12. William Thom, *The Motives which have determined the University of Glasgow to desert the Blackfriars Church and betake themselves to a Chapel* (Glasgow, 1764), 9.

13. To fund salaries which would secure for the professors 'that status in society, which was essential to their respectability and usefulness' was the primary purpose of the 1747 Union (though not one immediately achieved), according to *Report into the State of the Universities of Scotland*, 390; see also Ronald G. Cant, *The College of St Salvator* (Edinburgh and London: Oliver and Boyd, 1950), 187–8. The rise in the incomes of Scottish professors during the century, and the corresponding improvement of their position in relation to other middle-class groups, have been traced by Roger L. Emerson (see footnote 10).

14. Ronald G. Cant, *The University of St Andrews: A Short History*, 3rd edn (St Andrews: St Andrews University Library, 1992), 117–19; for the professorial view of the matter, looking back from 1827, see *Evidence*, iii. 67 and 109.

15. E.g. the monthly 'common schools', mentioned in 'Elegy on John Hogg', and the sort of pastoral befriending of student by professor to which Fergusson pays tribute in 'An Eclogue, To the Memory of Dr William Wilkie'. Both these poems are considered in more detail later in this chapter.

16. *Works of John Wesley*, ed. W. Reginald Ward and Richard P. Heitzenrater (26 vols; Nashville: Abingdon Press, 1982–95), xxiii. 18 (entry for 27 May). One Scottish educationist subsequently suggested that rather than go on from a Scottish university to Oxford or Cambridge, as sons of richer Scottish families often did, such students would do better to take advantage of the tutorial system at Oxbridge first, and then go to Scotland for the specialists: see Michael Russel, *Remarks and Explanations connected with the 'View of the System of Education at present pursued in the Schools and Universities of Scotland'* (Edinburgh, 1815), 75–6.

17. A difference of view in this matter is one of the points of contrast between Fergusson's poem 'The Farmer's Ingle' and Robert Burns's version of the same theme, 'The Cotter's Saturday Night'.

18. See Cant, *The University of St Andrews*, 117. Just possibly Fergusson (whose bursary was not paid from college funds) spent at least his first session in lodgings with a Mrs Gibson, mentioned as requiring payment for his board in a letter from Fergusson's father to the College (see *Poems*, i. 92), but this woman may have been a college functionary.

19. *The Matriculation Roll of the University of St Andrews, 1747–1897*, ed. James Maitland Anderson (Edinburgh and London: William Blackwood, 1905), 15. I am indebted to Dr Robert Smart of St Andrews University for the biographical information from which I have calculated these ages.

20. For a more extensive account of these marginalia, see Matthew Simpson, '*O man do not scribble on the book*: Print and Counter-print in a Scottish Enlightenment University', *Oral Tradition*, 15/1 (2000), 74–95.

21. For the different table-settings, see Minutes of the United College, 1765–73 (St Andrews University Library MS UC400/2), 469. For the other details of college life, see James Hall, *Travels in Scotland* (2 vols; London: J. Johnson, 1807), i. 117–19; quotation from p. 119.

22. This copy has the class-mark sG650.E5.

23. Fergusson's word 'skelp' commonly implies a blow with the hand: hence *skelp-doup* for a schoolmaster. For a description of caich, see John Burnett, *Sporting Scotland* (Edinburgh: National Museums of Scotland, 1995), 11–12. Caich balls dating from the later 18th or early 19th centuries have been found in St Salvator's College: they will eventually be described and pictured, among other University Museum possessions, on the Scottish Cultural Resources Access Network (www.scran.ac.uk).

24. Minutes of the University Senatus (St Andrews University Library MS UY452/7) 224. Gregory did not, then, retire at the end of the 1763/4 session (as McDiarmid says in *Poems*, i. 17), but died while he was still on

the University staff: so much the more pertinent and boldly improper Fergusson's poem.

25. P. 236, of the copy class-marked sDA30.R2D26. The Librarian in this case, to judge from other student writings in the book, was Laurence Adamson, although this nickname was also used for Adamson's successor.

26. There was some manoeuvrability in class attendance, but Maths was officially a second-year subject, and Fergusson's name does not appear in the list of pupils for 1764/5 in David Gregory's own notebook (St Andrews University Library MS QA35.G8L4), f. 21.

27. *The Memoirs of the Life, and Writings of Percival Stockdale* (2 vols; London: Longman, Hurst, Rees, and Orme, 1809), i. 175.

28. *Life of Robert Fergusson, the Scottish Poet* (Edinburgh, 1803), 11.

29. I do not take these three poems in order of their composition. However, they were all composed within a period of one year: October 1772 - September 1773.

30. According to James Hall, this morning 'perlustration' by the hebdomadar fell into disuse shortly after 1747, 'in the progress of time and luxury', though the evening version continued for some while longer (*Travels in Scotland*, i. 114).

31. James Boswell, *The Journal of a Tour to the Hebrides with Samuel Johnson*, ed. L. F. Powell (London: Dent, 1958), 34–5 (entry for 19 August).

32. *Memoirs of Percival Stockdale*, i. 203–4.

33. That it seemed emblematic in this way to Fergusson is evident in several of his poems, perhaps most notably in 'A Tavern Elegy', where that point of view easily prevails against the poet's criticisms of tavern life.

34. *The Epigoniad. A Poem*, 2nd edn (London: A. Millar, 1759), 'Preface', p. v.

35. For Fergusson's 'strong attachment' to Wilkie, and admiration for his learning, see Sommers, *Life of Robert Fergusson*, 11–12.

36. The English phrase comes from a translation into English made by Josiah Burchet, and called 'An Explanation of 'Richy and Sandy' ': see *The Works of Allan Ramsay*, i. 106–11.

37. *Poems*, ii. 269. Although the note is most reasonably attributed to Fergusson (as it is by McDiarmid), it may perhaps have been an editorial addition.

38. Hall, *Travels in Scotland*, i. 137.

39. See R. D. Anderson, 'The Scottish University Tradition: Past and Future', in Jennifer J. Carter and Donald J. Withrington (eds), *Scottish Universities: Distinctiveness and Diversity* (Edinburgh: John Donald, 1992), 67–78 (quotation from p. 72); also, in the same book, the editors' introduction, p. 12.

ROBERT FERGUSSON

To wander through these frosted leaves,
Scuffing, kicking, deceives
No one in the blue drift of days.
I feel the cold erase
Part of my life, as my shoes sift
Dead leaves for the dead gift,
For that lost thing. I play the sleuth
Searching for health, or youth.
Something about a coat is lonely,
"As if . . .", "If only . . ."

A V of geese has cracked the sky.
You would have seen them fly
Across St Andrews, Eden, Tay.
Those eighteenth-century
Fergussonian geese! Those feathered
Long-necked icons of instinct, weathered
Beyond endurance, fit
Too neatly into it,
This picture of madness, art,
Delighting the voice, breaking the heart.

High spirits, then the low, so low
You don't know where to go,
Or look, or say, or what to do
While the elusive clue
Stays secret in the rotting leaves,
The little land-star, the light that grieves
For human suffering
And the hope it can bring
Just by looking, turning
Leaves with a foot, the mind burning . . .

Another flight of geese goes by
With its communal cry.
Something about a shoe is lonely . . .

"As if" . . . "If only".
Such are the icons of the daft.
The dog sang, and the cat laughed,
And the cow jumped over the moon.
A half-remembered tune
Or half-forgotten song
Repeats "What's wrong? What's wrong? What's wrong?" . . .

Lyric oblivion! Earth-star,
I scuff for you. You are
Almost visible, like a cure,
Or lost, remembered thing, the lure
That leads me on, and through
Leathery chestnuts, and the blue
Frost-bitten sycamores.
Those who die mad, at twenty-four's
Door to the future, sing
For ever of their suffering . . .

I'm getting closer to you, working
My way to where you're lurking.
Under this pile? Here? There?
I scuff and sift them both. There? Where?
I can't go on like this.
Lovely woman, give me your kiss.
Robert, I hear your howl
In the ungraduated owl
Who sits so wisely on my summerhouse,
His prey already posthumous.

The winded leaves give up
Their multitude of ghosts
And huddle into wetness.
Do you hear? I've ceased to rhyme.
What good did it do you, keeping time,
Beat after neo-classical beat?
You wrote little of love . . .
You shouldn't have gone to Edinburgh.
I've made a fire in the rain
To keep the crow away.

Black dog? He stalks my dreams, and barks
Before breakfast, a patriarch's
Command, and my coffee cup
Shakingly taken up.
Too much Enlightenment brings forth
Snoring Reason. For what it's worth,
You should've stayed in Fife,
Or the Mearns, or taken a wife.
Something about a coat is lonely . . .
"As if", "If only" . . .

Bewigged by candlelight among
Auld Reekie's massed, unsung
Choristers of nibbed law,
You must have heard the caw
Croak in your mind, the ink-black rook
That perched on your half-written book.
By draughted candlelight
In tenemented night
You would have heard your first
Bird-whispers of the cursed –

Rough laughter from a distant close,
The way sounds, too, metamorphose
To audible shadows
Passing across windows
On the warlock wind. Ah, what ghosts
Blow in across our eastern coasts,
Whisky and syphilis
Each with its toxic kiss –
Visionary, vernacular,
The brain's beacon, the earth-star.

It's a condition of verse
That it should make life worse.
I'll lie down with the fox and hare,
Pheasant and mouse. A bluetit's prayer
Will speak my mind to feathered god,
For I'm one of the awkward squad
Who lives with the songthrush

In his dacha, in the hush
Between the road and evening
In the tree-swish when birds sing.

Douglas Dunn

Auld Breeks and Daft Days

DOUGLAS DUNN

Although his life was all too short, Robert Burns was awarded the kind of reputation no one can turn down – posthumous. That is said to have eluded his immediate forerunner, Robert Fergusson. What we are asked to believe is that while Burns roams in his posterity, in Scotland especially, but also in the recesses of a world which has almost everywhere revered and monumentalised him, Fergusson is noticed chiefly by enthusiasts and specialists. Yet he has a rooted place in the Scottish canon. Anthologists cannot and do not ignore him. But his brief career seems to pose problems. Poor Fergusson! Pity is, indeed, the temptation. Hold on, though. What could be more patronising than to feel sorry for Fergusson's reputation when the abrupt life and remarkable productivity of a man who died miserably and young did more than enough to forge a link between Allan Ramsay and Robert Burns, and did so with a poetry that blazes in its own triumphs? Literary histories are, of course, made up of works created by men and women who lived either short lives, lives of middle duration, or long lives, sometimes in relative obscurity, sometimes in the public eye, and sometimes enjoying a middling reputation subsequently revised in one direction or another. While obvious and true, it plunges us to the depths of banality. Like all histories, whether of nations, families, or human activities such as music, or the visual arts, or the sciences, that of literature is full of 'if onlys'. If only Robert Fergusson or Robert Burns had lived to a ripe old age and written consistenly well into their dotages, what then? If only Robert Louis Stevenson had lived to eighty-five, which would have taken him to 1935, then what would Scottish fiction be like now? Would Scott, Hogg and Galt have written exactly as they did were Burns to have been alive and a potent presence and reputation in their time? Can you imagine a meeting between Stevenson and MacDiarmid in, say, the late 1920s, preferably a meeting of Stevenson, Muir, Barrie, MacDiarmid and Lewis Grassic Gibbon, with Neil Gunn and Eric Linklater as guests also? 'Goodness gracious!' doesn't seem strong enough an expression of speculative delight. In fact, it's stupid.

Any country's poetry and literature are quantities of fluid and interpretable facts and mysteries, and therefore always controversial, always open to reinterpretation, misinterpretation, re-misinterpration, bluff, special pleadings, obtuseness, daredevil opinion-mongering, self-advertising, self-promotion, and sheer critical and political usage. It is a process known as 'revising the canon'. However, I would say this. Poets who die young like Fergusson, Burns, Keats, Shelley and Byron, – and there are many others, – deserve an eerie privilege: they are remembered and imagined as young, not as old, compromised, grand, or embarrassing. Or, as Sean O'Brien ends one of his poems, 'Before your talent bored you, you were dead'. Never to have to repeat yourself, nor find yourself facing self-parody, to have insufficient time to even care about your 'reputation' let alone calculate how it should be tended and perpetuated – poets who die young are spared these embarrassments. In the context of the work, there's a terrible rightness to these curtailed careers, just as with, say, Wordsworth, Tennyson, Browning, Pound, and MacDiarmid, longevity is worrying and scary.

What I like about Scots poetry is its verse.[1] As Burns was to do later, and as Ramsay had done before, Fergusson exploited characteristic Scots versification. Scots verse is like vernacular architecture – stepped gables, chiselled stone, with a touch of the fortified about it. Fergusson's poetic shove was an "emulating vigour" as much as the momentum of re-use and perpetuation which he inspired in Burns. Standard Habbie, the six-line elegiac stanza of Scots poetry which is in fact capable of many guises of mood – satiric, comic, epistolary, hortatory, what-you-will, and not just mock elegy – was used frequently by Fergusson. It's a difficult stanza when you come to squeeze it in the hope of exploiting its potential variousness while retaining the chances of originality or individual distinctiveness. It tends to make its poets sound similar if not exactly alike, as if it's a stanza dominated by an Ur-melody (as Montgomerie's stanza is also). Eighteenth-century poets liked Standard Habbie to be self-contained – rarely does one stanza run into the next. Not all lines are end-stopped in Fergusson and Burns, but most are. Rhymes are almost always full rhymes. In mastering it, the finest exponents of Standard Habbie and the other Scots stanzas seem to have steeped themselves in a lore of Scots verse that has been lost to us. In those earlier days, tuition in artistry in verse must have been passed on chiefly by word of mouth, as, indeed, it still is, although by now it is more accessible to those who want to attempt its acquisition, but without the memorising which I suspect was an essential part of the apprenticeship in those earlier days. Creative writing courses institutionalise that handing on of lore and the encouragement of instinctive taste. There need be nothing wrong with that if the teacher is the right one for the student. It is unlikely to happen very often.

The likeliest candidate for Fergusson's mentorship is William Wilkie (1721–72), Professor of Natural History at St Andrews, as the late Matthew P. McDiarmid mentions in the introductory volume to his STS edition.[2] 'The Hare and the Partan', one of Wilkie's *Moral Fables*, is in Scots,[3] but otherwise he was more known for verse in a form of Augustan English. Wilkie was eccentric – he rarely washed, and seems to have detested freshly laundered bed-linen and clothing as unhealthy. McDiarmid notes wittily that he inspired eccentricity in others, mentioning in particular David Hume's acclamation of him as 'the Scottish Homer'. To some extent this is unfair. Wilkie's posterity may by now owe more to Fergusson's than to his own achievements; but we tend to forget Wilkie's other activities. For example, he was an experimenter in agricultural science, and invented a new and more convenient plough. Whether it made ploughing any less laborious in eighteenth-century Scottish conditions is, of course, a matter for doubt.

Fergusson passed two summers at Wilkie's farm in the parish of Cameron, in North-East Fife, where he fair-copied the professor's lectures. At around eight miles from St Andrews, Cameron was well within eighteenth-century walking distance. Their acquaintanceship, or friendship, or whatever it was, makes a nice story. Dr Charles Webster, who was a student with Fergusson, reported to another that Fergusson 'was considered the best singer at the university, of consequence, he was oftener than he inclined, requested to officiate as clerk at morning and evening prayers.' Unhappy with what the good doctor Webster called 'this drudgery', Fergusson decided on mischievous measures as a way of possibly putting an end to it. 'It is usual,' said Webster, 'according to the Scottish mode of Presbyterian worship, to mention the names of persons, who are recommended in prayer; our poet, who, as usual, was in the precenter's desk, rose up with great composure, and with an audible voice, as if reading from a paper he held in his hand, said "Remember in prayer [John Adamson] a young man, (who was in the hall at that very instant) who, from the sudden effects of inebriety, there appears but small hope of recovery"'. Understandably, it brought the house down. Webster continued by saying that 'The indecorous behaviour had nearly cost young Fergusson his gown; and had not Dr Wilkie (the ingenious author of the *Epigoniad*) stept in between him and the displeasure of the rest of the professors, it may easily be conjectured what would have been the consequences'.[4]

While amusing in itself, what this anecdote tells, decisively, is that Fergusson was a self-confident young rogue, daringly witty, with a short fuse for officiousness and heavy-handed morality, and, of course, 'the best singer at the university'. There's a wonderful cheekiness to Fergusson's poetry, and it can be taken for granted that it was temperamental. It pervades his poetry. There's also a performerly poise to it, an assurance. Those traditional Scots stanzas are associated with merriment and music as well as in the case of Standard Habbie with elegy. Spirited elegy, of a kind that trades more on celebration than mourning, is characteristic of the male Scottish mind. We can imagine readily enough that the mood of this elegiac stanza and the way it is conducted stem from the old-fashioned presbyterian style of funeral, which can still be encountered. One after another, relatives and friends of the deceased rise to the front of the kirk or crematorium to deliver a few reminiscences or remarks. Not all of them will be grim or mournful. Some will be clear statements of affection. Others will be to the effect that so-and-so annoyed the speaker for his ability to grow bigger onions (or gladioli, or dahlias) than he could. Some will be candid recollections – the deceased never bought a round in his life. Or the deceased was the nicest man you could hope to meet, but . . .

What I call 'Montgomerie's Stanza', the verse of his great poem 'The Cherrie and the Slae', was written not only to be sung but to be danced to in a courtly style, as was made abundantly clear in August 1999 at the 9th International Conference on Medieval and Renaissance Scottish Language and Literature, held in St Andrews, and which I had the honour of organising. Poems of Fergusson's such as 'Hallow Fair' and 'Leith Races', the stanza of which is derived at least in part from 'Christis Kirk on the Greene' and 'Peblis to the Play' as well as Montgomerie's stanza (which was written to the tune of 'The Bankis of Helicon') would seem to me to enforce a connection between Scots verse and music, singing, and dancing.[5] Fergusson could sing. Burns was a collector of folk airs and lyrics, was himself a marvellous lyricist, played the fiddle, and I don't think it takes much imagination to conclude that he could carry a melody convincingly on his voice. Robert Louis Stevenson, a great admirer of Fergusson, and the author of fine poems in Scots, played the flageolet, and there's a photograph of him doing just that in David Daiches' *Robert Louis Stevenson and His World*. Another follower of Fergusson, Robert Garioch, was musical, too, but probably played the gramophone better than any other instrument, although he was a pianist. Hugh MacDiarmid didn't play an instrument, and I doubt if he could sing. As a Wagnerian theoretician of Scots music he, unfortunately in my opinion, applied his thoughts to the pibroch. As the late Sorley MacLean used to say, the Highland bagpipe is not a musical instrument; it is a weapon of war. If it wasn't the music of the spheres itself, the diapason chordon, then I doubt if MacDiarmid was interested. Norman MacCaig, too, was musical. He played the fiddle. Indeed, he once said to me that the best event of his literary life was that he got to share the same platform as Ally Bain, that wonderful exponent of the Scots fiddle. Hamish Henderson was, of course, a singer and songmaker as well as a celebrated scholar of Scots balladry. Iain Crichton Smith mentions Gaelic song frequently in his poems. Sorley MacLean used to say that he wrote poems because he couldn't sing.

On the nature and quality of Wilkie's mentorship, it is difficult to be anything other than imprecise. Fergusson, however, seems to have been indebted to him. In his 'An Eclogue', dedicated to Wilkie's memory, Davie, one of the two bucolic speakers in the poem, says,

> They tell me, Geordie, he had sic a gift
> That scarce a starnie blinkit frae the lift,
> But he wou'd some auld warld name for't find,
> As gart him keep it freshly in his mind:
> For this some ca'd him an uncanny wight;
> The clash gaed round, 'he had the second sight,'
> A tale that never fail'd to be the pride
> Of grannies spinnin at the ingle side.[6]

'Some auld warld name' for the stars could as easily be Greek or Latin as an indigenous term retrieved from the memory (or it could mean both). But as innovative farmer as well as poet and professor, and a man of his times, albeit an eccentric, Wilkie's knowledge of Scots vernacular would have been in any case both instinctive and thorough. It seems less than fanciful to suppose that Wilkie's attractiveness for Fergusson could have been a robust old-fashionedness that was both learned and vernacular. Certainly, in his forging of a poetic style in which a cultivated neo-classical surge met a deliberated and sparkling vernacular vocabulary and versification, the presence of the advice and instruction of one such as Wilkie can be imagined as indispensable.

What, though, of Wilkie's willingness to take Fergusson on as a helpmate and amanuensis at his farm in the parish of Cameron, a morning's walk from St Andrews? Nothing homo-erotic need be implied (and anyway, it is so long ago as to be meaningless). He must have seen something in Fergusson, and I suggest that it was a detection of precocious talent and ability. For all his mentioned and footnoted eccentricities Wilkie was a gifted and productive man. Youthful, way-ward Fergusson must have seemed to him a talent who could be advised to continue the blending of mid-eighteenth-century Augustan English with Scots verse forms and diction when necessary. As teachers are prone to do, he could have seen in a gifted pupil one whose superior talents would remember him.

Fergusson's two Eclogues struggle, I feel, with their pastoral con-ventions, even if they expose a prodigious young poet's fascination with rhetoric and pastoral decorum. His Eclogue in memory of Wilkie, however, reveals profound if also formalised sorrow and lamentation as well as intimate rural and agricultural lore which he must have learned on Wilkie's farm. Fergusson's mentor and Professor is lauded and commemorated by both speakers, Davie, and Geordie, for his Scot-tishness and his scientific mind. He taught Fergusson mathematics:

> 'Twas na for weel tim'd verse or sangs alane,
> He bore the bell frae ilka shepherd swain.
> *Nature* to him had gi'en a kindly lore,
> Deep a' her mystic *ferlies* to explore:
> For a' her secret workings he could gie
> Reasons that wi' her principles agree.
> Ye saw yoursell how weel his *mailin* thrave,
> Ay better faugh'd an' snodit than the lave;
> Lang had the *thristles* an' the *dockans* been
> In use to wag their taps upo' the green,
> Where now his bonny riggs delight the view,
> An' thrivin hedges drink the caller dew.[7]

'Elegy, on the Death of Scots Music'[8] practically sets up a convention of its own which has since become all too familiar. It is the conventional belief that anything that is good in Scotland is all in the past. This is a serious convention – in the sense, though, that there is something seriously wrong with it. Exaggerated woe for cultural and other losses made it all the more difficult for poets (and other interested parties) to lament depletions and distortions subsequently as Scottish concerns moved into more modern times. Sempill's lament for Hab Simpson is a mock-elegy for an individual or local character. Fergusson's elegy is for Scots music as a whole. An entire culture is seen as poised before extinction:

On Scotia's plains, in days of yore,
When lads and lasses *tartan* wore,
Saft music rang on ilka shore,
    In hamely weid;
But harmony is now no more,
    And *music* dead.

Round her the feather'd choir would wing,
Sae bonnily she wont to sing,
And sleely wake the sleeping string,
    Their sang to lead,
Sweet as the zephyrs of the spring;
    But now she's dead.

Mourn ilka nymph and ilka swain,
Ilk sunny hill and dowie glen;
Let weeping streams and *Naiads* drain
    Their fountain head;
Let echo swell the dolefu' strain,
    Since music's dead.

Whan the saft vernal breezes ca'
The grey-hair'd Winter's fogs awa',
Naebody than is heard to blaw,
    Near hill or mead,
On chaunter, or on aiten straw,
    Since music's dead.

Nae lasses now, on simmer days,
Will lilt at bleaching of their claes;
Nae herds on *Yarrow*'s bonny braes,
    Or banks of *Tweed*,
Delight to chant their hameil lays,
    Since music's dead.

There are six stanzas more, one of which goes:

    Now foreign sonnets bear the gree,
    And crabbit queer variety
    Of sound fresh sprung frae *Italy*,
        A bastard breed!
    Unlike that saft-tongu'd melody
        Which now lies dead.[9]

Even larks and linnets are said to be dead. We could mis-read the poem as one of an inflated, formalised but 'sincere' regret. However, what I think happens is that the Standard Habbie verse betrays its origins in mock elegy, through, almost certainly, the engineered condescension of its earlier authors in addressing persons and creatures 'beneath' them in the social or natural order. The poem seems a staged rather than actual admonition. For example, the violinist William Macgibbon, lamented in one of the stanzas – '*Macgibbon*'s gane: Ah! wae's my heart!' – may well have mattered to Fergusson, but he died when the poet was six. It's not impossible that he heard him play, or that he was familiar with his three volumes of *Scots Tunes*, or heard others play renditions based on them, but the loss can hardly be claimed immediate or deeply personal. Although referring to the past, almost relentlessly, Fergusson is perhaps warning a future generation of what could be lost of native Scottish culture were steps not taken to preserve it. The stanza bewailing Italian musical influence (and the reference to 'foreign sonnets' is part of Fergusson's ploys: 'sonnet' comes from Italian 'soneto', meaning 'a little song') hardly accords with the myth of Scottish sensitivity to influences from Europe, and which by the 1920s Hugh MacDiarmid would transform from 'sensitivity' to a muscular necessity paralleling, or, to use a MacDiarmidism, 'at one with', an even stronger aboriginal insistence. (Macpherson and Scott, and to a lesser extent, Burns, traded this influence back to Europe, and to America.) Instead, the mood of 'Elegy, on the Death of Scots Music' courts xenophobia. Its hostility to change and difference encourages the poet to feel insubordinate before the movement of time. Scots poetry, that is, poetry in Scots, in the eighteenth century seems to have been, by and large, peculiarly resistant to those European influences that enriched the poetry of the fifteenth and sixteenth centuries, although there were also significant if now largely forgotten translations, for example William Mickle's of Camões's *The Lusiads* (a bestseller in 1776). Despite his neo-classical outfit, Fergusson, and Burns after him to a more expansive, more thoughtful, more complicated degree, were determined to be local and loyal.

By the 1750s onwards, and even before, Scots merchants, entrepreneurs, financiers, manufacturers, businessmen, and adventurers, were engaged in a dynamic exploitation of the Union and the colonies. A poem like Fergusson's would seem to suggest that growth in economic activity was coincidental with a cultural entrenchment in native traditions. There was equally significant growth in intellectual, philosophical, historical, scholarly, scientific and academic disciplines, which would later become known, retrospectively, as the Scottish Enlightenment. I doubt greatly if someone as intelligent as Fergusson was unaware of these economic and intellectual movements in Scottish society. As a consequence, I doubt if 'Elegy, on the Death of Scots Music' should be read exactly as it seems. Something subtle is being demanded of 'mock elegy' in the poem. That emphatic refrain, with 'dead' rhymed eleven times – and Scots verse loves refrains and *emphases* – feels like it endorses a tongue-in-cheek deliberation of the mock mode as much as plangency pressed from the demise of Scots music. However, it is a subtlety which I fail to detect in a 'flat' or po-faced reading of Fergusson's poem. In exploiting an inherited form and manner, a very young poet perhaps lacked the resources to prime his expressions with irony. Or so it could seem. Instead, the topical contest between 'sound fresh sprung frae *Italy*' and 'that saft-tongu'd melody/Which now lies dead' led him to depict an overstated lamentation insufficiently ironic and satirical for the poet's intention to survive. Again, or so it could seem. But the satire and irony could live in the *performance* of the poem. Were it to be read aloud in a mood as iconised in recent times by the Scottish undertaker, played by John Lawrie, in the TV series *Dad's Army* – 'We're doomed. All doomed!' – were it read, that is, in an atmosphere of caricatured fatedness, then the irony and satire emerge, complicatingly, and amusingly. That is, the satire warns *against* xenophobic responses to 'crabbit queer variety' while at the same time *upholding* the value of traditional Scots music, and indicating the dissonance which can enter a culture when fashionable influences from elsewhere are permitted to go unexamined. James Robertson, in a note in his recent and very welcome edition, tells us that the fiddler William Macgibbon was also a violinist adept in the European repertoire. He finds that ironic. I wonder, though, if Fergusson did, despite the recurrence of the native assertion in 'The Daft-Days'? There's no way of knowing for sure; but Fergusson's intelligence strikes me as remarkable and a phenomenon that we can trust. The epigraph from Shakespeare's *Twelfth Night* could be pointed to as an indication that I'm wrong in my reading of the poem:

> *Mark it, Caesario; it is old and plain,*
> *The spinsters and the knitters in the sun,*
> *And the free maids that weave their threads with bones,*
> *Do use to chant it.*

Epigraphs are printed, literary devices. But, if my notion of 'Elegy, On the Death of Scots Music' as a piece for performance (and I believe this to be true of many, perhaps all of Fergusson's poems in Scots) is more than an exercise in personal interpretation, then I can see how such a preface to a histrionic performance would work, and I mean an actorly, over-the-score, ham performance. It would wrong-foot the listener and free the poet/actor for fun and games with the audience. Shakespeare was big guns then, and is big guns now. By firing them ostensibly on the side of his subject, Fergusson would have complicated a poem which is assured in its verse but by our times seems uncertain in its attitude or meaning. He is sporting with the High Culture of his epigraph from Shakespeare by playing it off against the hameil vernacular of his poem and its stanza. ('Grannies spinnin at the ingle side', from 'An Eclogue', is a version, but perhaps also a reduction, of 'The spinsters and the knitters in the sun'.)

What I need to emphasise is the inherent need of Scots poetry for performance. It is encouraged by the traditional Scots stanzas and verse forms, as used by Fergusson and Burns after him. Performance is encoded in them like an indigenous verse DNA. (Try 'performing' Fergusson's poems in English and feel the difference.) Burns's ex-pertise and passion as a writer of lyrics and as a collector of songs serves to underline my point, to say nothing of 'Holy Willie's Prayer' or 'Tam O' Shanter' or many others of his poems with astonishing narrative drive and voice. Within the indigenous context, Fergusson's formal range is satisfying although not as complete as Burns's in that there is no poem in Montgomerie's Stanza. 'Leith Races' and 'Hallow-Fair' are simpler shapings of the 'Christis Kirk on the Greene' stanza, while there are many poems in Standard Habbie, and 'Auld Reikie' and 'To my Auld Breeks' are in the tetrameter couplets favoured by the Scots language and its poets. Propulsion, narrative wickedness, voice and its characterisation, were among the features of verse in Scots which Fergusson exploited and preserved and which Burns learned from him.

'Auld Reikie' is a performance poem in that it is a descriptive and celebratory address to the city of Edinburgh. Its rhetorical volume is prominent from the very first lines – 'AULD REIKIE, wale o' ilka Town/ That SCOTLAND kens beneath the Moon; . . .' By virtue of being one iambic foot shorter than pentameter, the lines are speedier and the rhymes introduced sooner. Although that's obvious enough, I think we should ask *why?* of preferred poetic forms peculiar to a national poetry, and ask *why*? also of the preference of Scots poetry for performance. Just as the songs in Shakespeare's plays are trochaic, hinting at a poetry prior to that of the high-culture iambic pentameter of the blank verse surrounding them, the poetry of the Green World, of Arden, perhaps of Stratford-upon-Avon, then so, I believe, is the shorter line of Standard Habbie, Montgomerie's Stanza, the Christis Kirk stanza, and tetrametric verse in couplets, a gesture of loyalty to a community, to the people of a nation, and to their preferences in poetry. The Green World, a Scottish Forest of Arden, is only intermittently present in Scottish poetry, which is not so much botanical as geological. Andrew Young is one of the few exceptions. Norman MacCaig is another, but he was creaturely rather than botanical or stony. MacDiarmid is mineral and geological ('On A Raised Beach' and *Stony Limits*), or liquid ('Water Music'). Poets and readers (or, rather, listeners) in Scotland prefer their poetry to be sociable and audible.

Fergusson's steadfastness, his loyalty to aboriginal forms, is exemplary; and I suspect that this is what recommended him so strongly to Burns. But in a longer view of Scottish poetic history it can only be described as a stasis resulting from a triumphant recuperation. It is a tragedy, or at at least a disappointment of Scots poetry, that in its popular acclaim it can hardly be said to have outlived its obsession with forthrightness and fast tempo, direct address, and a relative disregard of mystery and the spiritual outside of orthodox or oppositional religiosity. You will look in vain in Fergusson, and in most of Burns for that matter, for *figurative* energy, for ingenuity or spontaneity of imagery and metaphor. That epigraph introducing 'Elegy, on the Death of Scots Music' is very instructive. 'The spinsters and the knitters in the sun' is exactly the sort of line of which Scots poetry, that is, poetry in Scots, is incapable, and which, in terms of the poetics of Scots since the second half of the seventeenth century, is shunned as inappropriate. It is a line of very wide and beautiful pictorial resonance delivered off-handedly in a play – as if in conversation – with Shakespeare's bewildering genius. Edwin Muir pointed to an absence of figuration in Scots poetry in his *Scott and Scotland*, and as long ago as 1936. His examples of lines improbable or impossible in Scots were from Shakespeare's *Sonnets* – 'And peace proclaims olives of endless age', and 'Bare ruined choirs where late the sweet birds sang'. But Muir was writing as a modern poet very much fascinated by imagery, fable, allegory, and mystery, and, increasingly, with the spirituality of poetic art. Ever since, his book and its arguments have been criticised, dismissed and ridiculed. I find it astonishing that one of the most interesting and provocative critical works in Scottish literature should be pushed to one side, or deliberately misunderstood, or seen as a 'document' in relation only to Hugh MacDairmid's very low opinion of it. As all true books are, Muir's *Scott and Scotland* is inconvenient.

There's a passage or verse paragraph in Fergusson's 'Auld Reikie' that I adore. (Incidentally, I keep tripping over the fact that the poem was written by one so young.) He evokes Edinburgh's vegetable and flower market, and in doing so demonstrates not only the characteristic directness of his verse and Scots verse in general, but his ability to slow down his customary quick pace when it's required. Technical aspects of poetry, of course, are not what recommend a poem to its readers. What we enjoy is what a poem says, while how it is said is simply the way in which we're carried along by the writing, or, rather, by the saying as we hear it in our minds as we read:

> If Kail sae green, or Herbs delight,
> Edina's Street attracts the Sight;
> Not Covent-garden, clad sae braw,
> Mair fouth o' Herbs can eithly shaw:
> For mony a Yeard is here sair sought,
> That Kail and Cabbage may be bought,
> And healthfu' Sallad to regale,
> Whan pamper'd wi' a heavy Meal.
> Glour up the Street in Simmer Morn,
> The Birks sae green, and sweet Brier-thorn,
> Wi' sprangit Flow'rs that scent the Gale,
> Ca' far awa' the Morning Smell,
> Wi' which our Ladies Flow'r-pats fill'd,
> And every noxious Vapour kill'd.
> O Nature! canty, blyth and free,
> Whare is there Keeking-glass like thee?
> Is there on earth than can compare
> Wi' Mary's shape, and Mary's Air,
> Save the empurpl'd Speck, that grows
> In the saft Faulds of yonder Rose?
> How bonny seems the virgin Breast,
> Whan by the Lillies here carest,
> And leaves the Mind in doubt to tell
> Which maist in Sweets and Hue excel?[10]

In the topicality of its descriptions, 'Auld Reikie' participates in the urban poetry of the eighteenth century which includes such works as John Gay's 'Trivia', or Samuel Johnson's 'London', as well as poems and passages of poems by Alexander Pope and Jonathan Swift. It's a crucial poem in the Scots canon in general and not only of the eighteenth century in that it is both urban and urbane, an assured work of robust, measured, vernacular Augustanism, close to satire but far from always satirical. Matthew P. McDiarmid was perceptive in stating that Fergusson's 'town poetry is local poetry':

> For Fergusson, as for Ramsay, the life of Edinburgh is the nation's life; the city is described in such zestful detail, not merely because it is a favoured locality, and it is a merely local audience that is being addressed, but because it is the country's capital, and it is the distinctively Scottish way of life that is its theme. Fergusson's local patriotism is the product of his nationalism.[11]

'Auld Reikie' relies heavily on the neo-classical poetic conventions of its time, and it is difficult to understand Fergusson's 'nationalism' except as located in his diction and in native preferences and choices ('Braid Claith' is another good example, perhaps a partner poem to '*To my* Auld Breeks'). When he addresses Nature towards the end of the passage I've quoted, 'keeking-glass' (mirror) delights a Scots ear, while 'empurpl'd speck' sounds as it were pilfered from standard poetic stock. That contrast between convention and vernacular relish and originality should alert us to the probability that Fergusson's poetic style was still in process of being formed, and that we can have no clear idea of where it might have led him (although '*To my* Auld Breeks is an indication, as I'll discuss). 'Mary's shape, and Mary's air' is one of the few references to feminine beauty or love in his work, an exception being the very conventional Scots song 'The Lee-Rigg', almost all of which comes from the warehouse where Scots poeticisms and diminutives are kept in waiting.

Robert Burns's daring and ingenuity owe much to Fergusson, and he is the greater poet, but he can hardly be said to have extended Scots poetry by very much more than Fergusson achieved in his even shorter lifetime. Burns did much the same thing, but did it better, in a different place. Burns theorised or explained his localism in his verse, and in his letters, and in the preface to the Kilmarnock edition (1786), which provides his work with a purpose or a cause, with, that is, the documentation that we lack almost entirely when we confront Fergusson's poetry. Burns, too, was a song-collector and lyricist, and dedicated to song as an act of national self-preservation to the extent that he refused to accept payment for his song-work. (His magnificent efforts can be said to have disproved Fergusson's 'Elegy on the Death of Scots Music'.) Conservation of national cultural resources – language, lyric, melody – was essential; but when poetry is foregrounded as an act of cultural or linguistic salvation or protection, then its subjects and procedures tend to be limited as a consequence. Subjects and attitudes to them become part of a national cause, or war by other means. It is, I believe, possible to see Fergusson and Burns as martyrs to the idiom they employed, and which they used in order to preserve it just that little bit longer, like the patches and re-stitching on Fergusson's auld breeks.

'*To my* Auld Breeks' is such an energetic and unforgiving meditation on poverty and its association with poetry that its robustness overturns the usual expectations of an address to something as domestic and 'low' as an old pair of trousers.[12] Trying to re-repair them is said to be as hopeless as attempts by the dying to stay alive on medicines (11–16). Nor need the breeks feel despondent or disappointed that their reward for good service is to be thrown from a garret window in the manner of eighteenth-century Edinburgh waste disposal (17–22). So long as the pockets could hold coin, he cared for his trousers, but this is foolish now that they're ragged and full of holes. On the other hand, everyone knows that a poet's pennies are few and have demands made on them; no poet can bear to lose coppers when he seldom enjoys their replacement (17–30). Fergusson then puts his personified breeks in the same position as those cadged by parasites to give credit or buy drinks, until they're skint, then despised, then forgotten (31–36). That passage, incidentally, could disclose the riotous if penniless milieu in which Fergusson lived:

> For weel we lo'e the chiel we think
> Can get us tick, or gie us drink,
> Till o' his purse we've seen the bottom,
> Then we despise, and ha'e forgot him.

There then follow a few lines of remorse and gratitude, in which Fergusson remembers composing verses while wearing his auld breeks (37–40) – and these breeks by now are becoming phantasmagoric or weirdly significant or a mid-eighteenth-century Scottish proto-symbol. (We could bear in mind that Pablo Neruda addressed Odes to such intimate items as his socks[13] – and he lived long and sanely.) 'The braes o' rime' suggests to Fergusson the financial and personal cost of poetry:

> Whare for the time the Muse ne'er cares
> For siller, or such guilefu' wares,
> Wi' whilk we drumly grow, and crabbit,
> Dowr, capernoited, thrawin gabbit,
> And brither, sister, friend and fae,
> Without remeid of kindred, slay.

It reads as an extreme declaration, and it is, even if 'slay' in Scots can sometimes mean to inflict blows short of fatal. It shows also something at least of Fergusson's mind, and its commitment. From that passage dismissing the source of drinking money the poem drops momentarily into a despairing candour. Continuing to address his 'auld breeks', he says how they've seen him carouse and then fall into despondency:

> But the niest mament this was lost,
> Like gowan in December's frost.

Fergusson was aware of his mood swings, whatever their biological or bio-mental causes, and it is instructive to remember that the poem appears in the STS edition after 'A Drink Eclogue. Landlady, Brandy *and* Whisky'[14] and before a poem purporting to be his his 'Last Will',[15] then a 'Codicile' to it,[16] an 'Ode to Disappointment',[17] an 'Ode to Horror',[18] 'On Night',[19] and a paraphrase of Job, chapter III ('Perish the fatal DAY when I was born' . . .).[20]

Fergusson's poetry is full of high-spirited celebrations of the carouse, and low-spirited remorse in the aftermath. Fergusson, Burns, and MacDiarmid, write about drink, extol drink, depend on drink to such an extent that you can wonder if at least some of the procedures and effects of much poetry in Scots rely on whisky for their forms and expressions. In the next passage (53–60) he says that if the tailor's skills could make clothes that would last for ever, then he'd wear the breeks now about to be discarded, whatever the circumstances or changes in fashion. It leads him into macaronics, with inventive rhyming and a quick display of high-spirited virtuosity of a kind to which Scots verse seems attracted, even on a theme like mutability which usually asks for softer notes than those of a shout:

> But, hegh! the times' *vicissitudo*,
> Gars ither breeks decay as you do.
> Thae MACARONIES, braw and windy,
> Maun fail – *Sic transit gloria mundi!*

That is, he implicates verse in the general vulnerability to change and failure which forms a large part of the poem's substance.

A proposed fate for the abandoned breeks is that they be worn by a virago under her skirts, not only in the familiar sense of 'wear the breeks' but as a chastity garment (61–68):

> Now speed you to some madam's chaumer,
> That butt an' ben rings dule and claumer,
> Ask her, in kindness, if she seeks
> In hidling ways *to wear the breeks?*
> Safe you may dwall, tho' mould and motty,
> Beneath the veil o' under coatie,
> For this mair faults nor yours can screen
> Frae lover's quickest sense, his ein.

Odd, and puzzling, the passage enforces the fantasia or anachronistic surrealism released by an imaginative address to a pair of outworn trousers. It is also sly, bitter, as if a mock elegy for commonplace breeks has burst its seams as it ends up mocking the human condition and the poet's position within it. Given its chronological place in Fergusson's work, we could consider the poem the result of a disordered but hyperactive mind, or a literary sensibility impatient with poetic conventions which he by now knew thoroughly if precociously. Johnson's celebrated regulations drawn from blankets and tulips, for example, are transgressed with eagerness. From a Johnsonian point of view the initial break with decorum would have been to have written in Scots in the first place.

Fergusson then enlists his auld breeks to serve as a warning to poets who make money and use it to behave with unseemly ostentation (69–76):

> Or if some bard, in lucky times,
> Shou'd profit meikle by his rhimes,
> And pace awa', wi smirky face,
> In siller or in gowden lace,
> Glowr in his face, like spectre gaunt,
> Remind him o' his former want,
> To cow his daffin and his pleasure,
> And gar him live within the measure.

'And gar him live within the measure' admonishes the poet of 'lucky times' (a notional future as well as a stroke of good fortune) and asks that he obey the demands of poetry ('measure'). More reductively, it hints at independent poverty as a natural condition of the poet or, more particularly, a Scottish poet. Wistfully, given what we know of Fergusson's habits, it suggests too that moderation ('measure') is a better way of life. But the probable double meaning of 'measure' (metre, moderation) is loaded in the direction of poetry itself. If moderation is implicated (and I think it is), then when we bear in mind the sacrifices and cost of poetry described in lines 37–46, it is at the level of a sour joke. It is an immoderate poem. Some of it, such as the passage quoted above, is momentarily unpleasant, chastening, vindictive, embittered.

How poems end is a fascinating subject in itself. How this poem ends is especially interesting in that it is unusual for a poem in Scots to close so obliquely. Fergusson delivers a narrative image of Philip of Macedon insisting on the limitations of kingship by asserting his humanity:

> So PHILIP, it is said, who wou'd ring
> O'er *Macedon* a just and gude king,
> Fearing that power might plume his feather,
> And bid him stretch beyond the tether,
> Ilk morning to his lug wad ca'
> A tiny servant o' his ha',
> To tell him to improve his span,
> For PHILIP was, like him, a MAN.

No cultural shift is involved in the 'translation' of the anecdote from antiquity to eighteenth-century Edinburgh or Fergusson's Scots posterity. It is possessed and domesticated into Fergusson's idiom. 'So PHILIP, it is said, who wou'd ring' can sound metrically inaccurate, though not if 'who wou'd' is pronounced 'who'd' in a Scots way, that is 'wud'. It is *written* 'who wou'd' which is presumably how Fergusson also spoke it – and his verse, like all good verse in Scots, is very speakable. On my ear, that extra syllable finds its compensation in the spondee of 'gude king'. However, it is lines like 'Ilk morning to his lug wad ca' / A tiny servant o' his ha'' that proclaim Fergusson's masterly conversion of the ancient and distant into the immediate and close tones of his vernacular.

From its jaunty, mock-elagiac beginning, '*To my* Auld Breeks' moves through verse paragraphs expressing various moods, and only by the penultimate verse does it start to discover the subject with which it will end. It does so with a narrative image which obliterates the poet's self and introduces a sentiment better known from Burns's poetry ('A Man's a Man'). Along the way the subjective wrestle has been humorous (1–10), routinely satirical in the manner of *memento mori* (11–16), wittily dismissive but also affecting (17–36), in lines 37 to 46 punitive on the sacrifices and selfishness of poetry, high-spirited then remorseful (47–53), bravura (53–60), prurient and bawdy (61–68), admonitory and perhaps sour (69–76), and then expansive. It is a hectic poem. It could even at times be a mad poem. Those contrasts of mood, manner and tone, the puzzling stroke by which the breeks' destiny is to be worn by a woman, and the unexpectedness of how it ends, could all have been part of an impatient struggle with poetic conventions as well as with self.

Notes

1. See my essay ' "A Very Scottish Kind of Dash": Burns's Native Metric', in Robert Crawford, ed. *Robert Burns and Cultural Authority* (Edinburgh: Edinburgh University Press, 1997), 58–85.
2. Matthew P. McDiarmid, *The Poems of Robert Fergusson*, 2 vols. (Edinburgh: Blackwood for the Scottish Text Society, 1956–56). See I, 18 *et seq.* All further references are to this edition.
3. The poem is reprinted in the first volume of David McCordick's copious and useful anthology, *Scottish Literature* (New York: Peter Lang, 1996).
4. Quoted in McDiarmid I, 18.
5. I've been known to wonder if Robert Sempill of Beltrees wrote his elegy for Hab Simpson, the Piper of Kilbarchan, to a tune in mind which has echoed down the years inaccurately but embodied in the stanza.
6. McDiarmid II, 84.
7. McDiarmid, II, 84.
8. McDiarmid, II, 37–39.
9. McDiarmid II, 37–39.
10. McDiarmid II, 115.
11. McDiarmid I, 163.
12. McDiarmid II, 215–17.
13. Pablo Neruda, *Twenty Poems*, trans James Wright and Robert Bly (New York: The Sixties Press, 1967), 90–95.
14. McDiarmid II, 210–214.
15. McDiarmind II, 217–221.
16. McDiarmid II, 221–223.
17. McDiarmid II, 224–226.
18. McDiarmid II, 226–228.
19. McDiarmid II, 228.
20. McDiarmid II, 228–230.

THE AULD ENEMY

There they are, bonny fechters, rank on tattery rank,
Murderer-saints, missionaries, call-centre workers, Tattoos,
Bunneted tartans weaving together
Darkest hours, blazes of glory,
Led by a First Bawheid, rampant, hair fizzin, sheepsheared,
Scrumming down, pally wi their out-of-town allies,
Wallace fae Califaustralia, Big Mac, an Apple Mac,
Back from the backwoods, wi Rob Fergusson, Hume, Sawney
    Bean –
See how yon lot yawn and yell and stretch
Right owre from Blantyre tae Blantyre, Perth to subtropical
    Perth!
Wait till ye catch the whites o their eyes, aye,
The specky, pinky-flecky whites o their eyes
Worn out from ogling down a Royal Mile o microscopes, or fou
Wi dollars and yen signs, or glaikit wi bardic blindness. Wait
Till ye hear their 'Wha daur meddle wi me', their hoochs
And skirls of 'Rigour!' Wait till ye smell
Through coorse, dauntless, distilled Jock courage,
The wee, trickling smell of their underdog-on-the-make fear
Dribbling down greaves, rusting nicked, spancelled armour.
Wait till you hear the start of those whispers,
'We're fine, thanks, Tony.' 'Don't rock the boat.'
'Oh, thank you, thank you, Secretary of State.'
That's the time, eyeball-to-eyeball,
To face them down, the undefeated
Canny Auld Enemy, us.

                                        Robert Crawford

Fergusson's Edinburgh

IAN DUNCAN

I. Tales of two cities

'Fergusson is to Edinburgh as Villon is to Paris, or Dickens to London, or Joyce to Dublin', wrote Sydney Goodsir Smith in 1952.[1] It is striking how natural these equivalences seem – as though the city is unfinished until a poet writes it into our imagination. Alasdair Gray's meditation on the claim has become a *locus classicus*:

> 'Glasgow is a magnificent city', said McAlpin. 'Why do we hardly ever notice that?' 'Because nobody imagines living here', said Thaw . . . '[T]hink of Florence, Paris, London, New York. Nobody visiting them for the first time is a stranger, because he's already visited them in paintings, novels, history books and films. But if a city hasn't been used by an artist not even the inhabitants live there imaginatively. What is Glasgow to most of us? A house, the place we work, a football park or golf course, some pubs and connecting streets. That's all.'[2]

Here is a secular healing of the Augustinian split between the fallen, mortal, alienated city, where we spend our lives, and the ideal or celestial city, the New Jerusalem, gleaming on an apocalyptic horizon. The artist, by creating historical and aesthetic associations that are surplus to the needs of everyday life, invests the visible city with its visionary double: and the imagination finds itself at home. In Fergusson's case, such work entails less, perhaps, a sublimation of the material city than an art that makes the visionary ordinary, mundane, even (as we shall see) *dirty*.

Fergusson was proclaimed 'Laureat' of 'Auld Reikie' within months of the publication of his first poem about Edinburgh, 'The Daft-Days', in Thomas Ruddiman's *Weekly Magazine, or Edinburgh Amusement* on 2 January, 1772. 'The Daft-Days' was also Fergusson's first published poem in Scots; indeed, Fergusson contributed just about the only writing in Scots to appear in *The Weekly Magazine* (one of the running concerns of which was the teaching of proper English). Among the very few exceptions are a couple of poems addressed to Fergusson by other writers, which dialogically assume the vernacular in order to drive home its fitness for the accurate representation of city life. 'Whae'er has at *Auld Reikie* been, I And King's birth-days exploits has seen,' writes 'J. S.' on 3 September 1772, 'Maun own that ye hae gi'en a keen I And true description'; while F. J. Guion (October 22) hails Fergusson as Allan Ramsay's successor and 'The LAUREAT of [our] CITY'.[3]

In his most ambitious poem, Fergusson boasts that the development of the Edinburgh New Town will wrest the laurels of urban splendour from – Glasgow:

> Nae mair shall GLASGOW Striplings threap
> Their City's Beauty and its Shape,
> While our New City spreads around
> Her bonny Wings on Fairy Ground.[4]

These couplets close the 1773 version (published as 'Canto I') of 'Auld Reikie'. They specify the first of two epochs in which the modernising transformation of Edinburgh coincided with the city's representation in works of literature. In 1767 the Town Council had approved James Craig's plans for an extensive residential development on the far bank of the North Loch – spreading, with the fashionable South Side squares, the 'bonny Wings' of Fergusson's metaphor. The North Loch Bridge, linking the Old Town with the site, was opened to traffic (after a disastrous collapse) in 1772. The foundation stone of Robert Adam's Register House, the first public building in the New Town, was laid on the other side of the bridge in June 1774.

Four months later Fergusson was dead. His dismayingly brief poetic career coincided with the years in which the New Town – planned, surveyed, partially feued, but not yet built – was still a visionary project, on the brink of realisation; while the Old Town remained the dense, vital centre of Edinburgh's social as well as administrative and business life.

It was in these years too that the city became a significant site of literary attention, for the first time since the Act of Union – indeed, since the Union of Crowns. 'It is now become fashionable among the English to make a tour into Scotland for some few weeks or months,' commented the *Weekly Magazine* on 9 January 1772.[5] The tour was not just a social ritual but a major literary genre. The previous year Tobias Smollett had brought the cast of his epistolary novel-cum-travelogue *Humphry Clinker* to Edinburgh, and let them linger for several lively instalments before sending them on to Loch Lomond. In 1773 Samuel Johnson visited, also on his way to the Highlands, although he would pass over Edinburgh as 'too well known to admit description' in his *Journey to the Western Islands of Scotland* (1775). Undeterred by the dismissal, Edward Topham, an English Captain of Life-Guards, published impressions from his 1774 and 1775 visits in two volumes of *Letters from Edinburgh*, giving vivid descriptions of the city's social life and customs. The close of the decade was marked by the appearance of Hugo Arnot's *History of Edinburgh* (1779), a work of self-consciously monumental scope, which reports the completion of St Andrew's Square and the rapid progress of building along Princes Street. Arnot devotes less than half his book to the chronicle of past events, from the earliest times to 1778; of more urgent historical import, clearly, is what occupies the rest, a detailed account of the city's 'Progress and present State'.

More subtly and profoundly than any of these writers, Fergusson imagines an Edinburgh on the historical threshold between Old Town and New. This threshold came into retrospective focus during the second epoch of Edinburgh's modernisation, in the decade or so following the Napoleonic wars – the epoch of the 'Modern Athens', Scott's Waverley novels and *Blackwood's Edinburgh Magazine*, solemnised in the 1822 state visit of George IV. Where the first phase of representing Edinburgh had coincided with the founding of the New Town, this second phase marked that project's realisation. By the mid-1820s the city was consolidating its renovation in a series of spectacular public and monumental works. Edinburgh had assumed a form fit for modernity, reclaiming the metropolitan grandeur lost through the succession of Unions.[6] Intensely conscious of their historical situation, Edinburgh intellectuals looked back across the half-century of modernisation – made topographically literal in the view of the Old Town from Princes Street across the chasm of the North Loch. 'The ancient part of EDINBURGH has, within the last fifty years, experienced a vicissitude scarcely credible to the present generation. What were, so late as the year 1775, the mansions of the higher ranks, are, in 1823, the habitations of people in the humblest degrees of life': Robert Chambers opens his *Traditions of Edinburgh* (1824) by noting the opening and closing dates of the era of transformation. He adds, sounding the characteristic note of his epoch: 'The contemplation of this change is at once melancholy and gratifying'.[7]

Traditions of Edinburgh typifies the dominant approach to reading the city over the next century and three quarters: as an antiquarian text. Its principal archive is the Old Town, the former habitat of an ancient, 'organic' social world, characterised by a vertically stratified mixture of ranks (gentry, professionals and tradesmen dwelling in the same buildings, but on different floors) and a wealth of eccentric types (preserved, like images of a vanishing fauna, in John Kay's *Edinburgh Portraits*). That world is now hastening to extinction. The city's horizontal extension has torn it in two, so that the North Loch marks a modern alienation of the classes – the quality have migrated to the terraces and squares of the New Town, and 'Auld Reikie' decays into a slum. A proto-Victorian middle-class sensibility, itself a product of this modernisation, expresses the major theme for imagining early-modern Edinburgh: its sociability. Nostalgia for lost couthy ways is mingled with a polite disgust at their excesses. The figures of Old Town conviviality range from David Hume dispelling 'philosophical melancholy' in a game of backgammon, through well-born ladies dancing reels in oyster-cellars, to the drunken, brawling, puking mob of Fergusson's urban eclogues. Merchants, advocates, even judges, themselves in a permanent state of inebriation, transact their business in the same howffs fre-quented by their clerks (of whom Fergusson was one) and less re-spectable types, not so far down the scale to bullies and whores. The organic character of this social life, in short, gives it its disgraceful as well as its alluring charge.[8]

Fergusson's poems, replete with the colourful ethnography of Old Town life – City Guard, ten o' clock drum, Cape Club, trusty cadies, chamberpots emptied out of windows, and the rest – form a significant portion of the archive of Chambers's Edinburgh. The poet himself makes a symptomatic appearance, in a discussion of 'Auld Reikie':

> In apostrophising the capital of Scotland, we might have expected some allusion to its romantic history or picturesque localities, such as that of Burns, perhaps, in his beautiful 'Address to Edina.' But, instead of this, the first and prominent idea of the poet turns out to be, that Edinburgh is a choice place for drinking and merry-making. It is also remarkable, that, throughout the whole of 'Auld Reekie,' he is perpetually recurring, in the midst of general descriptions, to the subject of tippling. Taverns, clubs, reeling drunkards, and the Town-guard, with whom these gentlemen came so often into contact, are the staple themes of the poem. Wherever he indulges in allusion to other matters, it is only by way of digression. He occasionally, as it were, steps out into the fresh air, to see

'–Morn, wi' bonnie purple smiles,
Kissin' the air-cock o' Saunt Giles;'
but, quickly finding the air a little keen, and taking no interest in
what he sees abroad, he turns again down the close, to his favourite
tavern.[9]

Chambers is obliged to admit that this obsessive 'bacchanalianism'
constitutes 'a faithful picture of the common manners of the period',
however tinged by the poet's 'own propensities and peculiar turn of
mind'. It is left to Burns, a stranger, to produce a polite discourse of
'romantic history or picturesque localities', more amenable to a generation that looks back from the horizon of a completed modernisation
– from the sober precincts of the New Town. Fergusson, personifying its
lethal excesses, lies sunken in the misery and bliss of an extinct way of
life.

Chambers takes many of his cues, including the at once melancholy
and gratified contemplation of progress, from the Waverley novels,
which themselves stock the antiquarian trove of a vanishing Scotland.
Scott's great Edinburgh novel *The Heart of Mid-Lothian* (1818) makes
an early and prominent citation of Fergusson to establish its Old Town
setting. 'The Daft-Days' supplies a motto for the third chapter, which
goes on to quote stanzas from 'Hallow-Fair' and 'The King's Birth-Day
in Edinburgh'. Scott's Fergusson more emphatically represents the city's
public life: 'Poor Fergusson, whose irregularities sometimes led him into
rencontres with [the City Guard], . . . mentions them so often that he
may be termed their poet laureate'.[10] The poet's 'irregularities', in other
words, fit him for the central, mock-heroic rite of those 'occasions when
a holiday licensed some riot and irregularity' – the clash between the
Edinburgh mob and an incompetent police. Unrestrained conviviality
spills over from the taverns onto the public streets, where it signifies
political disorder and misrule.

Yet the main action of *The Heart of Mid-Lothian* takes place nearly
fifteen years before Fergusson was born. Scott detaches Fergusson's
poetry from its own historical moment, the moment of the founding of
the New Town, and pushes it back a generation, in order to embed it
more deeply in the lost world of a pre-modern Edinburgh. The poetry's
complex engagement with an epoch of modernisation sinks out of sight.
Instead, the Romantic account of Fergusson as genius of a cosy but
reprobate Auld Reikie prevailed well into the twentieth century. Sydney
Goodsir Smith approvingly quotes the late-Victorian verdict of W. E.

Henley: 'the old Scots capital, gay, squalid, drunken, lettered, venerable, lives in his verses'.[11] The most recent book-length study of Fergusson reproduces this Romantic account – and gives it historical and ideological substance – through an impressive scholarly development of the theme of Edinburgh as two cities. Situating the poet in a Scots Tory, Episcopalian tradition of classical humanism, R. W. Freeman invokes a scheme of antithetical contrasts – at once Augustan and Augustinian – between 'an ideal, imagined city of the past' and the modern city of 'chaos, dirt, noise, broken communication, luxury, disorder':

> The two cities embody two quite different Scottish cultures: Auld Reikie, the pastoral, civilised, humanist culture; and Edina, the Athens of the north, but more often, Babylon, the counterpastoral, brutal, Whig culture.[12]

Now life-affirming conviviality belongs to the Old Town, while dirt and disorder attend the growth of the New. The antithesis is sustained through powerful readings of, on the one hand, Fergusson's celebration of primordial values of shelter and sociability ('The Daft-Days') and, on the other, the satire of political corruption in the modern Whig city ('Mutual Complaint of Plainstanes and Causey', 'To the Tron-kirk Bell', 'The Election', 'The Ghaists'). Freeman concedes that the poet's relish for 'animal energy' may subvert this ideological opposition; while Fergusson's masterpiece, 'Auld Reikie', reconciles antagonistic principles of energy and order in the traditional humanist scheme of the *concordia discors*. (More of this in a moment.) The concession warns us how readily didactic frameworks can obscure something crucial, the poetry's (and thus the reader's) *enjoyment* of the riot and squalor invoked in 'Leith Races' or 'The King's Birth-Day in Edinburgh'.

It is worth pausing for a moment over the issues involved here: the imaginative sympathy with Dionysian or Blakean outbursts of 'energy', the distinction between cultural categories of disorder and misrule. Disorder means a negation of order; but misrule belongs to a larger, long-durational idea of order which it dialectically confirms. Fergusson's 'brawl' poems identify occasions marked as festivals on the local calendar, and with which their publication in the *Weekly Magazine* coincides: the Daft Days (January), the King's Birthday (June), Leith Races (July), Hallow Fair (November). This calendrical order, binding specificity of place to an immemorial, seasonal temporality, designates the riotous outbreaks as ceremonial, 'carnivalesque', culturally functional and productive. Some of these festivities are ancient, like the saturnalia of 'The Daft-Days', and others relatively new, like the King's Birthday (4 June) – in which the fermentation of popular high spirits proves satirically explosive. The dialectic between order and misrule is written into the traditional Scots genre that Fergusson (following Ramsay) is reactivating, the so-called 'Christ's Kirk on the Green' poem.[13]

Even that view of the matter, though, may impede the rhetorical and cognitive movement of Fergusson's poetry. 'Hallow-Fair', 'Leith Races' and 'The King's Birth-Day' rejoice in misrule for its own sake rather than for its endorsement of some invisible, antithetical cultural order; and their rejoicing is a capacious kind of excitement, with room for bouts of moral and political sermonising as well as glee and fury. To read 'disorder' as 'modern', the antithesis of an ancient (Tory) order, is to impose a premature ideological definition upon the apprehension of modernity in, especially, 'Auld Reikie' – a poem that impressively ignores the Romantic opposition between tradition and modernity. The identification of Fergusson with the Old Town at the expense of the New misses much of the vitality and complexity with which this poetry attends to its historical moment.

Freeman's analysis helps us to interpret a set of critical, linked problems confronted in Fergusson's city poems. What kind of order is represented by the city, which is a man-made world, an artefact? How might a poem, a second-order artefact, represent that order? What constitutes an authentic representation of the city: the impression of a vivid, fleeting scene or moment, or the vision of a totality? – the city as a system, an organism or machine. The dialectic between union and fragmentation, identified by Susan Manning as the predicament of modern Scottish representation, seems written into the challenge of depicting city life.[14] Such poems as 'Hallow-Fair' and 'Leith Races' seem to revel in their fragmentariness, as the condition of the truthful force with which they grasp experience. When, in one of his lesser-known works, Fergusson does attempt the programmatic representation of Edinburgh as a unified system, he resorts, interestingly enough, to English, and to Augustan mock-heroic – in other words, to an 'imperial' rather than a 'national' linguistic and literary formation – and to the satirical logic of counter-pastoral.

'The Bugs' (10 June, 1773) unfolds an ecological fable: urban improvement has caused a reckless deforestation of the surrounding countryside. The 'rude ax, long brandish'd by the hand | Of daring innovation', evicts the local 'Dryads' (146: 29–30). These pastoral nymphs are metamorphosed into swarms of tree-dwelling parasites which invade the city in search of new quarters.[15] Colonising alike 'the rich trappings and the gay attire | Of state luxuriant' and 'the bed | Of toil'd *mechanic*' (147: 47–8, 52–3), the bugs provide a unifying medium for Edinburgh's complex, fragmented society; they reconstitute it as an ecosystem. At the same time, the infestation specifies the separate ranks by assuming a form peculiar to each. Edinburgh is revealed as one in the lowering, antithetical discourse of satire; and this dystopian totality is enunciated in a language drawn from outside the city's speech and life – the language of Union, performing the colonisation it describes. In other poems we find Fergusson practising a virtuosic blend of Scots, English, classical and vernacular languages and genres. Far from being pitched against one another, historically or ideologically, these styles work together, in complex integration, to express a native culture that, entering into dialogue with the English, is fully confident of its traditional integrity and sophistication. 'The Bugs' represents a different mode of unification – that of a formal purification – as won at the dire cost of an antithetical dismemberment, which cuts off the kindly styles of pastoral and vernacular from the language of the city.

II. Edina's Roses

Modern neoclassical convention assigns to the city the 'counter-pastoral' discourse of satire, framing it as a disorder, a realisation of human depravity in the breach of nature. 'The King's Birth-Day in Edinburgh' ends with a mock-heroic *praeteritio* as the Muse turns away in disgust from the excitements of the mob:

> She'll rather to the fields resort,
> Whare music gars the day seem short,
> Whare doggies play, and lambies sport
>   On gowany braes,
> Whare peerless Fancy hads her court,
>   And tunes her lays. (55: 91–6)

Fergusson mocks the logic of pastoral that confects an idyllic countryside out of a distaste for city life. The poem's opening has invoked this namby-pamby Muse as the thoroughly conventional medium of the hired effusions of laureates; the poet has to make her tipsy on whisky before she can sing Edinburgh's raucous enjoyments.

But the Muse, all the same, has deserted the city. If this is a conventional predicament, it is also – for the poet, who deals in convention – a real one. How to entice her back? The opening lines of 'Auld Reikie' suggest a solution:

> O'er lang frae thee the Muse has been
> Sae frisky on the SIMMER'S Green,
> Whan Flowers and Gowans wont to glent
> In bonny Blinks upo' the Bent;
> But now the LEAVES a Yellow die
> Peel'd frae the BRANCHES, quickly fly . . . (109: 7–12)

As the season changes at this northern latitude, the scenery of pastoral withers; the Muse, like everyone else, must move indoors. In a wonderful deepening of the opening stanzas of 'The Daft-Days', the city provides a refuge from winter conditions. Here pastoral values of social mirth may prevail until summer comes round again:

> Thanks to our DADS, whase biggin stands
> A Shelter to surrounding Lands. (109: 21–2)

Fergusson recasts the pre-modern, immemorial city of 'The Daft-Days' in a relation to pastoral of dialectical complementarity, articulated by the cycle of the seasons, rather than of crude negation.

This is all very well; but the promise, or threat, of satire, the discourse fit for the city, remains potent. Fergusson's view of urban conviviality will not avert its eyes from the drunken 'Macaroni', sprawled in the gutter:

> Ah, Legs! in vain the Silk-worm there
> Display'd to view her eidant Care;
> For Stink, instead of Perfumes, grow,
> And clarty Odours fragrant flow. (113: 127–30)

As in 'The Bugs', Fergusson draws on an Augustan rhetoric of antithetical substitution ('Stink, *instead of* Perfumes') and ironical contradiction ('*clarty* Odours *fragrant* flow'). This rhetoric is trained, as in Swift and Pope, on dirt, dirt registered in the primitive, instinctual sense of smell. Dirt, Mary Douglas has taught us, is 'matter out of place'[16] – and as such a specifically urban as well as a satiric concept, the sign of categorical disorder in a man-made world. There is no dirt in the country.

Early in 'Auld Reikie' the ironical epithet 'Edina's Roses' provides for a complex meditation on the question:

> On Stair wi' TUB, or PAT in hand,
> The Barefoot HOUSEMAIDS looe to stand,
> That antrin Fock may ken how SNELL
> Auld Reikie will at MORNING SMELL:
> Then, with an INUNDATION BIG as
> The BURN that 'neath the NORE LOCH BRIG is,
> They kindly shower EDINA'S Roses,
> To QUICKEN and REGALE our NOSES. (110: 33–40)

The stench caused by the emptying of slop-pails into wynds and closes supplied the main satiric topos of Old Town life, remarked by just about every commentator. Fergusson's rhetorical alchemy transmutes even this into a source of civic pride:

> Now some for this, wi' Satyr's Leesh,
> Ha'e gi'en auld Edinburgh a Creesh:
> But without Souring nocht is sweet;
> The Morning smells that hail our Street,
> Prepare, and gently lead the Way
> To Simmer canty, braw and gay:
> Edina's Sons mair eithly share,
> Her Spices and her Dainties rare,
> Then he that's never yet been call'd
> Aff frae his Plaidie or his Fauld. (110: 41–50)

Slyly the poet repudiates satire's lash. In doing so he shifts from a simple kind of irony, based on the logic of antithetical substitution (in which a word signifies its excluded opposite), to a more complex one – an irony which has complexity for its theme. 'But without Souring nocht is sweet': foulness does not negate sweetness, it is a component of it, it achieves it. How? The morning smells prepare and gently lead the way to the pastoral season of summer. They make Edinburgh citizens more fit to inhabit that season – to savour its spices and dainties – than the traditional denizen of pastoral, the shepherd. The contrast between urban refinement and rural dullness draws lightly upon a metropolitan discourse of aestheticised consumption, or 'luxury' ('spices', 'dainties'), and at the same time (anticipating the last lines of the poem), a Presbyterian discourse of election ('never yet been call'd'). The migration from country to town is a type of effectual *calling*, marked by an accession of *taste*. The witty – and 'dirty' – yoking together of such disparate cultural registers instantiates Fergusson's theme: in Edinburgh there's room and time for everything.

Later in the poem, the pastoral season arrives for which Edina's roses have been preparing her citizens:

> Glour up the Street in Simmer morn,
> The Birks sae green, and sweet Brier-thorn,
> Wi' sprangit Flow'rs that scent the Gale,
> Ca' far awa' the Morning Smell,
> Wi' which our Ladies Flow'r-pats fill'd,
> And every noxious Vapour kill'd.
> O Nature! canty, blyth and free,
> Whare is there Keeking-glass like thee? (115: 203–10)

Summer's presence invites the eye beyond the city, to the rural views that Edinburgh's hilly setting affords, and admits sweet scents that banish the noxious morning smell. The epithet 'Flow'r-pats' now reasserts the simpler antithetical mode: while 'Edina's roses' *were* in a sense roses, in that they contained the potential of sweetness (as blossoms spring from dung), these flower-pots are named for what they negate, or, rather, for what negates them. The passage retrospectively reinterprets the earlier one through a logic of purification: Foulness (like suffering) prepares us to enjoy more keenly a sweetness *that will take its place.* The formula smooths over the piquancy of the earlier suggestion – that foul odours can be relished in themselves, as part of the complex bouquet of urban sensations. Just as Fergusson's verse, at its most energised, relishes the city's squalor and chaos for their own sake, rather than for any grander order they might endorse.

With this hint, that a position or formulation achieved at any point in the text may be undone or reconfigured at another, the poem requires us to keep reading. The substitution of sweet smells for foul 'kills' smell altogether; its place is taken by the more exalted sense of sight, which mediates the very tropes of purity. Fergusson turns around – in a sudden reversal of cultural history – a standard metaphor for representation, the mirror held up to nature. Now, for a moment, nature itself is a mirror – a representation:

> Is there on Earth that can compare
> Wi' Mary's Shape, and Mary's Air,
> Save the empurpl'd Speck, that grows
> In the saft Faulds of yonder Rose? (115: 211–14)

The sublime rather than earthly figure of this Mary (all shape and air) ushers back into the poem the 'Rose', likewise transfigured, at once erotic and celestial. Traces of a pre-Reformation spirituality and an 'archaic' (allegorical, typological) model of signification invest the temporal haze of the city's collective mentality: but as a 'structure of feeling', attached to a love-lyric overheard in the street or tavern, rather than as a doctrinal system, a theology or (even) an ideology. This is crucial. Fergusson's verses open a profound insight into the imaginative life of cities, in which large numbers of people of heterogeneous backgrounds and beliefs come to share an accumulated, complex, shifting and uneven subjectivity, compiled from different cultural times and spaces. Ideological unity is as alien to this world as are other modes of purification – sensory or linguistic, for example. Paradoxically, then, it is at this moment of rapture, displaying the topoi of purity, that Fergusson's poem of the city is culturally at its 'dirtiest'.

And so this extraordinary sequence – the afterglow of a metaphysical or Dantesque sensibility, and the extremity of the poem's wit – is succeeded by an abrupt vertical plunge back downward, to note (once more) 'Smells I That buoy up frae markest Cells' (115: 221–2). Stink of offal from underground, more 'unclean' than even a 'Hottentot' could imagine (116: 227–30; even the Hottentot is a figure conjecturally available in the city, thanks to Edinburgh's place in a global empire rather than a 'nation'). The movement of the poem performs, as it so often does, the antithetical substitution it represents, collapsing a mystic-erotic *altitudo* back into the satiric register of low foul stench it had so ardently sublimated. There is, in short, no 'resolution', no synthesis – least of all around Mary and the Rose. The poem swerves off again, this time horizontally, to 'an alter'd Scene' (116: 231), the Sunday recreations of the citizens, where satire and eulogy continue their chop and change.

'Edina's roses' represents, I suggest, a principle of *transition* rather than of resolution or synthesis. Transition – temporal and spatial, sensory and metaphysical, cognitive and rhetorical – is the animating theme as well as scheme of 'Auld Reikie'. In this principle the poem grasps its own historical condition, as it explores (it tastes) the textures and forms of urban experience. Its lines rehearse modes of continuity and discontinuity, juxtaposition, modulation, transformation, contrast and antithesis: the movement across categories and registers, rather than any arrival in one of them, keeps the verse alive. Synthesis features as just one possibility, rather than a master-category that absorbs – and purifies – all the rest. Like them, it remains subject to the sequential form with which the poem imitates secular time and holds our reading.

In the revised ending of 'Auld Reikie', the poet sees the city whole –
when he is outside it:

> Aft frae the *Fifan* coast I've seen,
> Thee tow'ring on thy summit green;
> So glowr the saints when first is given
> A fav'rite keek o' glore and heaven;
> On earth nae mair they bend their ein,
> But quick assume angelic mein;
> So I on *Fife* wad glowr no more,
> But gallop'd to EDINA'S shore. (120: 361–8)

The couplets blend a familiar Scots ('keek o' glore') with literary English
('assume angelic mein') in the wonderful vision of Edinburgh across the
Forth as the City on the Hill, Zion, the New Jerusalem. At last we glimpse,
in Freeman's phrase, the archetype of 'the Scots humanist city . . .
embodying the universal principle of *concordia discors*', glossed as 'the
ancient humanist – later Tory – view of harmony through variety and
opposition'.[17] This figure of a total, apocalyptic order is only visible,
however, from certain angles, when the city is seen from a distance, across
the water. The poet gazes longingly on Edinburgh from Fife, much as the
saints, vouchsafed a glimpse of heaven, avert their eyes from earthly things
and begin to 'assume angelic mein'. Thus Fergusson evokes the temporal
threshold of a final transition – from life to death, from time to eternity –
for the view of Edinburgh in its apocalyptic form. But where the saints step
into eternity, the poet goes the opposite way: hastening back to immerse
himself once more in the dense, squalid, teeming life of the city, in its
complex rhythms of daily and historical and seasonal time.

III. Invisible city

Far from looking back in nostalgia – the moment for that has not come
yet – or fixing the city in a timeless stasis, 'Auld Reikie' is remarkable for
the confidence with which, fully inhabiting its transitional time, it looks
towards the future. Edinburgh may be the old town of 'our DADS,
whase biggin stands | A Shelter to surrounding Lands'; but it is the city's
future, rather than its past, that accommodates a visionary unfolding of
the present:

> While our New City spreads around
> Her bonny Wings on Fairy Ground.

The city is a butterfly, emerging from the chrysalis of the ancient Royalty; and as it spreads its wings it enchants the surrounding fields. The figure of metamorphosis itself performs a reflexive shift of register, from the natural-historical to the magical. The movement reverses the elegiac charge of modern pastoral, according to which the growth of the city has disenchanted the green world. We saw Fergusson put the topos to satirical work in 'The Bugs'. Henry Cockburn provides a famously poignant version in the next century:

> How glorious the prospect, on a summer evening, from Queen Street! We had got into the habit of believing that the mere charm of the ground to us would keep it sacred, and were inclined to keep to our conviction even after we saw the foundations digging. We then thought with despair of our lost verdure, our banished peacefulness, our gorgeous sunsets. But it was unavoidable. We would never have got beyond the North Loch, if these feelings had been conclusive. But how can I forget the glory of that scene! on the still nights on which, with Rutherfurd and Richardson and Jeffrey, I have stood in Queen Street, or the opening at the north-west corner of Charlotte Square, and listened to the ceaseless rural corn-craiks, nestling happily in the dewy grass.[18]

Cockburn looks back, with the requisite blend of gratification and melancholy, at the Moray estate developments north of Charlotte Square in the 1820s. The contrast with Fergusson, which could hardly be more striking, marks the difference of their epochs. Fergusson glances across the North Loch at a New Town which is yet – for the last possible moment – imaginary: the site of an uncanny or fantastic threshold of possibility.

The past, to be sure, provides the occasion for Tory nationalist elegy. The poet contemplates a dilapidated Holyrood,

> Lamenting what auld SCOTLAND knew
> Bien Days for ever frae her View;
> O HAMILTON, for shame! the Muse
> Would pay to thee her couthy Vows,
> Gin ye wad tent the humble Strain
> And gie's our Dignity again:
> For O, waes me! the Thistle springs
> In DOMICILE of ancient Kings,
> Without a Patriot to regrete
> Our PALACE, and our ancient STATE. (117: 275–84)

The ruined palace supplied a Jacobite topos, while complaints about the Duke of Hamilton's neglect of the property were standard.[19] The lack of a patriot who will care for Scotland's past and restore, if only symbolically, its lost national dignity is answered, however, by the appearance of a patriot who provides instead for Edinburgh's future. While Fergusson is ready to indulge in Jacobite melancholy, as part of the repertoire of sentiments and sensations available in the city, he is also ready to drop it for a very different kind of patriotic utterance.

'Auld Reikie' hails George Drummond, six times Lord Provost of Edinburgh (1725–7, 1746–8, 1750–2, 1758–60, 1762–4), as the presiding genius of the city's transformation: 'wale o' Men' for this 'wale o' ilka Town | That SCOTLAND kens beneath the Moon'. Fergusson praises Drummond for charitable institutions such as the Royal Infirmary, founded during his first term of office. This was part of a greater achievement. A. J. Youngson, calling Drummond 'the most influential citizen of Edinburgh in the eighteenth century', gives him full credit for the New Town development, largely realised after his death.[20] In the later addition to 'Auld Reikie', Fergusson denounces Drummond's corrupt successors on the Town Council for neglecting his 'sacred' legacy.[21] Freeman points out that Drummond's disinterested civic patriotism, which sometimes brought him into opposition with his fellow magistrates, made him something of a hero to Tory commentators.[22] Yet Drummond was also the city's foremost opponent of Jacobitism, having raised volunteers to defend Edinburgh in 1715 and 1745 and gone out himself to the fields of Sherrifmuir and Prestonpans. David Daiches sums up his political character as 'an enlightened Whig anti-Jacobite who did not look back to Edinburgh's violent independent past but forward to its great British future'.[23] One of Drummond's contemporaries recalled a conversation with him as the two stood gazing across the North Loch from the Old Town in the early 1760s. The passage forms a kind of chronological book-end with Cockburn's reminiscence of the rural corn-crakes:

> 'Look at these fields', said Provost Drummond; 'you, Mr Somerville, are a young man, and may probably live, although I will not, to see all these fields covered with houses, forming a splendid and magnificent city. To the accomplishment of this, nothing more is necessary than draining the North Loch, and providing a proper access from the old town. I have never lost sight of this object since the year 1725, when I was first elected Provost.'[24]

Provost Drummond, like the poet, creates imaginary cities that make real ones possible. But where 'fields covered with houses' fill Drummond's vision, Fergusson's is filled – now that the plans have been drawn, ground broken, lots put on sale – with their transitory and pregnant emptiness.

Drummond died in 1766, one year before the approval of Craig's plans. He lived to oversee the drainage of the North Loch, which began in 1759, and in 1763 he laid the foundation stone for a bridge across it. The North Loch Bridge, specified in Fergusson's early lines on 'Edina's roses', would be Drummond's chief monument – leading to a New Town that did not exist yet:

> The spacious *Brig* neglected lies,
> Tho' plagu'd wi' pamphlets, dunn'd wi' cries;
> They [Drummond's successors] heed not tho' destruction come
> To gulp us in her gaunting womb. (119: 333–36)

Fergusson refers to the scandal ensuing from the bridge's partial collapse in 1769. William Mylne, the contractor, had founded the south abutment on what turned out to be a mass of loose earth and rubbish dumped there from earlier construction up on the High Street. On 3 August part of the vaults and side-walls gave way, burying five people. Arnot blames the disaster on the 'wonderful infatuation' of the city magistrates, who refused to appoint an overseer to superintend the work.[25] Although the bridge was repaired and opened to traffic in 1772, it had grown ominous to the Edinburgh citizens. One of them wrote to the *Weekly Magazine* (6 May 1773) complaining of the Town Council's continuing neglect of 'our new bridge, which indeed is a great ornament to this city, but, in its present situation, is the means of exposing many of its inhabitants to imminent danger. [. . .] The sinking of the pavement, the large rents, cracks, and departure of the side walls from off the streight line, are evident to every one who has an eye in his head'.[26] '[S]o great was the fear it occasioned amongst all ranks of people', reports Edward Topham, 'that many of them look upon it with terror even to this day, and make it an objection to residing in the New Town, that they must necessarily pass over it.'[27] Not without relish, he tells the story of an elderly lady nearly blown over the side by winds gusting along the North Loch.

Such 'cries' cast the Bridge as edifice of a ruinous and fatal modernity, leading nowhere but a vacant, windblown heath – a counterpart to the decaying Holyrood Palace. But Fergusson's poem refuses this Gothic characterisation. His apocalyptic figure of destruction – the drained North Loch become a 'gaunting womb' – threatens not the Bridge itself but those who undermine the project of modernisation it represents: the birth of a new city. 'The spacious *Brig* neglected lies': the line evokes a habitable grandeur, waiting to be filled, to be used. Fergusson's bridge, opening onto the uncanny ground of the future, is no bad emblem of the historical moment that his poem occupies, and makes its theme.

Notes

1. Sydney Goodsir Smith, ed., *Robert Fergusson 1750–1774* (Edinburgh: Nelson, 1952), p. 12.
2. Alasdair Gray, *Lanark: A Life in Four Books* (London: Granada, 1982), p. 243. A decade after Fergusson's death, in his verse-epistle 'To William Simpson' (1785), Robert Burns complained that poetic neglect of his native district had left it a *terra incognita*:

   > Nae Poet thought her worth his while,
   > To set her name in measur'd style;
   > She lay like some unkend-of isle
   >   Beside New Holland,
   > Or whare wild-meeting oceans boil
   >   Besouth Magellan.

   Whereas 'Ramsay an' famous Ferguson | Gied Forth and Tay a lift aboon', setting those rivers in the world-historical company of 'Illissus, Tiber, Thames and Seine'. (Burns is referring to Fergusson's eulogy of the Tweed in 'Hame Content', ll. 75–92).
3. J. S., 'To Mr Robert Fergusson', *Weekly Magazine, or Edinburgh Amusement*, XVII (3 September 1772), 305–6; F. J. Guion, 'The Muses' Choice', *Weekly Magazine*, XVIII (22 October 1772), 214. See John W. Oliver, 'Fergusson and "Ruddiman's Magazine"', in Smith, ed., *Robert Fergusson 1750–1774*, pp. 84–98.
4. 'Auld Reikie', in *The Poems of Robert Fergusson*, ed. Matthew P. McDiarmid (2 vols; Edinburgh: Blackwood, 1956), II, 119, ll. 325–28. Future citations to volume II of this edition will be given in the text.
5. *Weekly Magazine*, XV (9 January 1772), 139.
6. See Ian Duncan, 'Edinburgh, Capital of the Nineteenth Century', in *Romantic Metropolis: Cultural Productions of the City, 1770–1850*, ed. James Chandler and Kevin Gilmartin (Cambridge: Cambridge University Press; forthcoming).
7. Robert Chambers, *Traditions of Edinburgh* (2 vols.; Edinburgh: W. & C. Tait, 1825), I, 1.
8. For this view of Old Town conviviality, see, in addition to Chambers's *Traditions of Edinburgh*, Walter Scott, *The Provincial Antiquities and*

Picturesque Scenery of Scotland (1819); Henry Cockburn, *Memorials of his Time* (1856); Edward Ramsay, *Reminiscences of Scottish Life and Character* (1858). The catalogue of Old-Town topoi in Alexander Smith's poem 'Edinburgh' (1857) demonstrates how far they had settled into a conventional repertoire by the mid-nineteenth century.

9. Chambers, *Traditions of Edinburgh*, II, 239–40.

10. Sir Walter Scott, *The Heart of Mid-Lothian*, ed. Tony Inglis (Harmondsworth: Penguin, 1994), pp. 32–33.

11. Smith, *Robert Fergusson*, p. 48; quoting W. E. Henley, *Robert Burns: Life, Genius, Achievement* (1898).

12. R. W. Freeman, *Robert Fergusson and the Scots Humanist Compromise* (Edinburgh: Edinburgh University Press, 1984), p. 179. There is an uncharacteristic note of anachronism here: the nickname 'Modern Athens' did not become current until the second, Romantic epoch of the New Town. Historically acute criticism of Fergusson can also be found in David Daiches, *Robert Fergusson* (Edinburgh: Scottish Academic Press, 1982). For a detailed account of eighteenth-century Jacobite traditions, assimilating this view of Fergusson, see Murray G. H. Pittock, *Poetry and Jacobite Politics in Eighteenth-Century Britain and Ireland* (Cambridge: Cambridge University Press, 1994), esp. pp. 132–62.

13. See Allan H. MacLaine, ed., *The Christis Kirk Tradition: Scots Poems of Folk Festivity* (Glasgow: Association for Scottish Literary Studies, 1996), 'Selected Bibliography', pp. 209–13.

14. See Susan Manning, *Fragments of Union: Making Connections in Scottish and American Writing* (Basingstoke: Palgrave, 2002).

15. McDiarmid suggests that the poem is based on the deforestation of the Burghmuir after 1508 and the Edinburgh plague of 1513, as reported in William Maitland's *History of Edinburgh* (Edinburgh, 1753); if this is so, Fergusson decisively obliterates a historical setting in the ominous era of Flodden. In any case the application to contemporary 'innovation' and lavish building is unmistakeable. (*Poems of Robert Fergusson*, II, p. 289.)

16. Mary Douglas, *Purity and Danger: An Analysis of Concepts of Pollution and Taboo* (New York: Praeger, 1966).

17. Freeman, *Robert Fergusson and the Scots Humanist Compromise*, p. 191.

18. Henry Cockburn, *Memorials of his Time*, ed. Karl Miller (Chicago: Univ. Chicago Press, 1974), p. 377.

19. See Freeman, *Robert Fergusson and the Scots Humanist Compromise*, pp. 205–7; Hugo Arnot, *History of Edinburgh* (1779; repr. Edinburgh: West Port Books, 1998), pp. 178–9.

20. A. J. Youngson, *The Making of Classical Edinburgh* (Edinburgh: Edinburgh University Press, 1966), p. 15.

21. On this corruption and neglect, see Arnot, *History of Edinburgh*, pp. 182–5.

22. Freeman, *Robert Fergusson and the Scots Humanist Compromise*, p. 209.

23. David Daiches, *Edinburgh* (London: Hamish Hamilton, 1978), p. 125.

24. Thomas Somerville, *My Own Life and Times, 1741–1814* (Edinburgh,

1861), pp. 47–8; quoted in Youngson, *The Making of Classical Edinburgh*, p. 17.

25. Arnot, *History of Edinburgh*, p. 182.
26. 'An Inhabitant of Edinburgh', *Weekly Magazine*, XX (6 May 1773), 168–9.
27. Edward Topham, *Letters from Edinburgh; Written in the Years 1774 and 1775, Containing some Observations of the Diversions, Customs, Manners, and Laws of the Scotch Nation* (2 vols; Dublin: Watson, Chamberlaine, etc., 1775), I, 26–7.

AT ROBERT FERGUSSON'S GRAVE

March 2000

A bleary chiel, monger o targes and dirks
redds his windae. Neist Holyrood Kirk

a shop chock fu o fudge. Taxis
judder on the setts. Naething mixter-

maxter here; some douce sea-maws
tak these white-washed wa's for a new Bass Rock;

a kiltie tour-guide on an open top bus
intones 'Mary, Queen of Scots . . .'

to a wheen toorie-hattit tourists,
huddlt and snell. The wan sun sclims

up stanes, tenements, turrets, crags,
to draw the chill fi the city's banes.

*

I' the kirkyaird, doos flap an rise
amang the tombs. Did these wierd

carved cherabim cam fleucherin
roon you, in your mad room? See –

a dosser's blanket, drapt in a mausoleum
– we live and dee, and while leeving,

heap stane on stane. Ootbye,
cranes turn, navvies big wir pairliament,

a birth in stane. And when we're deid
they gie us – stane, like this:

85

a 'simple stone', whaur all Scotia
'Should pour her sorrow o'er her poet's dust.'

*

Whit's wrang wi dust? I've no min' here
to flyte wi Burns, but staunin

under the Calton Hill, Embro's 'disgrace',
amang these smeekit monuments,

I'm thinking – poets are dust, or should be,
– free tae blaw a' tapsalteerie

aboot this brave, clean-swepit Canongate.
– Let dust be your memorial, not stane

then maybe Scotia' grund-doon specks
and mites could fin in your name

a champion; a constant irritant, alive.
– So when the wind pipes up a reel

and lowly grit affronts the eye
or marks the cloth of oor weel-cut macaronies,

politicos, hacks and hoors,
let them a' tak tent –

o the poet, Fergusson,
oor brilliant mote, oor breengin stoor.

Kathleen Jamie

Robert Fergusson and Eighteenth-Century Poetry

SUSAN MANNING

In December 1774 the London *Monthly Review: Or Literary Journal* picked up *Poems by Robert Fergusson* (1773). Its notice read, in full,

> Mr. Fergusson's muse appears in the different characters of a Lady of Quality and a Scotch Moggy. In the former she is sometimes tolerably graceful; as in stanzas against repining at Fortune, for instance:-

> Can he, who with the tide of Fortune sails,
>   More pleasure from the sweets of Nature share?
> Do zephyrs waft him more ambrosial gales,
>   Or do his groves a gayer livery wear?

> To me the heavens unveil as pure a sky;
>   To me the flowers as rich a bloom disclose;
> The morning beams as radiant to mine eye;
>   And darkness guides me to as sweet repose.

> But take her upon the whole, and she is more in nature when she is *lilting o'er the Lea.*[1]

Journalism accomplished its brief efficiently, and without expending much critical effort. The *Review*'s readers would have known what to look out for: a new poet from the provinces, competent in English, but truly at home in his native Doric idiom. In 1774 this was a safely familiar and conventional designation for such a volume. The 'revival of vernacular Scottish Poetry' was well underway, Allan Ramsay's *The Tea-Table Miscellany* (1724 - 37) and *The Ever Green* (1724) having been succeeded by more recent poems in Scots by Alexander Nicoll, Alexander Ross, John Skinner and others.[2] Fergusson may well have written the best Scots vernacular in the 1770s, but he was by no means the only poet experimenting with the possibilities of the idiom: poets adopted, augmented and absorbed elements from folk literature collected by antiquarian editors, and responded to renewed interest in the linguistic and political dimensions of idiomatic forms. Fergusson was impeccably up to the moment as much as he was rebelliously Scots or anti-Unionist in adopting the idiom. The acceptability of this 'vernacular revival' (which also comprehended collections of ancient ballads and Scots songs by Percy, Herd, and Pinkerton, and might more properly be described as the restoration of the Scots element to the Anglo-Scots dialectical balance, following the seventeenth-century trend towards anglicisation) was premised on its products having either primarily antiquarian or predominantly local reference. Either way, the 'Scots Moggy' was a primitive: she might speak charmingly from the heart, with the 'voice of Nature', but she did not aspire to engage actively with the sophisticated aesthetic of post-Union Britain.

Variations on this view have prevailed in subsequent accounts of Fergusson's poetry, which uniformly assume an absolute distinction between the sterile competence in English and the 'discovery' of a 'natural' Scots idiom. Through successive phases of his biographical and literary reputation three interwoven strands have entangled the body of poetry with the cultural work to which the life of the poet has been put. James Robertson, his most recent editor, begins his introduction to a selection of the poetry, 'There is no escaping the tragedy of Robert Fergusson'.[3] This story, entangled with the poet's equally tragic 'last moment' discovery of his true poetic vocation in Scots, has itself become a near-inescapable starting point for critical evaluation. I want to suggest that the 'tragedy of Robert Fergusson' is a creation of the cultural politics of sentiment which has had the – sometimes intentional, more often inadvertent – effect of diminishing the ambitiousness of the *oeuvre*; its re-assessment on different grounds is heavily overdue.

First, the story: Fergusson is an exemplary eighteenth-century poet in a certain tragic mode. Like Christopher Smart, he suffered manic delusions and depression, and died penniless in confinement (Fergusson in 1774, Smart three years earlier). Like Smart, too, and like their contemporary William Cowper, his delusions had a strongly religious cast; both Cowper and Fergusson seem to have suffered phases of Calvinist despair in which they feared damnation; both expressed their fears in verse paraphrases of the Old Testament. Like Thomas Chatterton, another contemporary, Fergusson died tragically young; though he survived twenty-four years, to Chatterton's seventeen, the published output of both is slender to a similarly poignant extent, and similarly full of unfulfilled promise. William Collins, in particular, who wrote what Roger Lonsdale has described as 'a poetry of excited aspiration rather than of final achievement' and all of whose poetic output belongs to his teens and twenties, seems a close compeer of Fergusson.[4] Another version aligned Fergusson with Burns, his fellow Scot: impoverished, misunderstood and unappreciated by the North British Establishment whose esteem he craved. Burns's own Fergusson was the product of his suspicion and distrust of the real extent of the benevolence of the literati who hailed his *Poems in the Scottish Dialect* as the work of a 'Heaven-taught Ploughman' and induced his removal to Edinburgh on the promise of patronage and preferment:

> O *Fergus[s]on!* thy glorious *parts,*
> Ill-suited *law*'s dry, musty arts!
> My curse upon your whunstane hearts,
>   Ye Enbrugh gentry!
> The tythe o' what ye waste at *cartes*
>   Wad stow'd his pantry![5]

In disappointment, so the story went, both took solace in drink and dissipation, thereby, apparently, hastening untimely and sordid ends:

> Fergus[s]on, dissipated and drunken, died in early life, after having produced poems faithfully and humorously describing scenes of Edinburgh of festivity and somewhat of blackguardism . . .
> [Burns's] great admiration of Fergus[s]on shewd his propensity to coarse dissipation.[6]

The 'Enbrugh gentry's' mad, dissipated Fergusson said less about the poet than about their anxiety over the negation of the promise of Moderatism and Enlightenment which seemed manifest in the resolutely unreconstructed world of his poetry. The tragedy could be intensified (and safely distanced) by a moralising gloss that located an explanation in the poet's dissipation: this 'reminiscence' of forty-odd years' distance is coloured not only by the intervention of Fergusson's satirical 'The Sow of Feeling' (an extempore extravaganza on the Epilogue to Mackenzie's sentimental drama *The Prince of Tunis*), but by a series of biographies that had appeared in the interim, including David Irving's 1801 portrayal of Fergusson's death as hastened by drink and debauchery, and Alexander Peterkin's dark hint in 1807 that syphilis was the cause of the poet's madness. It is worth noting, too, that the pejorative eighteenth-century implications of 'Moggy' were primarily class-based.

Like Keats (to continue the Romantic parallel of tragic genius),

Fergusson enjoyed an *annus mirabilis* of mature poetic productivity that seemed to herald future greatness; in both cases, this flowering was abruptly truncated by illness and death. Visual representations have had an eerie tendency to suggest that Fergusson somehow became increasingly like Keats after his death, with exaggeratedly intense and soulful features capitalising on the premonition of premature extinction. A portrait supposed to have been by Alexander Runciman was exhibited at the Scottish National Portrait Gallery in 1897 from the collection of Sir Henry Raeburn's granddaughter; though perhaps of later provenance, another 'Ruciman' portrait was exhibited as a contemporary likeness by the Gallery in 2000, featured in the poster of the City of Edinburgh's 250th anniversary exhibition, and appears on this book's cover.[7]

A second phase of Fergusson's posthumous reputation was prompted by the cultural nationalism of the Scots modernists, who read Fergusson as a 'true' Scots poet, possessed of an idiom purer, less parochial and folksy than Burns, an anti-Enlightenment figure whose poetic roots lay at once in Scots folksong tradition and in the sophisticated Scoto-Latin forms of the Makars. Celebrant of the city streets and the multifarious, anarchic, amoral life they supported, this Fergusson was the preserver of 'the old Scottish organic community', or, in F.W. Freeman's terms, Scots classical humanism.[8] The oppressors in this story were the cultural forces of gentility and anglicisation which seduced the young genius into wasting his talent on derivative English verses, and failed – as Establishment always fails – to recognise the true voice of national expression. Only his Scots poems matter; the English verse is nugatory apprentice-work which became redundant on his discovery of a 'true' poetic vocation as Scotland's great urban poet. In this reading, as in the mythography of Chatterton's medievalising Rowley poems, neo-Augustan conventions represented cultural oppression, against whose decorum a challenging idiom from the provinces interjected its rejuvenating poetic idiosyncrasy. 'In Scots,' as John Speirs put it, 'Fergusson is a poet of genius; in English he fails to be a poet at all.'[9] This phase of Fergusson-reading was focused by the bicentenary of his birth in 1950, and responsible for what until now has remained the only volume of essays on his work, edited by Sydney Goodsir Smith and containing pieces by Hugh MacDiarmid, Douglas Young, John Speirs, William Montgomerie and others, as well as Robert Garioch's distinguished poetic tribute to Fergusson. The bicentenary also produced, a little later, Matthew McDiarmid's authoritative two-volume Scottish Text Society edition of the poetry.

The linguistic nationalism impelling these readings implicitly consigned Fergusson's work to a prophetic and proleptic position in a teleological story following the hints thrown out by Allan Ramsay and leading to the glorious flowering of Burns. Each is the saviour, incomplete, imperfect, tragically abbreviated (in the case of Fergusson and Burns), of a moribund linguistic tradition which their genius resuscitated for a new generation. Anticipating his own early death, R.L. Stevenson would later cause his name to be inscribed on the symbolic shared gravestone of the 'three Rabs' in Canongate kirkyard in Edinburgh. In the first biographical sketch of the poet, probably by his friend Thomas Ruddiman, Fergusson's poetic achievement and promise clearly belong to the realm of preservation and recuperation rather than innovation or originality: 'Had he enjoyed life and health to a maturer age, it is probable he would have revived our ancient Caledonian Poetry, of late so much neglected or despised'.[10]

The third phase of Fergusson's reputation, though more diffuse, has been continuous with earlier readings. This Fergusson has been in various ways complicated by theory: information about eighteenth-century print culture, gender studies (Edwin Morgan recently, and quite plausibly, proposed a gay Fergusson, in his essay in *Gendering the Nation*), and Bakhtinian or post-colonial approaches.[11] New impulses in Scottish political and cultural nationalism are inclined to construct Fergusson less as a doomed Chattertonian 'marvellous Boy' than as a sophisticated exponent and exploiter of genre and poetic convention – though still, usually, within a nationalistic aesthetic, as a preserver and rejuvenator of community, tradition and Scots idiom.

The history of Fergusson's reception, I would suggest, has been primarily driven by cultural and political agendas which have had an interest in agreeing that Fergusson wrote conventional English poetry in his apprenticeship, and burst into creative Scots idiom in 1772 with the publication of 'The Daft-Days' in Ruddiman's *Weekly Magazine* (where most of his poems first appeared). From the perspective of linguistic nationalism, really nothing in these 'English' poems prepares a reader for the rapid mastery and technical innovation which accompanied Fergusson's shift to Scots in 1772. His contemporary 'Andrew Gray of Whistle-Ha' wrote an appreciative verse-epistle published in the *Weekly Magazine*, based on the fiction that sophisticated Doric idiom was in fact untutored natural utterance:

Ye've English plain enough nae doubt,
And Latin too, but ye do suit
Your lines, to fock that's out about,
   'Mang hills and braes:
This is the thing that gars me shout
   Sae loud your praise.[12]

Well before Wordsworth's Preface to the second edition of *Lyrical Ballads* (1800) derided 'what is usually called poetic diction' and claimed instead 'the real language of men' as the natural idiom of the true poet, critics and readers were constructing the crude equations which we find, still, extraordinarily hard to shake off: 'Augustan diction = artifice = bad;' 'vernacular idiom = naturalness = good'.[13] We have inherited a Burnsian (and subsequently Wordsworthian) model of the Romantic poet – in each case a self-construction designed to obscure the poet's extensive neoclassical reading and rhetorical training. They have been powerful constructions, nonetheless, sanctioned by the comparisons I've suggested, and hard now to circumvent because of the unfamiliarity into which they have cast eighteenth-century conventions of poetic decorum.

What posterity, like the cultural arbiters of their own generations – Mackenzie, Hugh Blair, and their counterparts in the South – has failed or refused to do is to take the poetry of either Burns or Fergusson seriously in terms of the aesthetic to which they themselves subscribed, as serious exercises in contemporary poetics. So the 'ploughman Poet' and the 'mad boy' have become canonical. But though it is hard to dispute, the evidence for the story doesn't quite hang together. For one thing, Fergusson's poetry is not preoccupied with any of the versions of Romantic self-consciousness or melancholy decline. For the most part, on the contrary, it suggests quite a different kind of eighteenth-century poetic persona: a satirist, an urbanite, a member of a literary coterie and frequenter of clubs and coffee houses whose affinities would seem to lie with Pope, Gay and Swift rather than with the lonely delusions of Collins, Cowper and Smart (if we accede to this version of *these* poets). Matthew McDiarmid sensibly warns against reading Fergusson's employment in the Commissary Office 'in the spirit of post-mortem investigation, as if it were a direct cause of the dreadful circumstances in which his life closed'(*Poems*, I, 23). The poet's employment as a copyist may have been drudgery in itself, but as an occupation it did not over-task his energies; it did position him in a densely literary Edinburgh milieu, with plenty of evening leisure for conviviality and writing. The Cape Club (at whose meetings he was an almost daily participant from 1772) included amongst its fellow members Herd the antiquarian and ballad collector, to whom, as 'Knight of the Noble Order of the Cape', Fergusson addressed a song, and the painter Alexander Runciman.[14] This convivial homosocial environment whose detail scholars have recently begun to address was clearly a formative influence in Fergusson's development. Positioning itself in the cultural mainstream of post-Augustan Britain, the Cape Club especially honoured the anniversaries of Shakespeare and James Thomson, and its members entertained a sophisticated awareness of the cultural situation and expressive possibilities of the vernacular.

Taking this as a point of departure, I would like to propose a different model for reading Fergusson's poetic *oeuvre*, one which takes its cues from the poetry rather than the biography, and that does not depend on a primary, and ideologically motivated, separation of his poetry in English and Scots. Fergusson's *poetic* biography tells a different life, one which has very little to do with events and much more to do with vocation and genre. If we need a biographical parallel, Pope provides a better model and analogy than Chatterton, or Smart, or even (one might hazard) Burns. It's a reading that, for all his protestations, would have been perfectly evident to Burns himself, however, and which is indeed signalled in the epitaph he wrote for the tombstone erected at his expense on Fergusson's previously unmarked grave in the Canongate Kirkyard. The inscription on this large, otherwise blank stone might seem a strikingly odd epitaph, from one comic poet skilled in idiomatic mock-elegy to another:

> No sculptur'd Marble here, nor pompous Lay
> No storied Urn, nor animated Bust
> This simple Stone directs pale Scotia's way
> To pour her Sorrows o'er her Poet's Dust

The explanation – and it is also a way into Fergusson's own poetry which does not derive from biographical or nationalistic mythologising of the kind that Burns himself (and perhaps Fergusson *him*self) was wont to indulge – lies in poetic decorum. Quite simply, Burns knew, and commanded, the appropriate public register for poetic epitaph. Despite the element of poetic self-identification which led in 1796 to his re-inscription of two lines of Fergusson's 'Job, Chap. III Paraphrased' in a letter to George Thomson, Burns was clear that if Fergusson was his 'elder brother in Misfortune', he was 'By far my elder Brother in the muse.'[15] That Muse's wardrobe included the costumes of both Lady of Quality and Scotch Moggy – and a few more outfits besides, to be worn as occasion demanded.

Once we discard a crude binary reading of English and Scots diction, the *exemplariness* of Fergusson's poetic progression becomes evident. His poetic education and self-education were textbook stuff in eight-eenth-century terms, as he pursued a rigorous poetic vocation along neoclassical lines sanctioned by Sidney's *Defence of Poetry* and Pope's progression up the hierarchy of genres from pastoral to elegy to satire to tragedy and epic, taking in the loco-descriptive and the Ode. Fergusson's poetic range encompasses fluency, indeed virtuosity, in an impressively wide range of genres, his precosity and mastery perhaps only rivalled by that of Pope (who polished his *Pastorals* between the ages of sixteen and twenty-one). Fergusson received a better formal education than many eighteenth-century poets of more erudite reputation. A fairly rigorous Classical training at the Edinburgh High School, followed by an extension at the Grammar School in Dundee, led to four years at the University of St. Andrews, where he studied advanced Greek and Latin, Mathematics and Logic, and Moral and Natural Philosophy. Such preparation would have made him far more extensively conversant with the branches of humane understanding not only than Ramsay or Burns, but also Pope (who as a Catholic was barred from attending university). According to Alexander Grosart in 1851, Fergusson owned copies of the works of Shakespeare, Beaumont and Fletcher, Milton, Butler, Pope, Shenstone, Gray and Gay, as well as Allan Ramsay and Watson's *Choice Collection*.[16] Quite simply, he knew what he was about. He was ambitious, competitive, and exacting. And he did not design (or anticipate) a premature tragic death:

> Mr Fergusson being one day in company with two of his friends, and the discourse turning on poetry, one of the gentlemen who was a little self-conceited, observed, that he thought there was no difficulty in equalling, if not excelling, Gray's Elegy in a Country Church-yard, or any of Shenstone's pastorals. Upon which Fer-gusson and the other agreed that he should, in the first place, attempt the *pastoral* style; in which, if he succeeded, he should then be allowed to proceed to the *elegiac*, which the gentleman accordingly undertook to perform. Some time after, having produced his performance to Fergusson, our Caledonian bard

began to read it with great attention, till coming to a passage where the author supposed his mistress seated on an island in the middle of a river, and imagined himself to be writing love-sonnets, and throwing them into the stream which, he said, would bear them to his Dulcinea, 'By Jove,' said Fergusson, 'You are mistaken, for a river always throws its filth to the banks.'[17]

Apart from indicating Fergusson's exigent critical sensibilities, and his capacity for a witty put-down, the anecdote reveals the persistent currency of classical poetic apprenticeship in his literary environment. Pastoral was, traditionally, the genre appropriate to a great poet in his noviciate: Virgil, after all, had begun with the short, quasi-dramatic pastoral form of the *Eclogues*, and in the English tradition Edmund Spenser published *The Shepheardes Calendar* as a prelude to *The Faerie Queene*.

The scale of Fergusson's poetic ambition may be measured in another anecdote, of his beginning work while still a student on a full-scale dramatic tragedy:

During the last winter that he resided in St Andrews, our poet had collected materials for a tragedy on the death of Sir William Wallace, and had even completed two acts of the play; but having seen a similar work on the same subjects, he abandoned his design; 'because (said he to a friend) whatever I publish shall be original, and this tragedy might be considered a copy.'[18]

His early aspirations to poetic eminence appear to have led to a precocious experiment in the 'high' genre of tragedy and epic as well as the more usual apprenticeship modes of pastoral and eclogue. Despite his indigent and markedly unpromising personal circumstances, he showed notable reluctance to train for or follow any profession, and seems to have harboured unrealistic aspirations for a sinecure; from the beginning, it would seem, poetry was his only calling, exercised daily and with obsessional intensity:

he had not . . . got his copy half finished, when he cried out to his office companion, that a thought had just struck him, which he would instantly put into verse, and carry to Ruddiman's Magazine (on the eve of publication), but that he would instantly return and complete the extract. He immediately scrawled out "Verses on Mr Thomas Lancashire," and ran with them to the press. On his return towards the office, he called at the shop of Mr Sommers,

Print-seller and Glazier . . . where he found the shop-boy reading a poem on Creation. This circumstance furnished him with another topic for versifying, and he wrote a coarse epigram on his friend Sommers. These proceedings occupied him about twenty minutes; and having thus given vent to the effervescence of his fancy, he returned quietly to his drudgery.[19]

So Fergusson's poetic emergence in print in 1771 as a pastoral poet was very much a declaration of intent. Here was someone on the way up. His first published work was the three pastorals, 'Morning, Noon and Night', subsequently perhaps his most reviled poems: 'vapid' and 'tinkling', Matthew McDiarmid calls them (*Poems*, I, 28). Composed in the popular manner of William Shenstone, they were an exercise in taste and harmonious numbers which achieved some recognition in Edinburgh, as examples of the *politesse* and civility to which the city aspired. These allusive and polished pieces in fact assume a highly literate readership; 'Night', for example, draws heavily (and as one might expect) on Milton's 'Il Penseroso' and Pope's reconfiguration of twilight moods in his Ovidian epistle 'Eloisa to Abelard', but the verse also slips in sly allusions for the gratification of an educated reader on the alert: when 'Florellus' refers to 'The grassy meads that smil'd serenely gay' (II, 13), we may hear a light echo of Pope's supremely civilised 'Voiture,' who

> . . . wisely careless, innocently gay,
> Chearful, he play'd the Trifle, Life, away.[20]

And the providential optimism of James Thomson's seasonal cycle is compressed into a quatrain that aligns Fergusson's emergent Anglo-Scots idiom with that of his celebrated near-contemporary (and Cape Club hero):

> At his command the bounteous spring returns;
> Hot summer, raging o'er th' Atlantic burns;
> The yellow autumn crowns our sultry toil;
> And winter's snows prepare the cumb'rous soil. (II, 15)

So Fergusson, appearing in pastoral guise, was establishing his poetical lineage and his credentials, as well as advertising his vocation and the scale of his ambitions. The much-derided 'conventionality' of these poems is in a sense precisely their point, and gestures towards a well-developed (and continuous) tradition of Scots pastoral stretching back to Henrysoun.[21] But even at this stage, ideological blandness was not an option for Fergusson: pastorals have always carried a political charge, and in 'Noon', 'Corydon' laments the national antagonisms that separate him from his beloved:

> There have I oft with gentle *Delia* stray'd,
> Amidst th' embowering solitary shade;
> Before the gods to thwart my wishes strove,
> By blasting every pleasing glimpse of love:
> For Delia wanders o'er the *Anglian* plain,
> Where civil discord and sedition reign.
> There Scotia's sons in odious light appear,
> Tho' we for them have wav'd the hostile spear:
> For them my sire, enwrapp'd in curdled gore,
> Breath'd his last moments on a foreign shore. (II, 9)

Apart from the disconcerting lapse of 'curdled gore' (though it had respectable eighteenth-century antecedents, and was subsequently borrowed by Scott for *The Lay of the Last Minstrel*), this is very accomplished verse. Fergusson's early poems are evidently cognisant of debates which developed from Pope's and Gay's altercations with Ambrose Philips in *The Guardian* (1713) throughout the eighteenth century, about the place of verisimilitude in relation to poetic convention in pastoral form. Ramsay's polemical proclamation of a new Scottish naturalism participated in this larger contemporary development of pastoral theory:

> *The* Morning *rises (in the Poet's Description) as she does in the* Scottish *Horizon. We are not carried to* Greece *or* Italy *for a Shade, a Stream or a Breeze. The* Groves *rise in our own Valleys; the* Rivers *flow from our own Fountains, and the* Winds *blow upon our own Hills. I find not Fault with those Things, as they are in* Greece *or* Italy: *But with a* Northern Poet *for fetching his Materials from these Places, in a Poem, of which his own Country is the Scene; as our* Hymners *to the* Spring *and* Makers *of* Pastorals *frequently do.*[22]

It is notable that (despite their obvious national sympathies and other areas of shared poetic concern) Fergusson and Ramsay were at odds here: Fergusson's *Pastorals* clearly came down on the side of Pope rather than Philips or Ramsay, endorsing an anti-naturalistic aesthetic which acknowledged the Theocritan or Virgilian position that rural simplicity in poetry is always a consciously adopted convention for a sophisticated urban poet. Pope's *Discourse on Pastoral Poetry* (1717) was at once forthright and sly on the nature of the convention: 'If we would copy Nature, it may be useful to take this Idea along with us, that Pastoral is an image of what they call the Golden age. So that we are not to describe our shepherds as shepherds at this day really are, but as they may be conceiv'd then to have been; when the best of men followed the employment' (*Pope*, p. 120). The rejection of the everyday, the assertion of art over the constantly disintegrating processes of nature; the fiction of paradise in a very imperfect world – these were the currency of pastoral. Politically, it allowed for what John Barrell and John Bull have described as the 'mingling of the aristocratic and the plebeian', and it asserted the right of a North Briton to assume the cultural authority of Classical tradition.[23] Pastoral is in a sense the quintessential urban genre, always a product of sophistication and civility. Evoking national feeling in conventional pastoral diction, Fergusson was neither naïve, nor cringingly deferential to 'English' models; Ramsay had set 'Scots' poetic language off on a track towards bucolic rusticity and the kailyard which the younger poet's idiom resisted from the outset.

Fergusson's most substantial pastoral plays off one mode against the other and begins to suggest some of the real possibilities of idiomatic confrontation. The 'Eclogue, to the Memory of Dr. William Wilkie, Late Professor of Natural Philosophy in the University of St. Andrews', first published in the *Weekly Magazine* on 29 October 1772, is a tour de force of convention, mingling the traditional bucolic dialogue of the two shepherds Geordie and Davie with the more instructional Georgic forms recently revived by John Philips's *Cyder* (1708) and John Dyer's *The Fleece* (1757) – clearly an appropriate poetic mode to honour Wilkie's agricultural experiments – with the terms of pastoral elegy perfected in Milton's 'Lycidas':

> Ye saw yoursell how weel his *mailin* thrave,
> Ay better faugh'd an' snodit than the lave;
> Lang had the *thristles* an' the *dockans* been
> In use to wag their taps upo' the green,
> Whare now his bonny riggs delight the view,
> An' thrivin' hedges drink the caller dew. (*Poems*, II, 84)

Its use of the 'Doric' idiom derives from Spenser, but also responds to current debates about the language and decorum of pastoral. And several references to Ramsay's 'Richy and Sandy' cement its affiliations with a more local vernacular project. When Fergusson's 'Scotch Moggy' puts in an appearance, she is quite plainly dressing down. But a return to high diction and the final Virgilian allusion make the conventional association between the lost subject and classical fame, and leave no doubt as to the poem's affiliations:

> Scholars and bards *unheard of yet* shall come,
> And stamp memorials on his grassy tomb,
> Which in yon antient kirk-yard shall remain,
> Fam'd as the urn that hads the MANTUAN *swain.* (*Poems,* II, 85)

The poet's calling is primary in the shaping of the verse. This writing-in of the elegist's own activities as ensuring the future reputation of his subject had recently been elegantly – and outrageously – perfected in Pope's 'Eloisa to Abelard':

> And sure if fate some future Bard shall join
> In sad similitude of griefs to mine,
> Condemn'd whole years in absence to deplore,
> And image charms he must behold no more,
> Such if there be, who love so long, so well;
> Let him our sad, our tender story tell;
> The well-sung woes will sooth my pensive ghost;
> He best can paint 'em, who shall feel 'em most. (*Pope,* p. 261)

The publication of 'The Daft-Days' in the *Weekly Magazine* on 2nd January 1772 came, in McDiarmid's words, 'with the startling effect of a stone breaking the windows of the hot-house and letting in a gust of fresh air', and was followed in rapid succession by the 'Elegy on the Death of Scots Music', 'The King's Birth-Day in Edinburgh', 'Caller Oysters', and 'Braid Claith' (*Poems,* I, 32). One immediate problem with this reading is that Fergusson had written poems in Scots at least back to his days in St. Andrews, and continued to write in English even after the 'breakthrough' of 1772. His poetry never definitively abandoned one poetic register for another. We should be grateful for that; had he merely indulged a fondness for local idiom and traditional metres, and abandoned his rhetorical education and aesthetic training, the poems in Scots would be, at best, antiquarian exercises, 'imitations' of a kind that became the currency of populist vernacular revival. As it is, they employ the full range of genre, of decorum and of idiom available to his contemporaries throughout Britain; adding mastery of vernacular art-speech to these forms, Fergusson expanded their potential, not only for Burns, but for all subsequent Scottish poetry, in Scots or English. Failure to take his poetic choices seriously enough has promoted various inimical and unnecessary 'divisions' in Scottish writing. Since 1807, for instance, collections of his poetry have segregated the poems in Scots from those in English, thereby doing both a disservice, as well as misunderstanding the significance and sophistication of the aesthetic decisions involved in adopting one or the other.

When Fergusson turned to Scots, it was not in any sense to express a 'folk self', or with the shattering *éclat* of a man at last discovering a Keatsian 'true voice of feeling'.[24] Throughout Fergusson's poetry the choice of 'English' or 'Scots' diction is dictated by the demands of poetic decorum: the match, or clash, of subject to style that defines tone and intention. The 'Elegy on the Death of Scots Music', for example, is a sophisticated lament for the loss of simplicity in song; this formal elegy cast in what Burns would call the 'Doric' mode is also a virtuoso performance of a favoured stance of classical satire: the poet speaking as a lone defender of tradition against degeneration. Lament –

> Now foreign sonnets bear the gree,
> And crabbit queer variety
> Of sound fresh sprung frae *Italy*,
>   A bastard breed!
> Unlike that saft-tongu'd melody
>   Which now lies dead –

– prepares the way for exhortation:

> O SCOTLAND! that could yence afford
> To bang the pith of Roman sword,
> Winna your sons, wi' joint accord,
>   To battle speed?
> And fight till MUSIC be restor'd,
>   Which now lies dead. (II, 39)

But Fergusson (a talented singer, whose Cape Club soubriquet was 'Sir Precentor') also composed lyrics for the Italian tenor Tenducci to sing in Thomas Arne's opera *Artaxerxes*.[25] As with Ramsay's (and later Burns's) polemics against 'foreign' music, the positive relationship between Scottish Enlightenment poetry and the complex mix of contemporary European musical taste is obscured by literalising verses which really serve a complex poetic purpose, at least part of which was to align Fergusson, in his reader's minds, with Milton and Dryden, and the 'Scots muse' – semi-ironically – with the gentility of St. Cecilia (in whose honour the concert hall of the Edinburgh Musical Society for which Tenducci sang was named). *The Jolly Beggars* alone makes plain that Burns, too, understood and absorbed the conventions of both oratorio and cantata with sufficient sophistication to employ and explode them in a single gesture.[26]

Further, few of Fergusson's poems employ one register to the exclusion of the other. 'The Daft-Days' is not a vernacular poem, but an impeccably neo-classical set piece whose formulae are lent a mock-heroic edge by macaronic juxtaposition. The opening gestures immediately towards a compound poetic backdrop that does not differentiate along national lines:

> Now mirk December's dowie face
> Glours our the rigs wi' sour grimace,
> While, thro' his *minimum* of space,
> > The bleer-ey'd sun
> Wi' blinkin light and stealing pace,
> > His race doth run.
>
> From naked groves nae birdie sings,
> To shepherd's pipe nae hillock rings,
> The breeze nae od'rous flavour brings
> > From *Borean* cave,
> And dwyning nature droops her wings,
> > Wi' visage grave. (II, 32 - 33)

The Anglo-Latinic macaronics of both Drummond of Hawthornden and Swift sound through these lines; but Thomson's 'Winter', Pope's Pastorals, and Milton's elegy are also fully present, and Ramsay's *Gentle Shepherd* echoes through the second stanza. The verse derives enormous energy in crossing between Scots and English diction, exploiting idiomatic mismatches and gaps in understanding. As well as projecting a bravura linguistic display, this inflects new cultural and political sharpness into traditional divisions between 'high' and 'low' diction. Having established genre and association, and retained his poetic independence in the idiomatic leaps and twists, Fergusson modulates the diction towards broader Scots as the poem homes in to locality:

> *Auld Reikie!* thou'rt the canty hole,
> A bield for mony caldrife soul . . .

Loco-descriptive formulae validate direct address and personification of the city, in the manner of 'London!', 'Sweet Thames', and so on. Here too the poem places its concerns alongside such earlier urban pastoral as Gay's *Trivia*, and Swift's relocation of the classical eclogue: 'A Town Eclogue. 1710. Scene. The Royal Exchange', or 'A City Shower' (a clear antecedent of Fergusson's unfinished masterpiece 'Auld Reikie').

His experiments in the comic octosyllabics of 'A Tale' (*Poems*, II, 64 - 65) bear fruit almost immediately in the Swiftian epigram: '*On seeing a* LADY *paint herself*':

> When, by some misadventure cross'd,
> The banker hath his fortune lost,
> *Credit* his instant need supplies,
> And for a moment blinds our eyes:
> So *Delia*, when her beauty's flown,
> Trades on a bottom not her own,
> And labours to escape detection,
> By putting on a false complexion. (*Poems*, II, 74)

This little *jeu d'esprit* typifies the opportunistic miscellaneity of the *oeuvre*, as well as Fergusson's impressive poetic facility. To read his poetry for sustained themes or messages would imply an ideologically motivated coherence not supported by the dazzlingly various mastery of the verse. The purposive drive of Fergusson's poetry resides in the area of poetic vocation rather than consistency of subject matter; his ambition is clear in the projects embarked on and never brought to completion: *Wallace*, for example, or (more solidly) *Auld Reikie*, for which only the beginning survives, or his projected translation of Virgil. But in what (if my reading is right) he himself would have designated the period of poetic apprenticeship, Fergusson exercised and expanded his poetic versatility as occasion arose and subjects presented themselves. Debates and correspondence of current interest in the *Weekly Magazine* become opportunities for experiments in genre and diction. 'Braid Claith', for example, was clearly prompted by a series of articles on social pretension in contemporary Edinburgh, and is a fairly light exercise in burlesque satire of a kind that Burns would later employ with real animus, to much more devastating effect. Topical events like the agitation over the Mortmain Bill, on the other hand, prompted the more substantial, and darker, 'The Ghaists: A Kirk-yard Eclogue', where Scots is turned away from comedy and pulls back to the solemnity of Dunbar's 'Lament for the Makaris', sardonic and sinister uncanny voices from the Ballads, and the argumentative edge of the late sixteenth-century 'Flyting betwixt Polwart and Montgomery'. But if these inform its tone and its emotional range, the eclogue form and regular iambic pentameter of the poem and its contemporary vocabulary provoke a tension with Augustan civility that prevents the spectres' protest against change from collapsing into nostalgia for a lost idealised Scottish past:

Whare the braid planes in dowy murmurs wave
Their ancient taps out owre the cald, clad grave,
Whare *Geordie Girdwood*, mony a lang-spun day,
Houkit for gentlest banes the humblest clay,
Twa sheeted ghaists, sae grizly and sae wan,
'Mang lanely tombs their douff discourse began . . .

HERRIOT.
I find, my friend, that ye but little ken,
There's einow on the earth a set o' men,
Wha, if they get their private pouches lin'd,
Gie na a winnelstrae for a' mankind;
They'll sell their country, flae their conscience bare,
To gar the weigh-bauk turn a single hair.
The government need only bait the line
Wi' the prevailing flee, the gowden coin,
Then our executors, and wise trustees,
Will sell them fishes in forbidden seas,
Upo' their dwining country girn in sport,
Laugh in their sleeve, and get a place at court.

WATSON.
'Ere that day come, I'll 'mang our spirits pick
Some ghaist that trokes and conjures wi' Auld Nick,
To gar the wind wi' rougher rumbles blaw,
And weightier thuds than ever mortal saw:
Fire-flaught and hail, wi' tenfald fury's fires,
Shall lay yird-laigh Edina's airy spires:
Tweed shall rin rowtin' down his banks out o'er,
Till Scotland's out o' reach o' England's pow'r;
Upo' the briny Borean jaws to float,
And mourn in dowy saughs her dowy lot. (II, 141; 144–5)

There is nothing 'natural' or homely about the Scots of this poem: its effects require 'Edina's airy spires' and the 'briny Borean jaws' every bit as much as the 'douff discourse' of ghaists 'sae grizly and sae wan'. Different freights of solemnity and portentousness are mutually intensifying in the compound idiom. There are no easy equations to be made between contemporaneity and anglicisation, or tradition and Scots: the opening couplet of the poem announces the inextricable hybridity of a poetic diction that commands the capaciousness of a vernacular able to reach without distinction or apology into courtly, neo-classical and contemporary post-Augustan 'graveyard' forms.

It is part of the profession of an art-poet to conjure poetry from minimal subjects; in this respect Fergusson is exemplary, and triumphantly defiant: the valedictory 'To My Auld Breeks' revels in making something of nearly nothing, in the manner of Swift, or Rochester. Formally, it combines self-mocking valediction with a Horatian verse epistle on the model of Pope's to Dr. Arbuthnot: an old friend is addressed in immediately engaging informal terms:

> Now gae your wa's – Tho' anes as gude
> As ever happit FLESH and BLUDE,
> Yet part we maun – (II, 215)

Fergusson's ear for spoken rhythms fuses the tonal possibilities of both the vernacular 'gae your wa's' (Scott's Meg Merrilees would address Ellangowan in similar style) and Pope's ' "Shut, shut the door, good *John!*" fatigu'd I said.'[27] Auld breeks are old friends; nobody need stand on ceremony here. The meanness of the subject allows for the play of burlesque and makes the vernacular an appropriate idiom; but the subject of parting also invokes elegiac tones, and an opportunity to indulge the classical trope of *memento mori*:

> Or if some bard, in lucky times,
> Shou'd profit meikle by his rhimes,
> And pace awa', wi smirky face,
> In siller or in gowden lace,
> Glowr in his face, like spectre gaunt;
> Remind him o' his former want,
> To cow his daffin and his pleasure,
> And gar him live within the measure. (II, 217)

As in the eclogue to Wilkie, subject finally gives place to the controlling poetic voice ('some bard') in communication with a readership sufficiently attuned to convention to appreciate the perspectival play of artistry. Fergusson's chosen poetic forms are, pre-eminently, conversational and sociable: Epistle, Eclogue, Satire, Elegy, Ballad and song; they are 'public' in an earlier eighteenth-century understanding of the terms of poetic vocation.

It is hardly surprising that Fergusson should have contributed to the revival of the Ode which took place in British poetry from the middle of the century. Both his musical training and ear for poetic number would have rendered this highly formalised verse form accessible and congenial. Odes are poets' poetry: intricate and demanding in form, highly allusive artefacts; the renaissance of the form signals a post-Popean aesthetic which turned away from satire to emphasise the poet's calling. As Thomas Warton put it in the 'Advertisement' to his *Odes on Several Subjects* (1746), 'the fashion of moralising in verse has been carried too far'; the 'right channel' for poetry lay in 'the imagination'.[28] Warton's, Gray's and Collins's experiments had tended to re-orientate the public classical form towards expression of private existential and vocational crisis, while Collins's 'Ode on the Popular Superstitions of the Highlands, considered as the Subject for Poetry' (1749) explored the imaginative possibilities of Scottish 'faery' beyond the reaches of 'English' poetic convention. Literary history notwithstanding, this was not exclusively an 'English' revival; it engaged Anglo-Scots poetic energies with notable intensity, though this dimension has been seriously neglected: Tobias Smollett, for example, wrote an irregular Pindaric 'Ode to Independence', James Beattie produced several, including 'To Peace', with its 'noble savage' motif, and Burns himself experimented with the form in the Pindaric 'Despondency', the Horatian 'Delia. An Ode', and the patriotic 'Bruce to His Men.' The implications of this revival among Scottish poets are tantalising, and hitherto unexplored. The exhortatory and dramatic aspects of the form exude cultural confidence, and demand a high degree of aesthetic literacy from both poet and reader; these are not the products of an impoverished, servile or decaying literary milieu. In such company, Fergusson's Odes 'To Pity' and 'To Hope' are properly, and exquisitely, conventional; nor do they appear less accomplished than Gray's or Collins's more celebrated exercises in the genre:

> Lo! Where the rosy-bosom'd Hours,
> Fair VENUS' train appear,
> Disclose the long-expecting flowers,

And wake the purple year!
The Attic warbler pours her throat,
Responsive to the cuckow's note,
The untaught harmony of spring:
While whisp'ring pleasure as they fly,
Cool Zephyrs thro' the clear blue sky
Their gather'd fragrance fling.[29]

Hope! Lively chearer of the mind,
In lieu of real bliss design'd,
Come from thy ever-verdant bow'r
To chace the dull and ling'ring hour;
O! bring, attending on thy reign,
All thy ideal fairy train,
To animate the lifeless clay,
And bear my sorrows hence away. (*Poems*, II, 77)

The first is from Gray's 'Ode on Spring', the second, Fergusson's 'Ode to Hope'. In this context, the poet's late 'Ode to Horror' should be read not (as it usually has been) as hectic, overstrained and euphuistic posturing, but – in its progression of octosyllabics through Epode, Strophe and Antistrophe – as something more akin to the formal exercises in poetic intricacy that Cowper and Smart set themselves to in their days of melancholy, in the belief that ordered activity has power to soothe a troubled mind:

To ease his sore distemper'd head,
Sometimes upon the rocky bed
Reclin'd he lies, to list the sound
Of whispering reed in vale profound.
Happy if *Morpheus* visits there
A while to lull his woe and care;
Send sweeter fancies to his aid,
And teach him to be undismay'd;
Yet wretched still, for when no more
The gods their opiate balsam pour,
Ah, me! he starts, and views again
The Lybian monster prance along the plain.
Now from the oozing caves he flies,
And to the city's *tumults* hies,
Thinking to frolick life away,

106

> Be ever *chearful,* ever gay:
> But tho' enwrapt in noise and smoke,
> They ne'er can heal his peace when broke;
> His fears arise, he sighs again
> For solitude on rural plain;
> Even there his wishes all conveen
> To bear him to his noise again.
> Thus tortur'd rack'd, and sore opprest,
> He constant hunts, but never finds his rest.
>   ANTISTROPHE.
>   Oh exercise! thou healing power,
> The toiling rustic's chiefest dower;
> Be thou with parent virtue join'd
> To quell the tumults of the mind . . . (*Poems,* II, 227).

This is intricate verse, and the thickness of its allusive texture is immensely sophisticated. 'Il Penseroso' is fundamental to its evocation of mood; Wyatt lurks in the hunting image; as do Gray and Collins in the formal experiment. References to current medical thinking on Spleen or Melancholy – including the prescriptions of Fergusson's countryman Cheyne, whose *The English Malady* (1731) prescribed movement to counteract stasis, and the exercise of public powers – inject contemporary particularity into the abstracted poetic situation. Most subtle and suggestive is the spectrum of echoes from Pope, beginning with 'To Miss Blount, with the Works of Voiture', where the re-working of the couplet lightly traced in Fergusson's early pastoral 'Night' by 'Florellus' takes on in this context a near-desperate edge which makes manifest its implausibility:

> Thinking to frolick life away,
> Be ever chearful, ever gay:
> But . . .

Pope's other 'Miss Blount' epistles, 'On Leaving Town after the Coronation', and 'Epistle to a Lady', play around the verse too, keeping its allusive surface mobile, but the tone is coloured also by the terrible restlessness of Eloisa, and of the caged socialites in 'To a Lady':

> But what are these to great Atossa's mind?
> Scarce once herself, by turns all Womankind!
> Who, with herself, or others, from her birth
> Finds all her life one warfare upon earth (*Pope,* pp. 563 – 4)

The range and precision of the ode's recall of Pope's women in their variously passive plights suggests that the 'Horror' ode has absorbed their complex symbolic shading with unique empathy. The most interesting gendered reading of Fergusson would need little recourse to biography. Public diction and private experience are fused, and turn aside any simple 'application' of the expressed emotions to the poet's own case. But the referential range, much of it lurking like an iceberg within the controlled surface, redeems the 'Ode to Horror' from emotional sterility. This poem alone suggests that Fergusson, like Burns, had the power and versatility to be, if not a great poet in English, certainly a very considerable one.

For all its complexity of implication, the 'Ode to Horror' is not, in any confessional sense of the term, 'personal'. One of the most striking things about Fergusson's poetry is its rejection of egotism: more squarely than Burns's, it claims an earlier eighteenth-century under-standing of the obligations of poetic decorum. Most of this slender *oeuvre* seems directly opposed to the popular Whig 'graveyard school', whose excesses Fergusson mocks in 'The Canongate Play-house in Ruins', 'Rob Fergusson's Last Will', and 'On James Cumming', just to take a few of the more explicit instances. These poems affirm comic vitality against the self-consuming melancholy of productions like Robert Blair's lugubrious 'The Grave'; they set no store by sensibility as the cement of society. In consequence, there is no exploitation of pathos to provoke sympathy for the physical frailty of the poet, his poverty, the hardness of his lot: the evidence of the poetry scarcely lends support to the story of the Romantic doomed youth tragically cut short in his prime.

There is one possible exception to this, the poem whose message Burns applied to himself near the end of his own life in that letter to Thomson. 'Job, Chap. III Paraphrased' appears to have been one of Fergusson's last poems; it was not, like 'Braid Claith' or 'The Ghaists', stimulated by current events or debates, and it is his only surviving Biblical paraphrase and belongs to the period of declining health and religious terror. It would be perverse in this case to side-step the association between choice of subject and the poet's immediate personal circumstances and state of mind. The poem is a dramatic monologue in standard English diction, uttered by Job at the moment when, rendered almost mad by unmerited suffering, he curses the day of his birth. The exercise of poetic paraphrase, like the rhyming pentameter couplets, creates a structure, a container, for the evocation of anguish:

108

Why have I not from *mother's womb* expir'd?
My life resign'd when life was first requir'd?
Why did supporting knees prevent my death,
Or suckling breasts sustain my infant breath?
For now my soul with quiet had been blest,
With kings and counsellors of earth at rest . . .
Or, as untimely birth, I had not been,
Like infant who the light hath never seen;
For there the wicked from their trouble cease,
And there the weary find their lasting peace . . . (II, 229).

The poem inhabits fully a transitional space between (as Paul Fry has put it) 'personal and impersonal voicing', the monologue form allowing for both identification and distance.[30] This most 'personal' of cries is no extempore effusion of release, but an exercise in taut aesthetic control – which is, indeed, the final word of the poem. All the echoes of the earlier imitations are firmly in place: the shadows and gloom of 'Il Penseroso', the formal lament of 'Lycidas' and the elegies, the graveyard sublime of Young's 'Night-Thoughts', the great speeches of Macbeth as he wearies of life beyond pity and mercy. This is a virtuoso performance not only of allusion, but of metrical mastery, and it attains a near-Miltonic stature and solemnity:

Lo! Let the night in solitude's dismay
Be dumb to joy, and waste in gloom away;
On it may twilight stars be never known;
Light let it wish for, Lord! but give it none . . . (II, 229)

Neither the mad, tragic boy, nor the vernacular genius, nor the urbane anti-Unionist composed this poem. Perhaps they all lent their hands to it, but this is the work of a craftsman who had served a disciplined apprenticeship to the forms of British poetry, who (like the compositor of his model, the Book of Job) could choreograph a highly conventionalised poetic diction into a powerful expression of poetic immediacy. Our reading of Fergusson's poetry is immensely impoverished if it does not comprehend his writing in English.

Notes

1. 'Monthly Catalogue. Poetical,' vol li (December 1774).
2. See John Butt, 'The Revival of Scottish Vernacular Poetry in the Eighteenth

Century', in Frederick W. Hilles and Harold Bloom, eds., *From Sensibility to Romanticism* (Oxford: Oxford University Press, 1965), pp. 219 – 38.

3. *Robert Fergusson: Selected Poems* (Edinburgh: Birlinn, 2000), p. 1.

4. 'Introduction', *Thomas Gray and William Collins: Poetical Works* (Oxford: Oxford University Press, 1977), p. xx.

5. 'To W. S****n, Ochiltree', ll. 19 - 24, *Poems and Songs of Robert Burns*, ed. James Kinsley (Oxford: Oxford University Press, 1969), p. 73. Subsequent references to this one-volume edition are incorporated in the text.

6. *The Anecdotes and Egotisms of Henry Mackenzie 1745 - 1831*, ed. H.W. Thompson (London: Oxford University Press, 1927), p. 150.

7. On the earlier 'Runciman' portrait, see Appendix 2: Notes on the Illustrations', in Sydney Goodsir Smith, ed., *Robert Fergusson 1750 – 1774* (London: Nelson, 1952), p. 203f.

8. John Speirs, 'Tradition and Robert Fergusson', in Goodsir Smith, ed., p. 104; *Robert Fergusson and the Scots Humanist Compromise* (Edinburgh: Edinburgh University Press, 1984).

9. Goodsir Smith, ed., p. 99.

10. Preface to 1779 edition of Fergusson's *Poems*, cited by Alexander Law, 'A Note on the Bibliography and "Lives" of Robert Fergusson', in Goodsir Smith, ed., p. 160.

11. See, for example, Christopher Whyte, 'Competing Idylls: Fergusson and Burns', *Scottish Studies Review* 1:1 (Winter 2000), pp. 47 – 62.

12. Quoted in *The Poems of Robert Fergusson*, ed. Matthew McDiarmid, 2 vols. (Edinburgh: Scottish Text Society, 1956), I, p. 43. Subsequent references to this edition are incorporated by volume and page number in the text.

13. Eds. R.L. Brett and A. R. Jones (London: Methuen, 1963; rpt 1971), pp. 251, 241.

14. See Hans Hecht, *Songs From David Herd's Manuscripts* (Edinburgh: William J. Hay, 1904), pp. 48 – 9.

15. *The Letters of Robert Burns*, ed. J. De Lancey Ferguson, 2nd edn, ed. G. Ross Roy, 2 vols. (Oxford: Clarendon Press, 1985), II, p. 378. For Burns's poetic tribute, see *Poems*, p. 258.

16. Goodsir Smith, ed., p. 200.

17. *The Weekly Magazine*, 22 Feb 1776, quoted by McDiarmid, I, p. 29.

18. George Gleig, *Supplement to the Third Edition of the Encyclopaedia Britannica*, I (Edinburgh, 1801), p. 647.

19. [Alexander Peterkin], 'Sketch of the Author's Life', *The Works of Robert Fergusson* (1807), facsimile reprint (Edinburgh: James Thin, 1970), p. 31.

20. *The Poems of Alexander Pope*, ed. John Butt (London: Methuen, 1963; rpt. 1973), p 169. Subsequent references to Pope's poetry are taken from this one-volume reprint of the Twickenham edition and incorporated in the text.

21. For examples of this tradition, see *The Mercat Anthology of Scottish Literature 1375 – 1707*, eds. R.D.S. Jack and P.A.T. Rozendaal (Edinburgh: Mercat Press, 1997; 2000), pp. 373 – 89.

22. Preface to *The Ever Green,* 2 vols. (Edinburgh: Thomas Ruddiman, 1774), I, p. xix.

23. 'Introduction' to *The Penguin Book of English Pastoral Verse* (London: Penguin Books, 1974), p. 7.

24. *The Letters of John Keats,* ed. Maurice Buxton Forman, 4th edn. (Oxford: Oxford University Press, 1952), p. 385 (to John Hamilton Reynolds, 21 September 1819).

25. The songs were 'Braes of Ballenden' (or 'Balandine'), 'Roslin Castle', and 'Lochaber No More'; according to Hans Hecht, the publication of this opera by Herd's printers Martin and Wotherspoon in 1769 was the first appearance of Fergusson's name in print. See Hecht, ed., *Songs from David Herd's Manuscripts,* p. 45.

26. R.D.S. Jack points out that the bardic voice of *The Jolly Beggars* condemns artifice and Castalian pedantry, yet the narrator opens the poem in the virtuosic Heliconian stanza employed by the late 16th-century Castalian poets. I am grateful to Professor Jack for his comments on an earlier version of this chapter.

27. *Guy Mannering* (1815), ed. P.D. Garside (Edinburgh: Edinburgh University Press, 1999), p. 44; Pope, *Poems,* p. 597 ('An Epistle from Mr. Pope to Dr. Arbuthnot').

28. Quoted by Roger Lonsdale, Introduction to *Thomas Gray and William Collins,* p. xviii.

29. Thomas Gray, 'Ode to Spring', *Ibid,* p. 18.

30. *The Poet's Calling in the English Ode* (New Haven and London: Yale University Press, 1980), p. 101.

FOUR VARIANTS OF 'CALLER WATER'

> *A caller burn o' siller sheen,*
> *Ran cannily out o'er the green,*
> *And whan our gutcher's drouth had been*
>   *To bide right sair,*
> *He loutit down and drank bedeen*
>   *A dainty skair.*
>
>   *Robert Fergusson, 'Caller Water'*

I

If I remember anything at all
of how we spent this winter, I'll recall

the afternoon we found a woodland spring
of caller water; how, as we drove home,

the scent of it still lingered on your hair
and, like a distant music, I could hear

the burn's slow purl. It's what we listen for
that makes us who we are: snow on the air

above a hill-town; strays out on the rim
of ditch, or marsh; the silence of a room

the dead have not abandoned; this bright spill
of silver, or a whisper from the well

where blackness pools and gathers in the soil.
It's what we listen for that makes us whole:

the keenest ear finds order in a stone,
perfection in a wisp of nerve and bone,

a resurrection in each stream of clear
cold water - 'caller burn, beyond compare'.

We listen to retrieve the souls we are
from meek adjustment; and to know our power:

though nobody steps twice into the same
quick stream, we are more innocent of time

than we believe: as water graces all,
we dwell in grace, untainted by the Fall.

II

Whan first we walked the banks o' Eden,
We man hae wyt that we hae hidden
Deep in the bludstream, far in the brain,
    A froglike saul,
For we are animate, and in this frame
    A' life is haill.

Yence water must hae been our dwelling,
Siller and clean, through green yird welling
Up frae its origin and swelling
    Reed-bed and strand,
Or drawn into the air and falling
    Back to the land;

But now we manufacture poisons;
Tinctures of lead; strains of dioxin;
Cankerous smeek; toxic emissions;
    Lapper'd water;
We scart the land, and scad the oceans,
    Gleg in slaughter.

Yet, though it seems our weird is certain,
Our future sold by slee commissions,
Rookit and lair'd by politicians,
    Nothing is sure:
There's time enough for true physicians,
    To find a cure:

So we'll hae nae sick clitter-clatter,
And briefly to expound the matter,
It shall be ca'd good Caller Water,
   Than whilk, I trow,
Few drogs in doctors' shops are better
   For me or you.

III

> *The words of atonement I pronounce are too inept*
> *to offer me release. Or forgiveness.*
> *What is to be done with the desire for exculpation?*
> > *Barry Lopez: Apologia*

I remember that afternoon
in Oradea: birdsong and sun
and lotus pools, the antique gold
and ice-white of the blossoms pearled
with drops of water where a frog
had crossed the lily pads, its peg
fingers reminiscent of a child's;
and, hidden in the mud's thick folds
we knew there would be spawn, and eggs
and secret animals, all legs
and eyes; or some folkloric eel
out of your mother's ancient tales,
a sister-shadow, quick and green,
drawn from the realm of in-between.
But now I learn the frogs are gone,
the fish and birds, the purse of spawn
beneath each lily-pad, all dead;
a fairy tale in someone's head,
sea-eagle; osprey; sturgeon; deer;
the fish that gathered at the weir;
your border country dumb and still
and nothing left to save, or kill.

IV

The woman saith unto him, Sir, thou hast nothing
to draw with, and the well is deep: from whence
then hast thou that living water?

                    The Gospel of John: IV, xi

If it resides in anything, the soul
will favour hidden springs and waterfalls,
hollows where snow-melt gathers, like the pool
I found this morning, when I climbed the hill
amongst the birks. If it were personal
like memory, or grief, it might be still,

but all things change that last: only the dead
are wholly motionless.

                    And Lao Tzu said:
The Way of Tao is best seen in a burn
of caller water; as it flows and turns,
water is gentle, yet it cuts through stone;
as rivers find their way, so Tao seeps in

- the current, and the source. I cannot own
what gives me life; spirit is not contained:
no ordinary logic can explain
this shiver in the marrow of the bone;
sublunar shifts of gravity between
the ribcage and the stitchwork of the brain

or how a thread of fluid in the spine
answers to fish and frog, answers to rain,
becomes implicit in a ceaseless play
of echoes; how I live beneath the sky
with all that lives, and how the soul extends
through every life that water makes or mends.

                    John Burnside

'Wow' and other Cries in the Night: Fergusson's Vernacular, Scots Talking Heads, and Unruly Bodies

JANET SORENSEN

The exclusion of the word 'wow' from Samuel Johnson's *Dictionary of the English Language* (1755) is one of a number of remarkable omissions, all the more striking for the term's seeming ubiquity in post-eighteenth-century English. The word, which now functions as a linguistic tic in much spoken English, was originally a Scots term, and for Johnson this would, of course, be the first strike against its inclusion in his *Dictionary*. 'Wow' first circulated in written form in the late fifteenth century in places north, in no less learned a text than Gavin Douglas' *Eneados*. The *Oxford English Dictionary* tells us that it was then, as it is now, a term of exclamation 'expressing aversion, surprise, or admiration, sorrow or commiseration, or mere asseveration'. In its late-eighteenth-century incarnation in Britain the term took on a more disreputably embodied sense, as 'a bark or similar sound' and 'a waul'. In Scotland at the same time it meant 'a howl, deep-throated call or cry, bark'.[1] In terms of eighteenth-century British linguistic propriety, the connection to the physical body this exclamatory term suggests might count as a second strike against its appearance in Johnson's *Dictionary*. This was, after all, a world in which language was considered 'degraded and debased by its necessary connexion with flesh and blood'.[2] Alternatively, proper language's distance from 'flesh and blood' ensured the status of its users both as rational, abstract thinkers – as, in a sense, 'disembodied' and therefore disinterested participants in an Anglo-British public sphere. Alternatively, the very blurring of animal and human in words like 'wow' – where the line between animal cry and human language dissolves in onomatopoeic sound – poses the always present threat to which embodiment points. The categories between animal and human, their boundaries often marked in the eighteenth century by the capacity for language, cannot remain distinct in a word like 'wow', and the claims of humans as rational creatures become compromised in that indistinction. 'Wow', then, was freighted in the eighteenth century with several layers of cultural and political significance, not least of which were the intersection of Scottishness and the blurred boundaries between rational 'disembodiment' and irrational, ineluctable embodiment that foreclose one's ability to participate in a disinterested public sphere and question the logic that defines political membership in those impossible terms.

Any reader of Fergusson's poetry knows his proclivity for the word 'wow', and in at least some instances there is little room for doubt about the swipe at notions of 'proper' English language – and perhaps even that Anglo-British public sphere – intended in this term. 'The King's Birth-Day in Edinburgh', for instance, brandishes the word in the first stanza, 'But wow! the limmer's fairly flung;/There's naething in't' (5–6), an observation about how little King George III's birthday inspires the muse.[3] In his poems that make use of Scots vernacular Fergusson appeals to the physicality that 'wow' hints at, invoking an unrepentant, often oral, embodiment through motifs of gorging on 'oysters and . . ./ haddock lug' in 'Caller Oysters' or drinking liquor that 'fires the mouth' in 'Caller Water' or smelling stench, in the observation in 'Auld Reekie' regarding 'how snell/Auld Reikie will at morning smell'. 'Wow' and its compatriot language, in phrases such as 'snell' smells and 'gusty gear' that makes 'stamacks fou', might be read, both in their distinct Scottishness and in their 'connexion to flesh and blood', as terms of resistance against the increasing dominance of an abstract, 'disembo-died' proper English language and culture within Scotland. Attention to competing linguistic practices and concepts of the period, however, reveals something far more than a simple English/Scots binary. Com-plex and contradictory itself, Fergusson's use of language in the Scots poems reveals the intricacies within Scottish/English and British cultural politics of the period. His linguistic choices, as well as the broader contexts of language theories and practices in which Fergusson's use of language intervened, remind us that there was no simple opposition even between such seemingly counterposed enclaves as Scots Humanists and Celtic Whigs in late eighteenth-century Britain. More generally, Fergusson's poetry cannily re-introduces the physical body to the public sphere of eighteenth-century Britain and its various manifestations within Scotland.

Often at variance with itself, Fergusson's urbane, dazzlingly distinct and rich lexicon is an explosive Scots all the more remarkable when considered in the context of the standardisation of English, which was taking place in grammar books, dictionaries and elocution lectures of mid- to late-eighteenth century Britain both north and south of the Tweed.[4] Central to that standardisation process was the eradication of 'provincial dialects', and Johnson's *Dictionary* stands as one important example of the many works operating under that principle. Underlying the rejection of provincial dialects was a longstanding neoclassical emphasis on the general over the particular. This rhetorical imperative had political reverberations in the period, for also underpinning the rejection of 'particular' provincial languages was the understanding of a new enlightened bourgeois subject. This subject's participation in an emerging public sphere depended upon his ability to suspend the differentiating particularities – and appetites – which might interfere with his ability to engage in discussions predicated on abstract, universal reason. The distinguishing particularism of 'provincial' languages not only prevented such languages as Scots from being considered public languages of universal reason. It also marked their speakers as inevitably embodied, incapable of transcending the particularities of place and place-related interest, rendering such speaking subjects, therefore, suspect.[5]

Access to the public sphere, or more specifically to the claim of disembodiment and disinterest, then, was geographically uneven. The public sphere's very formation, in fact, depended upon making spatial divisions between illegitimate, marginalised social spaces and a legitimate civic body. So the 'civic body is topographically reformed by the unceremonious exportation and dumping of libido in the countryside and in the colonies', amongst which Stallybrass and White include Edinburgh.[6] Edinburgh literati aspiring to full franchise in the public life of Britain thus faced a double burden, both in the onus of 'dematerializing' themselves, refining and policing their bodies, as their English counterparts were doing, and in the added encumbrance of overcoming an already topographically coded status as residents of a provincial site. Little wonder they worked in earnest to master the language ascribed with universalising potential, standard English. I want to pause a moment to consider what their resulting discourse looked like, both to provide a context for understanding the power of Fergusson's interventions in the arena of language and to note the ways in which there is no clear demarcation between the localism of Fergusson's vernacular poetry and the abstract discourse of some Scottish literati.

Even from the highest ranks of educated Scots there was some register of resistance to total linguistic abnegation. Fergusson was not alone amongst his fellow lettered Scots and learned Edinburgh citizens in taking umbrage at the eradication of all linguistic markers of Scottishness. Interestingly, the 'Society of Gentlemen in Scotland' produced their three-volume *Encyclopaedia Britannica* in Edinburgh in 1771, while Fergusson's earliest Scots poems appeared in the Edinburgh periodical the *Weekly Magazine* in 1772. In their entries for 'dialect' and 'dictionary' the Scots encyclopedia writers make an understated and rather prim case for the inclusion of some elements of Scots within the language of Great Britain. They do so in the detached language Stallybrass and White see as central to the eighteenth-century public sphere. Too polite to take on Johnson in any direct way, the writers aver that 'although it [Johnson's *Dictionary*] is executed in a masterly manner, yet . . . it cannot be expected that an undertaking of this nature could be brought to perfection by one man' (II, 434). It is Johnson's single vision ('one man') that is too limited, even too particular, to produce a compilation of the language with the scope that a group of writers might have given.[7] The *Encyclopaedia* writers provide new, improved entries for his *Dictionary of the English Language* in which they carefully suggest means for its improvement. Their gentle quarrel with Johnson's *Dictionary* is what they see as its lack of exactness in distinction between words. So they write, 'would it not have been an improvement if he had given an accurate definition of the precise meaning of every word . . . [I]t would have been necessary to exhibit the nice distinctions that take place between words which are nearly synonymous' (435).

Such distinctions between words within a language, although potentially infinite, are an important goal to enlightenment linguistics. What is most interesting about their tentative line of attack is the way in which it asserts that after full pursuit of these distinctions, the English language might be shown to be not exact enough. Provincial languages – such as Scots – might then be brought in to fill the gaps left by the absence of English words for specific ideas. The authors of the *Encyclopaedia* add, 'A dictionary cannot be reckoned complete without explaining obsolete words; and if the terms of the several provincial provincial [sic] dialects were given, it would be of great utility'. Under the standardisation process, provincial languages are the equivalent of obsolete languages, no longer in use, despite the fact that they might well be very much alive within the provinces themselves, as we see in Fergusson's poetry. They add that including 'obsolete' words would not 'take much time; because a number of these words need no other explanation than to mark along with them the words which had come in their place, when there happened to be one perfectly synonymous' (439). 'Provincial' and 'obsolete' have become synonymous in this discussion. There is no contest between a provincial and central term for the same idea – the central (English) term must necessarily supersede the provincial (Scots). The value of provincial languages is their ability to fill in the gaps in a rightfully dominant central language. The model on offer is a classical model of imperial inclusion, which elevates Scots to the ranks of the languages of Greek dialects. Thus, the encyclopedia's entry for 'dialect' reads 'an appellation given to the language of a whole province, in so far as it differs from that of the whole kingdom. The term, however, is more particularly used in speaking of ancient Greek, whereof there were four dialects, the Attic, Ionic, AEolic, and Doric, each of which was a perfect language in its kind, that took place in certain counties, and had peculiar beauties' (431). The encyclopedia writers promote, in very muted terms, the distinctness and self-enclosed quality and value of the local.

The Scottish encyclopaedists also mediate between local dialects and the nation, offering the terms upon which local words might be redeemed within the national language. They write, in 'cases where the same idea could not be expressed in modern language without a periphrasis it would be of use to explain them distinctly; so that, when a writer found himself at a loss for a term, and obliged to search for one beyond the bounds of our own language, he might take one of these, when he found that it was expressive and energetic, in preference to another drawn from a foreign language. This would at least have one good effect: it would make our language more fixed and stable; not to say more accurate and precise, than by borrowing from a foreign language'. The allegiance to Great Britain remains in place, and the importance of maintaining an insular national language becomes the basis of inclusion of terms from 'provincial dialects.' The two examples they offer do not veer from the tone of their discussion:

MOE or MO. adj. An obsolete term still employed in the Scotch dialect, and by them pronounced mae: denoting a greater number, and nearly synonymous with more; but it differs in this respect, that, in the Scotch dialect, mae and mair (English, more) are each employed in their distinct sphere, without encroaching upon one another; mae being employed to denote number, but never quantity or quality; and mair, to denote quantity and quality, but never number: thus they say mae, no mair apples, men, &c. See Mair. Both of these terms are supplied by the word more; which, in the English language, is applied indiscriminately to denote quantity, quality, and number.

and

THIR. pron. Obsolete; still employed in the Scotch dialect: the plural of this; and contrasted to these, in the same manner as that is to this. As there is no word in the English language equivalent to this, we thus shew the manner in which it is employed. In the English language we say, that stone or house, pointing at one at a distance, is larger than this stone or this house, which is supposed to be at hand. In the same manner, in the Scotch dialect, they say, these (or as it is pronounced, thae) tones are whiter then thir stones; denoting that the former are at a distance, and the latter are at hand.

These entries make the case in fairly bloodless terms. 'Thir' and 'Moe' provide a means of articulating more precise grammatical – abstract – relationships. They are not the names of local items that might assert local difference, nor do they invoke the affective body, as Fergusson's 'wow' does. The new public sphere of refinement and the ordered civic body in which the *Encyclopaedia*'s writers clearly hope to participate were based, in part, on a rhetoric distancing the public sphere from the 'grotesque body' with its physical appetites and often unrefined material presence. As they make a subdued argument for the inclusion of Scots terms within the standard English lexicon, they use a 'proper' standard English and steer clear of invocations of local places and particular moments of difference. The body, ushered in merely to observe and point, is distant and abstracted. And yet the case they make – for the value of a recognisably Scots term – is a radical one, not, obviously, adopted by the grammarians of the time, and the parenthetical reference to voice, as they note that the term 'these . . . is pronounced thae', offers a brief if well-mannered reminder of embodied difference.

The strategies of those interested in assimilating standard English reflect notions of a bourgeois public sphere as the basis of the British nation, a public sphere predicated on disembodiment and the eschewing of local interests when they are perceived to impinge upon one's ability to perceive and judge in general, disinterested terms. An encounter with the vernacular poetry of Robert Fergusson, on the other hand, is first and foremost an encounter with a singular language at once inviting in its ability to name with dramatic specificity elements of everyday Edinburgh public life and potentially alienating to any but the most local of readerships in its refusal to translate those terms – at least in their first appearance in the *Weekly Magazine* – even at their most idiosyncratic. This is not a redemption of 'provincial dialect' based on its ability to bolster 'our' 'modern language' of English through more precise terms to represent abstract, universal grammatical relations, but a revaluing of local terms that bespeak a distinct and untranslatable local experience. The speaker of Fergusson's 'Answer to Mr. J.S.'s Epistle' comments on the limited nature of his purview, without the hint of regret, noting 'it wou'd be news indeed,/War I to ride to bonny *Tweed*,/ Wha ne'er laid *gamon* o'er a steed/Beyont *Lusterrick*'. This poetry celebrates the local for locals and in that way achieves an exactness impossible to a more general, abstract language. 'Caller Oysters' brags of the size of the region's oysters, at specific times of year, and its sense of location is so strong that the poem boastfully refers to a locally well-known eatery, 'Whan big as burns the gutters rin,/Gin ye hae catcht a droukit skin,/To *Luckie Middlemist's* loup in'. Community is at once formed by and limited to readers familiar with that very particular reference, as also in the injunction in 'Good Eating', 'If appetite invite, and cash prevail,/Ply not your joints upon the homeward track,/Till LAWSON, chiefest of the Scottish hosts!/To nimble-footed waiters give command/The cloth to lay'. Equally specific references abound in 'Auld Reekie', where 'Gillespie's Snuff' makes an appearance, and landmarks of Edinburgh – from the 'Air-cock o' St. Giles' to the 'Luckenbooths' and 'Nore Loch Brig' reinforce the site-specificity of the poem.

This is a poetry of public spaces, but not of the disinterested sort of public sphere discourse. Rather, allusions to specific sensual experiences, including particular foods and 'The Morning smells that hail our Street', call up a resolutely particular regional community. This is a physically proximal community, emblazoned in the oral language of the poems. These poems, rather than hinting at vocal difference with a polite aside (as in the *Encyclopaedia*'s 'pronounced thae'), perform that vocal difference in their appearance on the page. Visual markers of oral pronunciation – and direct references to the grotesque body – abound, from familiar-toned advice to 'Ye tiplers, open a' your poses,/Ye wha are faush'd wi' plouky noses' in 'Caller Oysters' to allusions to a local community's standards of fashion in 'Waesuck for him wha has na fek o't!/For he's a gowk they're sure to geck at' in 'Braid Claith'.[8] Exclamations such as 'waesuck' approximate an oral outburst – here 'waesuck' and not 'wow' is the interjection of choice – in other poems ('The King's Birthday' and 'To the Principal and Professors of the University of Saint Andrews'). 'Oh willawins!' and 'Ah! Willawins,' respectively, serve as exclamations, and 'wae's heart!' features in 'Ode to the Gowdspink'. Unlike 'wow', however, these 'cries' do not slouch toward onomatopoeia. While onomatopoeia always carries the furtive promise of a universal language at the most basic and embodied points of communication – the 'waul' of pain, the cry of desire, the howl of lamentation – these exclamatory terms insist on regional specificity even at the least grammatical moments of speech.

If the representations of oral language and discrete pronunciations on the page aggressively assert a difference from any universal language and certainly from a standard English that disavows the oral, they also record regional differences within Scots. 'Hallow-Fair', for instance, includes the distinct pronunciations of Aberdonian and Highland dialects. The poem's Aberdonian stocking seller cries, 'I wyt they are as protty hose/As come frae *weyr* or *leem*'. As Matthew McDiarmid has noted, Fergusson draws from a recent issue of the *Weekly Magazine* in which an Aberdonian ('Philo-Orthologiae') had explained that Aberdonian dialect converts "the sound of oo into ee" (thus 'leem' for loom).[9] In the same letter, the image of London as standardising metropolis to provincial Edinburgh is recast, and instead Edinburgh stands as standardising, language-improving metropolis to provincial language communities such as Aberdeen. The letter's take on that spatially inflected linguistic improvement is ambiguous. Philo-Orthologiae writes of his efforts, 'The expedient succeeded almost to my expectation, but with exceptions too; for having called at Ab–n, where I had resided some time before, after spending some months in the metropolis, I was told by a gentleman of that city, 'Fat iver ye've impriv'd in, Sir, weel I wite, its ne I' your langige'.'[10] Whether the story comments on the impossibility of full linguistic assimilation or the undesirability of it, it alerts us to the chequered quality of language practices in Scotland, where oral pronunciation distinguishes linguistic communities in much more nuanced terms than a simple Scots and English binary.

Fergusson's language and the subject matter to which it refers is an altogether more embodied Scots than that of his predecessors, such as Allan Ramsay, and the next generation of his readers seems highly aware of and ready to locate Fergusson within a cultural political hierarchy that privileges language and literature so far as it offers distance from the material body. It is for that more lofty quality of language and topic that one commentator, Robert Cumming, 'staymaker in Edinburgh', celebrates Ramsay over Fergusson.[11] For Cumming, Fergusson's poetry appeals to the body: 'So true his colours rise, /They move the passions as they flash around' and 'we mark with pleasure and we feel with joy,/

Each pow'r pathetic in the flowing page,/When Ferguson [sic] attunes his solemn lyre'. Finally, however, Fergusson's more physically based verses 'only rouse the rougher powers of mind'. The goal of poetry, which Ramsay but not Fergusson achieves, is to leave the material word and body behind in eliciting elevated sentiment, a curiously disembodied phenomenon for Cumming, who writes that in Ramsay's poetry 'language disappears amidst the glow/ Of sentiment so beauteous, pure, and strong'. For Cumming, Ramsay's is a 'chaste' language that fades out of perception to make possible 'immortal' – and what immortal thing can be embodied? – 'sense'. Conversely, Fergusson's embodied 'wit' 'lives a while;/Then with the trivial subject dies away'.

Fergusson's is a poetry of the mortal body; the most intimate of bodily functions is fodder for this poetry, from folksy medical advice: 'for gin thou *art sick*,/The Oyster is a rare cathartic' in 'Caller Oysters' to a most indecorous image of a rash-plagued Dr. Johnson in the mock-polysyllabic question: 'Have you as yet,/With skin fresh rubified by scarlet spheres, /Apply'd BRIMSTONIC UNCTION to your hide,/To terrify the SALAMANDRIAN fire/That from involuntary digits asks/ The strong allaceration?'[12] Yet the insouciant tone of such passages belies their knowing response to linguistic and cultural political contexts. An itching Johnson inverts the common Scotophobic image of the scabies-prone Sawney. The localised, oral, and particular quality of the poetry contrasts with neoclassical and bourgeois public sphere criteria of standardised language and abstract themes. Fergusson is fully conscious of that contrast and of the transformation involved in print representations of such language. Even as he deploys this language in lively scenes very much of the moment, he is aware of their increasingly anachronistic and folksy connotations, writing in 'Answer to Mr. J.S.'s Epistle' that his muse 'can find a knack,/To gar auld-warld wordies clack/In hamespun rhime'.

We shall not be far off the mark here to recall Johnson's own reference to putatatively mortal, local, and in a sense embodied terms versus immortal, general, and disembodied words in the preface to his *Dictionary*, as he enumerates his criteria for including and excluding words. He writes, 'Of the laborious and mercantile part of the people, the diction is in a great measure casual and mutable; many of their terms are formed for some temporary or local convenience, and though current at certain times and places, are in others utterly unknown. This fugitive cant, which is always in a state of increase or decay, cannot be regarded as any part of the durable materials of a language, and therefore must be suffered to perish with other things unworthy of preservation'.[13] Those whose work, either with their bodies in manual labour or through their traffic in material goods, locates them more firmly in the realm of the material also speak an embodied language, 'always in a state of increase or decay'. In league with this physicality is a corrupting tie to specific, particular localities, and these qualities render such language unable to occupy the celebrated position of the abstract and general, unable, as Cumming might put it, to 'disappear'. For Johnson and for many writers on language at this time, Scots too was irredeemably local and its legible markers of distinct pronunciation designated it as troublingly physical. In an era when the idea of an abstract, general language held sway (however illusory such an idea might be), local, embodied language was perceived as a threat to the standard under construction and perhaps even to the disembodied discourse of the public sphere that used that standard as its currency.

In his poetry in Scots, Fergusson clearly revels in a 'fugitive' language, and part of the point of his description of that language as 'auld-warld wordies' is his reckoning of such language, in opposition to Johnson, as 'worthy of preservation'. Fergusson takes on Johnson, particularly critiquing the general/particular divide, in his 'To Dr. Samuel Johnson: Food for a new Edition of his Dictionary'. Like his compatriot *En-cyclopaedia* writers, Fergusson is interested in the notion of revising Johnson's *Dictionary*, but his tone is obviously scornful and satirical. The poem is in some ways, as others, including myself, have argued, a celebration of the material differences of Scotland in the face of a standardising English print culture.[14] The triumphant final lines attest to Scotland's superiority to England: 'Then hie you home,/And be a malcontent, that naked hinds,/On lentiles fed, can make your kingdom quake'. Yet the particulars offered up in this poem are not the specifics of local haunts of his other poems, the oysters of Luckie Middlemist's, the 'vegetative sweets' of 'Fair Duddingstonia' in 'Good Eating', or the snuff to be had at Gillespie's. Rather they are an inventory of the differentiating stereotypes, most associated with the Highlands, offered up by the likes of the Scotophobes to whom the epigraph alludes, John Wilkes and Charles Churchill (McDiarmid notes that Churchill is the author of *The Prophesy of Famine*, which depicts 'Jockey and Sawney' in an impoverished Scotland). Caves, kilts, and oats eaten from wooden bowls are not the particulars of Fergusson's – or his readers'–everyday life. This 'food' is not literal food, as in the 'famed' 'sheep's heads' of Edinburgh's inns in 'Good Eating', but rather this 'food' figures the discursively constructed images of Scots difference served up for consumption by Wilkes and others. It 'translates' those images into the high-blown Latinate language that would qualify it, the speaker suggests, for inclusion in Johnson's *Dictionary*, with its own out-of-touch language.

The poem attacks not English *per se* but the false valuation of a high-blown lingo, a ridiculous hybrid of English and Latin or Scots and Latin. It begins with a (fictional) quotation from 'Rodondo', William Pitt, who, as Matthew McDiarmid notes, had already made an appearance in a burlesque poem making 'fun of the high-flown oratory of the Earl of Chatham (Rodondo)'. McDiarmid provides a quotation from the earlier poem, which had appeared in a collection printed by Walter Ruddiman, 'The vulgar said equality;/But he parallelaity!', an assertion that the language of the vulgar is correct and appropriate, that of Rodondo inflated and inappropriate.[15] The parody of Johnson's Latinate language sounds much like that attributed to Rodondo, and thus it seems that the poem is satirising not just Johnson but also a 'false' language designed to secure the place of the 'high'. Complex politics are likely at work here. The poem Fergusson draws from ridicules Pitt's hours-long speech in Parliament against the peace plan brokered by the Earl of Bute, whose distinguishing marks of Scottishness provided no end of grist for the opposition's mill. Part of Fergusson's attack is perhaps a vindication of his fellow Scot, yet in appealing to 'vulgar' language, he operates on another, related level, one that reveals the double-sided meaning of Fergusson's seemingly resistant appeals to the body, the particular, and even the vulgar.

In his appeal to the body, to the oral, to Scots language, and to a striated local world, Fergusson stands apart from the Edinburgh literati's efforts at assimilation. Neither, certainly, Anglicising Scots moderate nor the type of Scots 'Celtic Whig' that Colin Kidd describes (these positions often held, it should be noted, by the same man), Fergusson occupies ground often under-represented in surveys of the cultural political map of eighteenth-century Britain.[16] He can be much more closely aligned with the countercurrent of a Scots Humanist tradition, and the appearance of his poems in the *Weekly Magazine*, published by Walter Ruddiman, the nephew of Thomas Ruddiman, a leading Scots Humanist, provides evidence of such an allegiance. In his study of Scots Humanism and Fergusson, Freeman has referred to Scots Humanism as 'an idiosyncratically Scots form of the Counter-Enlightenment' and as representing 'the Scotland of the old European Scot, the

Tory and Jacobite'.[17] Under the Scots Humanist world view, 'diversity meant not so much an order of greater and lesser cultures . . . but a sense of legitimate cultural differences'.[18] Thus, 'pride in the national language and literature was a great part of just such conservatism'. Recognising the counter-current of Scots Humanism at work in eighteenth-century Scotland demands that we interpret the seeming plebeian sympathies of Fergusson's poetry and those characteristics of his poems that would lend themselves to a reading of Fergusson as poet of 'resistance'. Refusal of the ethos of progress and linguistic standardization, opposition to politeness and the disembodied public sphere which politeness underwrites, and suspicion of the generalising claims of an improving Whig hegemony might represent a variety of counterposed political positions. Political positions from opposite sides of the political spectrum, from disenfranchised Tory to protesting peasant, overlap in the anti-Whig position.[19]

Influenced by Scots Humanism and its emphasis on classical learning and a conservative hierarchical social model, Fergusson's seeming appeal to the plebeian might then also be read as an appeal to Tory sensibilities. In his study of Humanist Latin culture of the eighteenth century, J.C.D. Clark writes that, in fact, 'on the Stuart side the culture of dynastic legitimacy displayed a marked ability . . . to include both the patrician and the plebeian.' Important in terms of the embodied and at times vulgar poetry of Fergusson is Clark's observation about the connection between 'the classical tradition and more earthy satire'. Similarly, F.W. Freeman locates Fergusson's 'earthy satires', his disrupted hierarchies, and grotesque bodies, within the Augustan tradition of Pope and Swift (and, related, Matthew McDiarmid has noted the influence of John Gay's *Trivia* on 'Auld Reekie'). Freeman sees Fergusson's poetry as performing the same conservative raillery as his Augustan predecessors. According to Freeman, Fergusson's relationship to a Scots Humanist tradition is in part responsible for his use of 'low life' subject matter. These observations about an embodied political rhetoric bring together and complicate notions of high and low constituencies and languages in Fergusson's vernacular poetry.

Yet Freeman's account of Fergusson, as useful as it is for reminding us of the lively intellectual communities not covered under discussions of a moderate Whig literati, falls short of capturing those complications of high and low so important to Fergusson's vernacular poetry. In Freeman's analysis, Fergusson increasingly resembles Clark's Tory Humanist Johnson, yet this leads us to wonder what to make of Fergusson's continuing antagonism toward Johnson. Here again, attention to language sheds some light on the question and reveals the ways in which simple binaries do not hold up. Just as the *Encyclopaedia* writers seem to act uncharacteristically in their attempt to negotiate a space for "local" language within the national standard, the Scots Humanist thinkers represented in the *Weekly Magazine*, perhaps surprisingly, paid tacit tribute to the learning and use of a general English language. Many of its weekly letters debate not the merits of linguistic assimilation but the most effective pedagogical methods for teaching English pronunciation. Even Fergusson's 'A Tale' ridicules not the learning of English pronunciation but the 'self-invented rules' characteristic of pedantry. In his lesson to pedagogues, he describes how one pedant loses out on getting his mutton when a student, taking to heart the pedant's 'self-invented rule' that 'H is but a breathing', eats the pedant's mutton when the pedant instructs him to heat it. Fergusson's vernacular poetry and the Scots Humanist tradition represented by the *Weekly Magazine* might not represent a resistance to English language so much as a struggle of position in the ongoing process of language valuation. Falsely elevated language and pedagogues, the corrupt mixing of Latin and vulgar languages – be they Scots or English – and the unnecessary erasure of the local and embodied from the linguistic scene altogether are the more specific points of resistance here.

Fergusson wrote in a non-uniform, wide-ranging Scots of impressive flexibility. Freeman links this use of vernacular to a centuries-old valuation of Scots and an Enlightenment cultural relativism which reclaimed rustic Scots language as the contemporary manifestation of an ancient poetic language, and he also notes Fergusson's sense of linguistic diversity – and hierarchy – between different registers of Scots. Yet the insertion of the speaker into the scenes of 'low' public spaces and the speaker's own use of Scots in a poem like 'Caller Oysters', as well as the use of the first person that accompanies the most humble of Scots registers (in 'Good Eating', for example) disrupts the clear sense of hierarchy that Freeman wants to ascribe to Fergusson. This is not a distanced disgust, a use of the low only as a symbol of the unworthy or a means of re-establishing hierarchies. Into our reading of these poems – and our understanding of the dense network of political and philosophical discourses of eighteenth-century Britain – it is important to add some of the 'low codes' to an interpretation of the cultural significance of Fergusson's poetry. Thus if, as Stallybrass and White have argued, an Augustan writer such as Dryden makes sure 'his audience knows that they much chose [sic] one or the other—that belonging comfortably to both realms is a monstrosity', Fergusson's ability to belong to both realms comfortably sets him apart from such Augustan writers. Further, if this cultural work of border constructing of high and low marks the work of early eighteenth-century writers such as Pope and Swift, the fact that such borders might be more securely in place at the point of Fergusson's writings changes the significance of his movement between them. The democratic promise of a "disembodied" public sphere gives way to its own hierarchies as such borders are more firmly established. Fergusson's vernacular poetry re-embodies its public subjects, suggesting, at the same time, the exclusions and inherent fictions of an Anglo-Scots bourgeois public sphere. Yet however tempting it might be to position Fergusson within an English/Scots binary or more generally within an authority/resistance binary through his use of language, more accurate is a reading of his work as representative of a third term, as exemplifying the complexities of late eighteenth-century cultural politics. Coming to an understanding of these complexities, in turn, provides a way to read back into related linguistic works of the period their own cross-hatched and intricate interventions in eighteenth-century Britain.

Notes

1. Ed. Mairi Robinson, *The Concise Scots Dictionary* (Aberdeen University Press, 1985).
2. Lord Monboddo, cited in Olivia Smith, *The Politics of Language* (Oxford: Clarendon, 1984), p. 22.
3. *The Poems of Robert Fergusson*, 2 vols., ed. Matthew McDiarmid (Edinburgh: Blackwood, 1956). All Fergusson poetry citations are from this text.
4. The rush to a kind of linguistic assimilationism has been noted in several important works, from Robert Crawford, *Devolving English Literature* (Oxford: Clarendon, 1992) to Thomas Miller, *The Formation of College English* (Pittsburgh: Pittsburgh University Press, 1997) and James Basker, 'Scotticisms and the Problem of Cultural Identity in Eighteenth-Century Britain,' *Eighteenth-Century Life* 15 (1991), pp. 81–95. These works note that some Scots writers, such as David Hume and James Beattie, went so far as to publish lists of Scotticisms for their countrymen to avoid in order to speak and write a more 'pure' and legitimate English.
5. Such notions of a 'universal' subject and concomitant language presuppose that a particular subject – the propertied English man and his language – might function in this universal capacity. For a critique of these notions, see Michael Warner, *Letters of the Republic: Publication and the Public*

Sphere in Eighteenth-Century America (Cambridge, MA: Harvard University Press, 1990) and Geoff Eley, 'Nations, Publics, and Political Cultures', in Craig Calhoun, ed., Habermas and the Public Sphere (Cambridge, MA: MIT, 1992), pp. 289–339.

6. The Poetics and Politics of Transgression (Ithaca: Cornell University Press, 1986).

7. Johnson of course had several assistants – several of them Scots. But he, of course, made the executive decisions regarding inclusion of words, often disregarding their suggestions. See Allen Reddick, The Making of Johnson's Dictionary (Cambridge: Cambridge University Press, 1990).

8. For a broader discussion of Fergusson's images of orality in relation to a transforming print culture, see my 'Dr. Johnson Eats His Words: Figuring the Incorporating English Print Culture', in Language Sciences 22 (2000), pp. 295–314.

9. Matthew McDiarmid, ed. The Poems of Robert Fergusson, Vol. II (Edinburgh: Blackwood, 1956), p. 270.

10. Weekly Magazine 22 October 1773 p. 101.

11. Essay Delivered in the Pantheon, on Thursday, April 14, 1791. On the Question, Whether have the Exertions of Allan Ramsay or Robert Ferguson [sic] done most Honour to Scottish Poetry (Edinburgh, 1791).

12. Matthew McDiarmid, ed., The Poems of Robert Fergusson, Vol. II (Edinburgh: Blackwood, 1956), p. 205.

13. Samuel Johnson, Dictionary of the English Language (London, 1755).

14. See Katie Trumpener, Bardic Nationalism (Princeton: Princeton UP, 1997), pp. 86–7 and my The Grammar of Empire in Eighteenth-Century British Writing (Cambridge: Cambridge University Press, 2000), pp. 99–102.

15. Matthew McDiarmid, ed., The Poems of Robert Fergusson, Vol. II (Edinburgh: Blackwood, 1956), pp. 309–10.

16. Colin Kidd, Subverting Scotland's Past: Scottish Whig Historians and the Creation of an Anglo-British Identity, 1689–1830 (Cambridge: Cambridge Univ. Press, 1993). Kidd's book has done much by way of revealing the complexities of the cultural political map of eighteenth-century Scotland.

17. For a discussion of Fergusson's place not only in respect to Scots/English geopolitics of the period but also in relation to philosophical and older political contests, see F.W. Freeman's Robert Fergusson and the Scots Humanist Compromise (Edinburgh: Edinburgh University Press, 1984).

18. In J.C.D. Clark's examination of this underexplored terrain, he relocates one of Fergusson's targets – a seemingly non-negotiable figure of opposition, Samuel Johnson, within a not unrelated milieu, a late Humanist Latin culture. Samuel Johnson: Literature, Religion, and English Cultural Politics from the Restoration to Romanticism (Cambridge: Cambridge University Press, 1994), p. xi.

19. Fergusson's use of traditional holidays as the subject matter of his poems represents a similarly complex cultural politics. See John Brewer, N. McKendrick, and J.H.Plumb, The Birth of a Consumer Society (London, Hutchinson, 1983).

IN THE CELLS

'The night is young,' they said, 'it's only nine.
We've brought a carriage for you, see, it's there.
What your blue devils need is a wheen wine.
Put on your coat, there's a nip in the air.'
They took him to the madhouse, not the club.
As the gate clanged behind him, he set up
A howl the inmates echoed in hubbub.
One more in hell! One more to drain the cup
Of horror, pick the sleepless straw! He sang,
He did, but it came out like the scream
That wakened him a week before: a cat
Had caught a starling in its playful fang,
Squeezing and rending its joy and the poet's dream:
A throat fluttering to death: it was like that.

Edwin Morgan

The 'Rhyming Trade':
Fergusson, Burns, and the Marketplace

CAROL MCGUIRK

There are indeed languages of minorities; often of minorities who are in that social situation because their country or place has been annexed or incorporated into a larger political unit. This does not make them 'minority languages', except in the perspective of dominance. In their own place (if they can resist what are often formidable pressures) it is their own language – a specific language like any other. – Raymond Williams, entry on Dialect, *Keywords*

Both Fergusson and Burns entered the marketplace with a single commodity to trade: their poems, 'chiefly' in Scots. Emphasising dialect precisely because it embodied national history and culture, they sought to remind their countrymen, in an era of rapid cultural assimilation, of what it meant to be Scottish. Both poets, in short, were also bards – a disquieting profession in later eighteenth-century Scotland, or so their poems suggest. Both shared a sense that bards can expect nothing material – nothing but applause and fame – in exchange for their writings. Nonetheless, their vision often darkens as their speakers stand, empty-handed observers, in Scottish scenes crammed full of imported luxuries and dainties.

Both set scenes of riotous urban consumption – displays of food, flesh, and finery – against scenes of quiet rural self-sufficiency. Addressing the world as Scotia's bards, they on occasion experiment with styles derived from such authors as John Gay, Alexander Pope, and John Milton.[1] Both were willing to learn what they could from English poets; it was English gold that they distrusted.

Contrary elements – pastoral and anti-pastoral, English and Scots, neoclassical and vernacular – contend in their vision of Scotland. Fergusson's *Poems on Various Subjects . . . In Two Parts* (1782) – this is the edition that Burns owned[2] – is even in mirrored sections. Part 1, with its timeless setting of love, song, and open, pleasant spaces, serves as an idealising counterpart to the teeming and clarty city of the Scots poems of Part 2, awash in discarded cess and foul with the detritus of consumer culture.[3] Burns must have marvelled at Thomas Ruddiman's evident editorial attempt in Part 1 to sedate the reader with neoclassical English before the surgical strike of Part 2 and the vernacular poems. 'Auld Reikie' in Part 2, for example, is a mock epic of city life that describes eating, drinking, and dressing up mainly in terms of such sequelae as spewing, passing out, and being spattered with dung. The poem's eye travels over brimming kennels to a sad prostitute, then moves on to a drunken dandy in the gutter whose silk stockings are raddled, his hair no longer 'slaister'd' with pomade, and his cheeks no longer ruddy with rouge.[4] A new day dawns, bringing only the shock of a sudden encounter with a gaily painted corpse being carried through the street to burial (II, 114).

The many portents of death in these poems, both in Scots and English, hint at Fergusson's own terrors. 'The surface is Ambrosia's mingled sweets', he writes in 'Tea', 'But all below is death' (II, 175). But Fergusson also warns of cultural deaths that he fears are imminent – of Scots music (subject of an early poem), Scots language, Scots self-respect, even Scots cuisine. From the outset of his brief career, Fergusson exhibits a hypersensitivity to change; one of his poems views a haircut as an '*amputation*' (II, 29). Burns learned much about understatement and comic balance – litotes and syllepsis – from the epistles and satires of Pope. But it was Robert Fergusson who taught him linguistic intensity, audacious hyperbole, and exuberant rhyme: '*Anacreontic*' and 'Pontic' (II, 106) in Fergusson's 'Caller Water', for instance, inspire Burns's 'fracas' and '*Bacchus*' in 'Scotch Drink'.[5] Fergusson also showed Burns saw how native and imported foods could be introduced as teaching devices in poems addressing deca-dence and virtue: new 'tastes' of all sorts attract their satire.[6] Burns's defence of Scots cuisine against foreign 'trash' in 'To a Haggis' and 'Scotch Drink' responds to such poems by Fergusson as 'Good Eating', 'Caller Water', and 'A Drink Eclogue' (in which imported Brandy debates with Scottish whisky).[7]

Among Fergusson's less heralded 'cuisine' poems is 'The Sow of Feeling', a burlesque in English that mocks Henry Mackenzie's best-selling sentimental novel *The Man of Feeling* (1771) and also Mack-enzie's grandiloquent play *The Prince of Tunis* (1773) (McDiarmid II, 284). The Sow decries in high style the new popularity of pork, which has led to the butchering of her husband and children. Denouncing fashion as only one of its victims can, she concludes by observing that Edinburgh's rage for culinary novelty is unlikely to stop at pigs:

> In early times the law had wise decreed,
> For human food but reptiles few should bleed;
> But monstrous man, still erring from the laws,
> The curse of heaven on his banquet draws!
> Already he has drain'd the marshes dry
> For *frogs*, new emblems of his luxury;
> And soon the *toad* and *lizard* will come home,
> Pure victims to the hungry glutton's womb:
> *Cats*, *rats*, and *mice*, their destiny may mourn,
> In time their carcases on spits must turn; . . . (II, 132)

Fergusson's speakers often stand apart in this way, critics rather than participants in the brawl or spree of late eighteenth-century Scottish urban life. 'Good Eating' describes an Edinburgh club banquet from the hostile perspective of the entrée, a side of beef:

> . . . Still are their tongues,
> While they with whetted instruments prepare
> For deep incision. – Now the *abscess* bleeds,
> And the devouring band, with stomachs keen
> And glutting rage, thy beauteous form destroy,
> Leave you a marrowless skeleton and bare,
> A prey to dunghills . . . (II, 100)

When considering the cost of new fashions and cultural innovations, Fergusson and Burns take the victim's side.

'The Ghaists: A Kirk-yard Eclogue' raises the spirits of George Heriot (d. 1624) and George Watson (d. 1723) to debate the Mortmain Bill of 1773 (II, 287). The estates of both men had endowed hospitals and schools, setting aside funds to educate the sons of needy Edinburgh burgesses and merchants. The proposed legislation would have required that these endowments be invested in government securities, reducing the national debt but guaranteeing a return of only 3 per cent (II, 287):

HERRIOT
> I find, my friend, that ye but little ken,
> There's einow on the earth a set o' men,
> Wha, if they get their private pouches lin'd,
> Gie na a winnelstrae for a' mankind;
> They'll sell their country, flae their conscience bare,
> To gar the weigh-bauk turn a single hair.
> The government need only bait the line

Wi' the prevailing flee, the gowden coin,
Then our executors, and wise trustees,
Will sell them fishes in forbidden seas,
Upo' their dwining country girn in sport,
Laugh in their sleeve, and get a place at court. (II, 144)[8]

The poem is characteristic of Fergusson in calling up Scotland's past in order to frame an argument about current and future public policy. As in 'The Sow of Feeling', he contrasts benevolence (former Scottish philanthropy and sociability) with newly imported evils: in this case, a pursuit of status ('a place at court') at the cost of the well-being of Edinburgh's poor. Self-serving English gold (or at any rate, new economic policy originating in London) is contrasted with the socially conscious 'Scottish' gold of Heriot, a benefactor of the poor though he had been a wealthy goldsmith. Heriot's and Watson's corrupt late eighteenth-century counterparts, the wealthy tradesmen who serve as the funds' trustees, are accused of betraying Scotland's spirit, literally personified in the poem by Heriot's and Watson's ghost-speakers.[9]

Parables of Consumption

'Yet, yet we swallow'–Fergusson's 'Tea. *A Poem*'

In 'Tea', Fergusson's speaker ascribes the cruel gossip of Edinburgh's fine ladies to their consumption from morning to midnight of 'Sushong, Congo, or coarse Bohea' (II, 174). A 'poison'd cup/From foreign plant distilled' (II, 176), tea is accused of infusing mainly bad temper and ill health:

O GOLD! Thy luring lustre first prevail'd
On MAN to tempt the fretful winds and waves,
And hunt new fancies. Still thy glaring form
Bids commerce thrive, and o'er the Indian waves
O'er-stemming danger draw the lab'ring keel
From CHINA's coast to *Britain's* colder clime,
Fraught with the fruits and herbage of their vales;
In them whatever vegetable springs,
How loathsome and corrupted, triumphs here,
The bane of life, of health the sure decay;
Yet, yet we swallow . . . (II, 175–76)

This is economic Jacobitism: the traditional and home-grown is preferred to the new-fangled and imported. And as in Jacobite discourses, it is again English gold that makes possible the 'triumph' of this 'loathsome' poison. In the printing of 'Tea', the words 'China' and 'Man' are rendered in small capitals, but Fergusson's bitter apostrophe to gold is printed in full size, suggesting his main satiric target. The final lines of 'Tea' call for a return to the consumption of wholesome native herbal beverages, including 'Green SAGE and WILD THYME' teas (II, 176).

The hostility of Fergusson to imported commodities and goods is logical, given his quest to find a Scottish audience for poems addressing Scotland. For like green sage tea, 'Scottishness' was falling out of fashion during Fergusson's early 1770s – and the situation had declined even further by Burns's 1780s and 1790s. The first edition of Fergusson's *Poems* sold about 500 copies in 1773, middling sales for Edinburgh at that time. He cleared fifty pounds from the volume, but little critical notice was taken – no 1773 review appeared (McDiarmid I, 39). James Boswell, under the spell of Samuel Johnson and the lure of Europe and London, never responded to the presentation volume that Fergusson sent to him in 1773 (McDiarmid I, 40), any more than sixteen years later he answered a tentative letter (sent through Bruce Campbell but addressed to Boswell) from Burns in November 1788 (*Letters* I, 335).

Even Allan Ramsay (1684–1758), Fergusson's commercially astute vernacular predecessor, had achieved his widest popularity with anglicised projects – the pastoral drama *The Gentle Shepherd* (1725) and songbook series *The Tea Table Miscellany* (1724–1737), which, as their titles indicate, had placed a selective use of Scots diction within a frame of standard English. The detailed Scots/English glossary that Ramsay compiled for his collected poems, which include some superlative poems in vernacular, suggests that Ramsay was confident during the 1720s that he addressed not only Edinburgh but a potential audience outside Scotland. Indeed, Richard Savage, Alexander Pope, John Arbuthnot, and Sir Richard Steele must have perceived no difficulty in Ramsay's use of Scots as 'Doric' counterpoint to Augustan English, for all of them subscribed to his 1721 *Poems*.[10] Nonetheless, Ramsay's most serious and sustained effort to revive a native Scottish literature, his projected four-volume modern edition of the Makars, *Ever Green* (1724), was his least profitable publishing venture: *Ever Green*'s first two volumes sold so poorly that the rest never were printed. (Fergusson did manage to find the first two volumes, and studied them closely.)

When Walter Ruddiman's *Edinburgh Weekly Magazine* – Walter was the father of Thomas, editor of Fergusson's collected poems – began to promote Fergusson's city satires between 1771 and 1773, poetry written in the vernacular must have seemed to people of fashion in Edinburgh a strangely retrograde idea, fetched from an earlier phase of that century of many changes. Between Allan Ramsay's most popular projects and the new work of Fergusson lay not only some fifty years but also the long shadow of 1745, a year during which Ramsay had left Edinburgh to avoid an invitation to attend Charles Edward Stuart at Holyrood Palace. No poet of conspicuous talent had addressed Scotland in Scots since a generation before Culloden. Tom Scott is eloquent on the difficulties that faced Fergusson when he sought to revisit Ramsay's patchy 'revival' of Scottish literary vernacular:

> The first point that we must grasp about Fergusson is that he inherited a desolation. He was the true heir of the great Scottish tradition in poetry, but his father's house was occupied by the enemy, his treasures and heirlooms were mostly locked up, himself dispossessed, the house desecrated, the servants ill-treated by the usurpers, and only the faithful old caretaker, Allan Ramsay, himself only semi-literate in his own or any culture, was there to tell him snatches of what had been. (16–17)[11]

When Fergusson sets scenes of decadent consumption against tableaux of simple, pastoral 'hame content', he is offering parables against consumerism. But he is also warning the Scots against being consumed (paradoxically) by the increase in post-Union economic trade. He urges Scotia to cleave to the home-grown, including her vernacular poets. Imported culture is to him an oxymoron. Fergusson knew that beyond the usual difficulties of bardic writing – finding images and words to affirm the idea of a Scottish community – he also had to find an audience. During the early 1770s, it was not a foregone conclusion that the Scots themselves would be sympathetic to the idea of Scottish subject matter, let alone Scottish dialect.

Sometimes Fergusson humours these reluctant readers, writing of Scotland in English even in some of his Edinburgh poems ('The Bugs', discussed below, is one example). When Tom Scott argues that these poems by Fergusson in English have "been grossly underrated and misunderstood", he writes against the grain of long critical consensus:[12]

> If he had not been a major poet in the medium of Scots, he would have been at least a good minor one in English . . . ['The

Canongate Playhouse in Ruins' is] a poem showing not only remarkable achievement in itself but promising greater things to come. [It] establishes Fergusson as a major poet, potentially, in English and the best Scottish one in English after Thomson. But while Fergusson was a discoverer in Scots, in English he was [still] only a seeker [at the time of his early death]. (23)

Scott remarks that an important legacy to Burns was Fergusson's re-invention of Scottish verse forms, especially the Standard Habbie stanza: 'Fergusson found it used only for comic elegy and left it fit for many other purposes' (24). But he maintains that Fergusson's command of language (including not only a range of regional Scots dialects but also the 'high' and 'middle' styles of neoclassical English) has been over-looked: 'His handling of blank verse was superior to that of any Scot writing in Scotland up to the present twentieth century' (24).

One of Fergusson's most celebrated poems, 'The Farmer's Ingle', describes in Spenserian stanzas the supper of a rural household. The buttered bannocks, oatmeal, cabbage, and strong ale are all served warm from the heart of the household, a blazing hearth-fire. Fergusson, however, maintains an ironic distance between the poem's peasant subjects, evoked in vivid dialect, and his imagined audience of urban sophisticates – who, the poem implies, no more speak the saturated Scots dialect of this poem than they eat the kind of rustic food set on the table by the farmer's wife. Fergusson implicitly contrasts older and newer (rural and urban) models of 'Scottishness', warning 'gentler gabs' or sophisticates that in abandoning native food and daily work, they make their nation vulnerable to more than culinary invasion:

> On sicken food has mony a doughty deed
>   By Caledonia's ancestors been done;
> By this did mony wight fu' weirlike bleed
>   In *brulzies* frae the dawn to set o' sun:
> Twas this that brac'd their *gardies*, stiff and strang,
>   That bent the deidly yew in antient days,
> Laid Denmark's daring sons on yird alang,
>   Gar'd Scottish *thristles* bang the Roman bays;
> For near our *crest* their heads they doughtna raise. (II, 138)[13]

'The Cotter's Saturday Night' is, as many have noted, Burns's attempt to trump 'The Farmer's Ingle'. It is, for one thing, among a very few poems by Burns written in Spenserian stanzas.[14] And as in Fergusson's poem, the description of a peasant family's meal is central to a final prescription for national values. Choosing cotters rather than Fergusson's prosperous tenant farmer (whose ploughmen and other helpers dine with the household), Burns paints a country family at their scanty supper of skim milk and oatmeal. (Shavings of homemade cheese, served last, are brought out in honour of Jenny's visiting admirer.)

Like Fergusson, Burns sees in the very spareness of his cotters' diet a symbol of Scottish self-reliance:

> O SCOTIA! my dear, my native soil!
>   For whom my warmest wish to Heaven is sent!
> Long may thy hardy sons of *rustic toil*
>   Be blest with health and peace and sweet content!
> And O may Heaven their simple lives prevent
>   From *Luxury's* contagion, weak and vile!
> Then howe'er *crowns* and *coronets* be rent,
>   A *virtuous Populace* may rise the whole,
> And stand a wall of fire, around their much-lov'd ISLE. (I, 151)

Simple Scotsmen nourished on self-denial (seen here as the bedrock 'Scottish' virtue) have always been strong enough to rise to the challenge of national defence. A 'wall of fire' repelling invaders, they are also a more passive barrier –a firewall that only stands and waits. The rural community's minimal contact with the larger world of cultural and economic exchange (here called 'Luxury's contagion', an image equating consumer goods with contamination and disease) allows the peasantry to stand as a buffer zone between Scotland and further cultural adulteration. Burns's curious imagination of Scotland as an island follows the poem's logic in equating virtue with an extreme insularity. Seeing in the contemporary Scottish social landscape all the signs of rapid cultural attrition – a vanishing 'Scotia' – Burns, like Fergusson, argues that what is left (mainly preserved among the poor, who, like bards, remain outside the loop of accelerating trade) should be vigilantly conserved.

The emerging Scotland of the later eighteenth century – that extraordinary landscape toured by Boswell and Johnson in 1773, the same year that Fergusson's first volume of collected poems was published – was in Samuel Johnson's imagining still awaiting the full growth of the newly planted tree of 'improvement'. Johnson's Scottish itinerary took in Edinburgh, the Northeast coast, and Ayrshire; it was much more comprehensive than is suggested by the title of his subsequent book, *A Voyage to the Western Isles* (1775).[15] Throughout his account of his

Scottish travels, Johnson sees a nation tamed not so much by military occupation – Johnson notes with satisfaction that by 1773 the soldiers at Fort Augustus are mainly employed in building roads (56) – as by commerce and trade, which have, he repeatedly asserts, finally connected all regions of Scotland to England. In an episode that appealed to eighteenth-century illustrators, a girl 'not inelegant in either mien or dress' (58) serves Johnson tea in a remote Highland change-house; he is amazed that the English custom is observed in a 'hut of loose stones . . . lined with turf and wattled with twigs' (57).

Johnson describes a Scotland that has shaken almost free of an oppressive past. Fergusson and Burns view the same scene, but with very different emotions. They both knew that, having no capital – only words, and those chiefly of a devalued Scots currency – they were excluded from the new improvements. They also knew that they spoke for many others in Scotland who had been left behind, or left to emigrate. They saw what was being lost in the cultural exchange that purchased the new 'improvements'. It is no accident that Johnson is the target of two of Fergusson's satires. That his former teachers at St Andrews should offer Johnson a 'magnificent treat' of foreign dishes symbolises to Fergusson the extreme deference to English authority (associated, as so often in these poems, with imported foods and tastes) that was vitiating Scottish self-respect.[16]

Fergusson and Burns often write in opposition, then, to eighteenth-century narratives of Scottish improvement; the emerging values that threaten old Scotia are specifically linked by both poets to commerce and trade. In Fergusson's 'The MUTUAL COMPLAINT of *Plainstanes* and *Causey*, in their Mother-tongue', the street and pavement of Edinburgh lament in Scots the dramatic recent increase in wheeled and foot traffic that has accompanied the city's growth. They debate who is taking more punishment from the high volume of traffic: the causeway, with its burden of 'clumsy carts and hackney-coaches' (II, 124), or the pavement, which daily endures the burden of 'tradesmen tramping o'er' its 'wamb' (125) as well as the 'teazing' 'stroaks' of ladies' '*patens*' (124) and the mincing tread of 'beaux and macaronies' (126). This increasing traffic is from their viewpoint an oppression: the constant circulation of bodies and goods-in-transit literally presses down on their consciousness. The nail-studded brogues of 'Gallic chairmen', laments Plainstanes, have stamped so heavily on his 'tender buke' that they have drilled him full of holes (123). Life was better a hundred years ago, they both agree; and those new veils over the ladies' faces are, like the other innovations, no improvement (123). This poem, like so many of Fergusson's best, evokes 'fundamental' Scottishness, captured in a moment of 'complaint' – both a legal and a lover's term – against the pressures of a somehow alien new prosperity, which (so far as plainstanes and causey can see) produces only wear and tear.

A close match in topic and setting to Fergusson's midnight dialogue is Burns's 'The Brigs of Ayr', in which the old fifteenth-century bridge, at leisure in the pre-dawn hours, engages in a spirited flyting with the new bridge, begun in May 1786, some six months before Burns's writing of the poem.[17] As in most such arguments in Burns and Fergusson, the old brig, who ridicules the inflated claims of the new one (significantly if bizarrely imagined as decked out in a fancy coat purchased in London), decisively wins the set-to:

> Conceited gowk! puff'd up wi' windy pride!
> This mony a year I've stood the flood an' tide;
> And tho' wi' crazy eild I'm sair forfairn,
> I'll be a *Brig* when ye're a shapeless cairn! (I, 285)

Burns follows Fergusson in often dramatising Scotland as a heated argument between 'then' and 'now'.

Fergusson's 'The Bugs', one source for Burns's 'To a Louse', focuses with a grotesque intensity on parasitic insects, illustrating a micro-economic vision of the new consumption. In 'To a Louse', to begin with the more familiar poem, the speaker observes (like Dr Johnson in his account of his travels) that the contagion of luxury has penetrated even into Scotland's smallest parishes. Jenny's finery follows a fad: so-called 'balloon' bonnets came in with the Italian aeronaut Vincenzo Lunardi, who was staging balloon ascents in Scotland during the mid-1780s.[18] Jenny has scorned the homemade flannel caps of the farm wives and purchased herself a 'fine Lunardi'. Yet her air-puffed 'balloon' signifies only her pride, about to be deflated as the parish laughs and points at an incongruity – a large louse on a fancy bonnet, a sight not visible to herself.

Fergusson's 'The Bugs' contains one likely inspiration for Jenny in its vignette of sleeping 'Cloe' and the bedbugs privileged to bite her bosom throughout the night. Cloe – unconsciously, like Jenny – entertains a select group of lucky 'reptiles' that

> . . . 'midst the lillies of fair CLOE's breast
> Implant the deep carnation, and enjoy
> Those sweets which angel modesty hath seal'd

From eyes profane . . .
    Even so, befalls it to this creeping race,
This envy'd commonwealth – For they a while
On Cloe's bosom, alabaster fair,
May steal ambrosial bliss – or may regale
On the rich *viands* of luxurious blood,
Delighted and suffic'd. (2, 148)

Both Burns's poem and 'The Bugs' consider what utopia might look like 'to a louse' (or bug). And both say that happiness resides in a minimum of strictly necessary transactions and exchanges. Lice do not need hats, underwear, or for that matter church services and sermons – only a little blood from time to time (which Jenny's poor nit will never extract from the gauze and lace of the bonnet). A host who sleeps soundly is also desirable, from the point of view of an insect. Other bugs, though,

. . . destin'd to an humbler fate
Seek shelter from the dwellings of the poor,
Plying their nightly suction in the bed
Of toil'd *mechanic*, who, with folded arms,
Enjoys the comforts of a sleep so sound,
That not th' alarming sting of glutting Bug
To mur'drous deed can rouse his brawny arm
Upon the blood-swoln fiend . . . (II, 147)

Burns's bumpkin speaker, trying to work out the stranded louse's problem, suggests that Jenny's bonnet be abandoned for the unwashed waistcoat of a small boy or perhaps the close-fitting woollen 'toy' of an older lady in the congregation (the poem takes place during a church service); but in an early stanza he has already thought of a better solution. If only the louse could find a beggar, it could emigrate, setting up a colony or plantation where its descendants could truly flourish:

Ye ugly, creepan, blastet wonner,
Detested, shunn'd, by saunt an' sinner,
How daur ye set your fit upon her,
    Sae fine a *Lady*!
Gae somewhere else and seek your dinner,
    On some poor body.

Swith, in some beggar's haffet squattle;
There ye may creep, and sprawl, and sprattle,

Wi' ither kindred, jumping cattle,
    In shoals and nations;
Where *horn* nor *bane* ne'er daur unsettle,
    Your thick plantations. (I, 193)

In an age when combs were routinely made of horn or bone, Fergusson's tiny 'cattle,' his bugs, never do move on, lingering in Cloe's bed until they are massacred in the flurry of spring cleaning that freshens her chamber. Burns seems to be reflecting throughout 'To a Louse' on the mock gravity of Fergusson's final *sententia*:

Happy the Bug, whose unambitious views,
To gilded pomp ne'er tempt him to aspire; . . .
He never knows at morn the busy brush
Of scrubbing chambermaid: his coursing blood
Is ne'er obstructed with obnoxious dose
By OLIPHANT prepar'd. (II, 149)

Burns's poem differs from Fergusson's in making its point in the vernacular and connecting his bug to the underclass: Fergusson's view down the social ladder stops at the working poor, the weary 'mechanic'.[19] Burns draws an analogy between nearly invisible biting insects and the hordes of homeless people in Scotland: both 'races' rate only as nuisances in middle-class and genteel eyes, and both are marked for extermination. Beggars (bypassed by improvement) are the only reliably hospitable hosts for a louse of 1785, for they will never have homes to clean, sheets to launder, or even combs to disturb the peace of any vermin who have taken up residence in their hair. As social outcasts, vagrants and lice have much in common.

Two of Burns's best known poems, then, 'The Cotter's Saturday Night' and 'To a Louse', carry on a conversation with a prototype poem by Fergusson that at least on one level addresses the Scottish economy. And notwithstanding differences in style, the message in all four poems is similar: peace and quiet are best found among the poorest Scotsmen.

Unlucky Poets

    . . . Tho' all the pow'rs of song thy fancy fir'd;
    Yet Luxury and Wealth lay by in state,
    And thankless starv'd what they so much admir'd.
  –Burns, epitaph for Fergusson, from additional stanzas
      unpublished in his lifetime

Walter Benjamin called the nineteenth-century Parisian *flaneur* 'the observer of the marketplace . . . He is a spy for the capitalists, on assignment in the realm of consumers' (427).[20] Fergusson, though an indefatigable urban stroller, and Burns (whose early speaker learned a stance of by turns playful and sardonic watchfulness from his 'elder brother in the Muse' [I, 323]) are not flaneurs in Benjamin's sense of wholly passive observers. They cannot move only through the opening landscape of their daily life. As Scotia's bards, however self-appointed and uncompensated, they are called to view the passing scene in the light of all of Scottish time. They know that as bards they play a vital role in the wellbeing of Scottish culture. Yet both, in by turns joking and bitter asides, also see the 'rhyming trade' as a series of 'luckless' tradeoffs: rich in feeling and thought, bards are in material terms (like 'reptiles', lice, or bugs) creatures of little substance.[21]

In a burlesque directly descended from such Fergusson poems as 'Tea', Burns describes the malignancy of fortune (and critics) towards that 'poor, . . . naked child – the BARD':

> Foil'd, bleeding, tortured in the unequal strife,
> The hapless Poet flounders on thro' life.
> Till fled each hope that once his bosom fired,
> And fled each Muse that glorious once inspired,
> Low-sunk in squalid, unprotected age,
> Dead, even resentment, for his injured page,
> He heeds nor feels no more the ruthless Critic's rage!
>   So, by some hedge, the generous steed deceased,
> For half-starved snarling curs a dainty feast;
> By toil and famine wore to skin and bone,
> Lies, senseless of each tugging bitch's son. (II, 587–88)

Retaining something of Fergusson's stylisation, Burns's lines show one of his major differences from his predecessor: Fergusson almost never directly appeals to his reader (for sympathy, as here, or for assent) as Burns's so often do.

Fergusson typically deflects to objects the articulate energy that Burns projects outward towards his audience. One of his best poems responds to the imagined reproaches of his threadbare breeches as he prepares to throw them out the window of his garret:

> You needna wag your DUDS o' clouts,
> Nor fa' into your dorty pouts,

> To think that erst you've hain'd my TAIL
> Frae WIND and WEET, frae SNAW and HAIL,
> And for reward, when bald and hummil,
> Frae garret high to dree a tumble.
> For you I car'd, as lang's ye dow'd
> Be lin'd wi' siller or wi' gowd:
> Now to befriend, it wad be folly,
> Your raggit hide, an' pouches holey . . . (II, 215)

Like their owner, the breeches must be discarded, for their pockets contain none of the coins needed to maintain them. Yet any bitterness is masked by humour. The speaker instructs the ghost of his deceased garment to search the city of Edinburgh for some 'lucky' poet to haunt:

> Or if some bard, in lucky times,
> Shou'd profit meikle by his rhimes,
> And pace awa' wi smirky face,
> In siller or in gowden lace,
> Glowr in his face, like spectre gaunt,
> Remind him o' his former want (II, 217)

The 'half-sarket' speaker of Burns's 'The Vision' also addresses the bard's impoverishment, but with more asperity. Beginning in close quarters (the speaker's smoky, rat-infested cottage), the poem becomes, after the arrival of the Lowland Muse, a panoramic survey of Ayrshire geography and history. But before Coila appears to change his mind, the speaker surveys a youth wasted in the pursuit of chimeras:

> . . . I had spent my *youthfu' prime*,
>   An' done nae-thing,
> But stringing blethers up in rhyme
>   For fools to sing.
>
> Had I to guid advice but harket,
> I might, by this, hae led a market,
> Or strutted in a Bank and clarket
>   My *Cash-Account*,
> While here, half-mad, half-fed, half-sarket,
>   Is a' th' amount (I, 103)

The mercantile reference to 'Cash-Account' is italicised, as if a term in some foreign tongue – and in Burns's view it is. (Similarly, line two of

'The Cotter's Saturday Night' denies its author is a 'mercenary Bard' – a highly rhetorical moment, as the speaker so clearly regards the phrase as an oxymoron [I, 145].) The creation of rhymes and accumulation of cash are antithetical activities in the minds of both poets.

Hugh MacDiarmid, writing of Fergusson and Burns, once declared that 'direct poetry' is the vital mode of Scottish literary genius.[22] Yet when these poets dramatise interactions (between the imported and the home grown, or between consumer products and freely circulating rhymes), they are more dramatic or dialogic than direct. Lively contrast – Scots versus English, country versus city, new versus old – is at the heart of these poems. Some of the best are outright dialogues: debates between two bridges, two dogs, two ghosts. But even poems not built around contending voices have a dialectic tendency to pose the material or 'real' (usually rejected) against its intangible bardic counterpart – an imagination, not description, of Scotland. 'The Vision' begins in a smoky hut, but daily life is transcended when the Lowland Muse appears.

Fergusson's 'A Tale' introduces another contrast between the real and the visionary, pitting the letter 'H' against a large joint of cold mutton. Pedantic Mr Birch maintains that the letter 'H' is 'but a breathing' (II, 65): '*Ergo* he saw no proper cause,/Why such a letter should exist' (II, 64). When Birch is given cold mutton for his dinner, he tells his servant to 'take and h - eat it'(65), scorning to voice the despised letter and thereby, as Fergusson notes with delight, author-ising the waiter Tom to eat his master's dinner. This stylised contrast between theory and practice, the word and the flesh, is offered as a joke, but on examination rather a grim one. To 'breathe' is in Latin also to inspire [*inspirare*], but Dr Birch's stand on inspiration or principle deprives him of his meat.

Benjamin writes of his detached urban stroller that 'the street conducts the flaneur into a vanished time. For him every street is precipitous. It leads downward . . . into a past that can be all the more spellbinding because it is not his own, not private' (416). Bards, too, view daily life while also travelling in time. Yet the echoes of history and possible futures they imagine are in fact experienced as private – belonging to them and appropriated to their bardic vision. Often they describe the world of their own day only to turn away from it and its inhabitants (in Burns's repeated scornful phrase, the 'warly race' [I, 59]) – and not only because the world and worldly people (pre-occupied with fine bonnets, cash-accounts, and consumption) reject bards as beings of little account. Both poets distance themselves from daily life in order to seek a larger perspective, a view of Scotland not as a collection of discrete objects and characters but as a coherent and rounded *subject.*

Hugh MacDiarmid, implying some oxymoron of his own, titled a mid-life memoir *Lucky Poet.* But Burns follows Fergusson in seeing the 'rhyming trade' as necessarily a 'luckless' business. The poems of both suggest that bards, dealing in improvised 'blethers', can expect only intangible benefits (fun, fame, good feeling, applause, notoriety) in exchange for their gift, to Scotland, of Scotland. The hands, pockets, and even 'stamacks' of bards must remain empty, even though they perform the crucial cultural work of integrating their passing scene with the storeyed Scotland of old and with all possible Scotlands to come. Increasing material prosperity and wealth cannot in themselves perform this work of cultural synthesis. Nor can newspapers: Walter Ruddiman of the *Weekly Magazine* was wise to be kind to Robert Fergusson.

In the view of Burns and Fergusson, the rhyming trade has its compensations; but they proceed from a dispersal of good feeling rather than an accumulation of wealth.[23] The poems of both show their awareness that the bard's Scotland, precisely because it is a matter of indirect and intangible breathings or words, can in theory circulate endlessly: poetry and song appreciate in cultural value to the extent that they *are* in circulation. Poems and songs are manufactured products, artifacts designed to be consumed. Yet they are not for sale, if to purchase a thing means to claim ownership, taking a commodity out of circulation. Strangely enough, poetic images, like the heart's blood of Burns's John Barleycorn (personification of whisky), show their vitality most dramatically following consumption:

> And they hae taen his very heart's blood,
> And drank it round and round;
> And still the more and more they drank,
> Their joy did more abound. (I, 31)

Still, both these self-called unlucky poets dramatise their sense that those who profess the rhyming trade purchase a speculative, remote possibility of endless circulation (a bard's eternity) at the cost of any hint of profit or material prosperity. They know they choose the 'breathing' at the expense of the dish of mutton, and that in one sense, the joke is on them.

Butterflies and Worms

Syne even poetrie becomes
a naething, an affair of thrums
of words, words, a noise that jumms
    wi leean skreed,
the purport tint, man's sperit numbs–
      as weill be deid. – Robert Garioch, 'To Robert Fergusson'

One central difference between the two poets is that Fergusson's pessimism drives his images downward. Sir Precentor strolls the streets of Edinburgh fascinated but at some level horrified by the city's daily and nightly orgy of consumption and waste: there is a hallucinatory quality in his poems. Burns, who can be as severe a critic of consumerism as Fergusson, nonetheless takes heart in such developments as the 'New Light' Calvinism spreading through his Ayrshire neighbourhood; he is comforted by signs of intellectual progress. One reason that Burns's 'The Brigs of Ayr' does not equal Fergusson's 'Plainstanes and Causey' is that Burns is simply not as afraid of the dark as Fergusson; he cannot with sufficient intensity evoke a haunted setting. He tries later to write of 'warlocks' in 'Tam o'Shanter' (like Fergusson's midnight dialogue, a poem in octosyllabics), and there he succeeds, for he divides the poem's viewpoint between a neoclassical narrator who spins out epic similes and a drunken protagonist who never trembles (indeed, shouts out loud approval) at the sight of dancing witches. In 'Tam o'Shanter', like the similarly constructed 'Address to the Deil', Burns writes brilliantly but sceptically of superstition. He has no thought of attempting to generate real fear.

Fergusson's Scots poems never open out, like so many of Burns's, into a vision of the better world that's 'comin yet, for a' that' (II, 763). Their very structure often traces a precipitous downward spiral. The concluding lines of 'Good Eating' gloomily predict the fate of the intemperate: 'misery of thought, and racking pain,/Shall plunge you headlong to the dark abyss' (II, 103). The final dismissal in 'Ode to the Gowdspink' is of life itself:

> Care I for life? Shame fa' the hair;
> A FIELD o'ergrown wi' rankest STUBBLE,
> The essence of a paltry bubble. (II, 178)

Burns tends to conclude his poems with an outward, upward movement: one example is the second verse-letter to John Lapraik, in which he and his fellow bard are taken up into poets' heaven. In Fergusson, a wilting or descent even can occur in the second line of couplets: '[Wine] maks you stark, and bauld and brave,/E'en whan descending to the Grave' (II, 113).

Burns cut his satiric teeth on William Auld, minister of Mauchline, and other Auld Licht men of the cloth. But religion is for Fergusson intertwined with thoughts of death; he is oppressed by a sensation of ineradicable guilt:

> . . . straight a painted Corp he sees,
> Lang streekit 'neath its Canopies.
> Soon, soon, will this his Mirth controul,
> And send Damnation to his Soul . . . (II, 114)

The satiric zeal with which Burns counterattacked the 'holy beagles', his oppressors, is not to be found in Fergusson, who reserves his most persistent animus for the Town Guard:

> And thou, great god of *Aqua Vitae*!
> Wha sways the empire of this city,
> When fou we're sometimes capernoity,
> Be thou prepar'd
> To hedge us frae that black banditti,
> The City-Guard. (II, 34)[24]

In 'Auld Reikie', the Edinburgh crowd pelt the Guard with dirt; and in 'Plainstanes and Causey', the roadway entertains a bizarre passing worry that he will be taken up by a sheriff's officer ('shelly-coat') for complaining so loudly about the traffic (II, 125). It is as if Fergusson insists only on poetic (not police) surveillance of the town.

Fergusson's Scotland is a darker place. He is less hopeful, more haunted, than Burns. It is much more difficult, as Edwin Morgan has observed, 'to see the man in his poetry' (76). Such poems as 'On seeing a Butterfly in the Street' suggest that he has taken the teachings of strict Calvinism too deeply to heart: he cannot rejoice in the rich gift of his talent, and in this he is more reminiscent of William Cowper than of Burns. The wings of poesy exist only to be stripped off by a cruel fate (II, 156). And the 'man's' not the 'gowd', as in Burns, but only a 'vile worm' tricked out as a butterfly:

> DAFT gowk, in MACARONI dress,
> Are ye come here to shew your face,

Bowden wi' pride o' simmer gloss,
To cast a dash at REIKIE's cross;
And glowr at mony twa-legg'd creature,
Flees braw by art, tho' worms by nature? (II, 154)

Metamorphosis into a thing of fluttering beauty (like a poem or a song) is seen by Fergusson mainly as an elaborate and fleeting imposture: 'Newfangle grown wi' new got form,/You soar aboon your mither WORM' (II, 155).

Burns's advantage over Fergusson, beyond possession of a more hopeful temperament, was simply time. Following his debut volume in 1786, published when he was twenty-seven, he had ten more years. During this decade, he moved beyond satire and narrative poetry, exploring the possibilities of lyric statement and Scottish song. He discovered and immortalised Highland speakers, Jacobite speakers, women speakers; he even learned from Jacobite song how to access the voices of aristocrats, from Robert Bruce to James II and Charles Edward Stuart. Burns's songs are (as he intended and envisioned) at the root of how Scotland is still imagined today.[25] He captured the soul of a nation – Scotland as comprised of Lowland and Highland, Jacobite and Presbyterian, aristocratic and democratic elements. But Robert Fergusson came first and showed him how, when he celebrated (and as a bard defined) Edinburgh, the city that is Scotland's vital heart.

Notes

1. A major Milton text for Fergusson is 'L'Allegro': 'But come thou goddess fair and free/In Heav'n yclep'd *Euphrosyne*/And by men, heart-easing Mirth' (Merritt Y. Hughes, *John Milton: Complete Poems and Major Prose* [New York: Odyssey, 1957], 68–69). Allusion can mark a single line, as in 'Auld Reikie': 'Gie to MIRTH the lee lang Day' (II,117). In 'Leith Races', the echo is extended, as the speaker invokes and is accompanied by Mirth. Burns's 'The Holy Fair', in which the speaker encounters and addresses 'Fun', is modelled on 'Leith Races', employing its 'Chrystis Kirk' stanza-form and its presiding spirit of glee (I,129–120). For further discussion of Fergusson and Milton, see Edwin Morgan, 'Robert Fergusson', in *Crossing the Border: Essays on Scottish Literature* (Manchester: Carcanet, 1990), 90–91.

2. Matthew McDiarmid, Fergusson's modern editor, believes that Burns first encountered Fergusson as late as 1784 or 1785 (I, 180); he is inclined to ascribe the outpouring of Scots poems by Burns in 1784–85 in large part to this first encounter. In his autobiographical letter to Dr John Moore, however, dated 2 August 1787 (the context there implies that his Irvine

crony Richard Brown may have introduced him to Fergusson's poems),
Burns himself sets the date in his 'twenty-third year', or around 1782.
Burns's letter to Moore does give his predecessor full credit for re-inspiring
him as a poet: 'Rhyme, except some religious pieces which are in print, I
had given up; but meeting with Fergusson's Scotch Poems, I strung anew
my wildly sounding, rustic lyre with emulating vigour' (J. DeLancey
Ferguson and G. Ross Roy, eds., *The Letters of Robert Burns.* 2 vols.
Oxford: Clarendon, 1985, I, 143). Subsequent citations are from this
edition.

    Burns purchased his own copy of Fergusson early in 1786. On 17
February he wrote to John Richmond, newly arrived in Edinburgh: 'Be so
good as to send me Ferguson [sic] by Connel and I will remit you the
money' (*Letters* I, 28). It is possible that he worked with an open copy of
Fergusson beside him as he arranged the contents and completed the
poems for his debut volume, *Poems, Chiefly in the Scottish Dialect,*
published at Kilmarnock in late July, 1786.

3. The order of poems in the first two editions is given in the Scottish Text
Society edition; but below are the contents as Burns encountered them
during the 1780s. The two sections are themselves curiously subdivided, as
the contents list reveals. Ruddiman's arrangement emphasises the dynamic
interplay of Scots with English elements:

English Poems
'Morning, A Pastoral', 'Noon, A Pastoral', 'Night, A Pastoral', 'The Complaint', 'The Decay of Friendship', 'Against repining at Fortune', 'Con-
science', 'Damon to his Friends, A Ballad', 'Retirement', 'Ode to Hope',
'The Rivers of Scotland, an Ode', 'Town and Country Contrasted, an Epistle
to a Friend', 'Ode to Pity', 'On the Cold Month of April', 'The Simile', 'Buggs
[sic]', 'A Saturday's Expedition', 'The Canongate Playhouse in Ruins',
'Fashion', 'The Amputation', 'Verses Written at the Hermitage of Braid',
'A Tale', 'The Peasant, the Hen, and young Ducks', 'Songs' [pp. 66–67],
'Extempore, On being asked which of three Sisters was the most beautiful',
'On the Death of Mr. Thomas Lancashire, Comedian', 'On seeing a Lady
Paint herself, an Epigram', 'On seeing Stanzas addressed to Mrs Hartley'.

Scots Poems
'Sandie and Willie', 'Geordie and Davie', 'An Eclogue, To the Memory of
Dr Wilkie', 'Elegy on the Death of Mr David Gregory', 'The Daft Days',
'The King's Birthday in Edinburgh', 'Caller Oysters', 'Braid Cloth', 'Elegy
on the Death of Scots Music', 'Hallow Fair', 'Ode to the Bee', 'On Seeing a
Butterfly in the Street'

PART II
'Ode to the Gowdspink', 'Caller Water', 'The Sitting of the Session', 'The
Rising of the Session', 'Leith Races', 'The Farmer's Ingle', 'The Election',

'To the Tron-Kirk Bell', 'Mutual Complaint of Plainstanes and Causeway [sic]', 'A Drink Eclogue', 'To the Principal and Professors of the University of St Andrews, on their superb treat to Dr Samuel Johnson', 'Elegy on John Hogg', 'The Ghaists: A Kirkyard Eclogue', 'Epistle to Robert Fergusson', 'Answer to the Epistle', 'To my Auld Breeks', 'Auld Reikie', 'Hame Content'

English Poems
'To the Memory of James Cunningham', 'The Delights of Virtue', 'A Tavern Elegy', 'Good Eating', 'Tea', 'The Sow of Feeling', 'An Expedition to Fife', 'To Sir John Fielding, on his Attempt to suppress *The Beggar's Opera*', 'Character of a Friend', 'To Dr Samuel Johnson', 'Epigram on seeing Scales used in a Mason Lodge', 'Epitaph on General Wolfe', 'On the numerous Epitaphs on Gen. Wolfe', 'Epilogue Spoken by Mr Wilson in the Character of an Edinburgh Buck', 'My Last Will', 'Codicil'

Posthumous Pieces
'Job Ch 3', 'Ode to Horror', 'Ode to Disappointment', 'Dirge', 'Horror Ode XI. Lib. I', 'The Author's Life', 'Song', 'Epigram on a Lawyer desiring one of the Tribe to Look with respect to a Gibbet', 'On the Author's intention of Going to Sea'.

Though the title identifies it as the second, this was actually the third edition of Fergusson's poems brought out by Ruddiman (*Poems on Various Subjects, by Robert Fergusson. In Two Parts, the Second Edition* [Edinburgh, T. Ruddiman, 1782]. The 1779 edition reprinted the 1773, which contained only eight poems in Scots, and collected many further poems; it is now considered the 'first' edition. See Alexander Law, 'The Bibliography of Fergusson', in *Robert Fergusson, 1750–1774: Essays by Various Hands to Commemorate the Bicentenary of his Birth*, ed. Sydney Goodsir Smith [London: Nelson, 1952], 150.)

4. Matthew P. McDiarmid, ed., *The Poems of Robert Fergusson*. 2 vols. (Edinburgh: William Blackwood for the Scottish Text Society; third series, vols. 21 and 24, 1954 and 1956), II, 112–113. Subsequent citations are from this edition.

5. James Kinsley, ed., *The Poems and Songs of Robert Burns*. 3 vols. (Oxford: Clarendon, 1968), I, 173. Subsequent quotations are from this edition.

6. A distaste for novelty extends to Burns's musical preferences. Millar Patrick considers Burns's account of the Scottish psalm settings in 'The Cotter's Saturday Night', for instance, noting with surprise that Burns praises only the old 'grave and slow-moving tunes' and entirely rejects the 'briskness of the new style that was just coming into use'. In Millar Patrick, *Four Centuries of Scottish Psalmody* (London: Oxford, 1950), 181.

7. The many parallels between the Kilmarnock poems and the Scots poems of Fergusson were systematically surveyed in 1925 by the *Scots Magazine*; there is also a very full account of echoes and parallels in Thomas

Crawford's *Burns: A Study of the Poems and Songs* (Stanford: Stanford University Press, 1960). Aside from 'Leith Races' and its influence on Burns's 'The Holy Fair', some other echoes noted by Crawford include Fergusson's 'Answer to Mr. J. S. Epistle' and its relationship to Burns's 'To J. S'. (Jamie Smith) and Burns's epistle to William Simson and its link to Fergusson's 'Hame Content' (96n). ('Hame Content' is also a strong influence on parts of Burns's 'The Twa Dogs' and 'The Cotter's Saturday Night'.) One further example from many possible: Fergusson's 'The King's Birthday in Edinburgh' not only influenced the Bard's song in 'Love and Liberty' (T. Crawford 142) but also Burns's 'A Dream'.

8. Burns's 'The Author's Earnest Cry and Prayer, to the right Honorable and Honorable, the Scotch Representatives in the House of Commons' evidently emulates Fergusson's 'The Ghaists'. The idea of the trustees betraying Scotland in order to 'get a place at court' is mirrored in Burns's lines on Parliament's abandonment of Scotland:

> Does ony *great man* glunch an' gloom?
> Speak out an' never fash your thumb!
> Let *posts* and *pensions* sink or swoom
>   Wi' them wha grant them:
> If honestly they canna come,
>   Far better want them. (I, 186)

9. George Heriot's fund was managed by the town council of Edinburgh, Watson's by 'a board of governors consisting of 'certain merchants and one minister of the city' (McDiarmid II, 287). Fergusson unfavourably compares the civic spirit of former and present men of business in the city.

10. For a detailed discussion of Allan Ramsay's relationship to London writers, see Carol McGuirk 'Augustan Influences on Allan Ramsay', *Studies in Scottish Literature* 16 (1981), 97–109.

11. Tom Scott, 'A Review of Robert Fergusson's Poems', *Akros* 2.6 (December 1967): 15–26. The title is misleading, for this is not so much a review as an overview and appreciation of Fergusson. Scott later surveyed Fergusson's bibliography in 'Robert Fergusson: A Bibliographical Review to 1966', *Scotia Review* 7 (1974), 5–18.

12. Marshall Walker summarises Fergusson's opus as 'thirty-three poems in Scots of consistently high quality and fifty comparatively pallid poems in English'(in *Scottish Literature Since 1707* [London: Longman, 1996], 73). Sydney Goodsir Smith begins an extensive overview of Fergusson with a similar dismissal of more than half of Fergusson's body of work: 'As in the case of Burns, we can neglect his English works. They were merely elegant exercises in the style of the period – of no literary value at all' (in *Robert Fergusson, 1750–1774, op. cit.*, 13). Alexander Kinghorn and Alexander Law reprint none of Fergusson's English poems in their selected edition, though they temper their critique of the non-vernacular writings: 'Of the fifty poems he published in English, only a handful are more than competent' (in *Poems by Allan Ramsay and Robert Fergusson* [Totowa,

NJ: Rowman and Littlefield, 1974], xix). Allan H. MacLaine begins his book on Fergusson with the observation that 'In no other Scottish poet of the century, including Burns himself, is the contrast between Scottish and English work so pronounced and striking as it is in Fergusson. His vernacular poems are usually fresh, original, and brilliantly executed; his poems in English, with few exceptions, are imitative, trite, and worthless as literature' (*Robert Fergusson* [New York: Twayne, 1965], 22). A final powerful voice is that of Hugh MacDiarmid, who writes that 'The consensus of literary critics holds that wherever Scottish writers have written both in Scots and in English, by far their best work has invariably been done in the former. Fergusson is no exception, and [J. Hepburn] Millar [in his essay on Fergusson] goes on to say [that]: "Fergusson's English verse, it need scarce be said, is poor and unimportant"' (*Robert Fergusson, 1750–1774, op. cit.*, 60).

Recent writers have questioned this assumption that Scots poets are doomed to mediocrity unless they employ vernacular. Robert Crawford, following quotation from Fergusson's satire on the banquet provided for Samuel Johnson by the faculty at St. Andrews, notes that 'It is tempting just to relish . . . the Scots, but the technically correct 'REGENTS' and the Latin 'ALMA MATER' remind us that the language-range of the poem is wide and that it deploys an insider's as well as an outsider's vocabulary and perceptions. Fergusson writes in and from the standpoint of the vernacular, but takes from the language of high culture and literary decorum what he needs in order to play these back to his Principal and Professors in a way that outflanks and mocks them' (in 'Robert Fergusson's Robert Burns', *Robert Burns and Cultural Authority*, ed. Robert Crawford (Edinburgh: Edinburgh UP, 1997), 5.

The poor quality of some (by no means all) of Fergusson's English poems might be considered in a light other than language *per se*: many are juvenilia, whose failure has to do with the poet's immaturity. But such confident burlesques in English as 'The Bugs' and 'Good Eating' are akin (in their hyperbole and grotesque imagery) to Fergusson's best poems in Scots.

13. One of Burns's songs, 'Caledonia', may echo these stanzas in 'The Farmer's Ingle' that celebrate an indomitable Scotia. 'Caledonia' is set to the air 'Caledonian Hunt's Delight' (familiar as the musical setting for 'Bonie Doon'):

> Thus bold, independant, unconquer'd and free,
>> Her bright course of glory for ever shall run;
> For brave Caledonia immortal must be,
>> I'll prove it from Euclid as clear as the sun:
> Rectangle-triangle the figure we'll chuse,
>> The Upright is Chance, and old Time is the Base;
> But brave Caledonia's the Hypothenuse,
>> Then, Ergo, she'll match them, and match them always. (I, 459)

The rhyming of 'chuse' and 'Hypothenuse' is reminiscent of Fergusson's geometric joking in 'Elegy, on the Death of Mr David Gregory, late Professor of Mathematics in the University of St Andrews': 'He could, by Euclid, prove lang sine,/A ganging point compos'd a line' (II, 1).

14. Burns's Spenserian rhyme in 'The Cotter's Saturday Night' differs from Fergusson's in 'The Farmer's Ingle'. Fergusson simplifies *The Faerie Queene's* rhyme-scheme (ababbcbcC) by introducing a d-rhyme (ababcdcdD). Burns adheres to the difficult rhyming pattern of Spenser, in the first stanza of 'The Cotter's Saturday Night' rhyming the words friend (a), pays (b), end (a), praise (b), lays (b), scene (c), ways (b), been (c), ween (C). In the twentieth stanza, quoted in my essay above, the 'c' rhyme is really a slant 'a' rhyme: soil (a), sent (b), toil (a), content (b), prevent (b), vile (slant a), rent (b), while (slant a), Isle (slant A). An extended explication of the cultural significance of 'The Cotter's Saturday Night' may be found in David Hill Radcliffe's 'Imitation, Literacy, and "The Cotter's Saturday Night"', in Carol McGuirk, ed. *Critical Essays on Robert Burns* (New York: Hall, 1998), 251–280.

15. Citations are from Samuel Johnson and James Boswell, *A Journey to the Western Islands and The Journal of a Tour to the Hebrides*, ed. Peter Levi (Harmondsworth: Penguin, 1984).

16. Fergusson must have learned about the fêting of Dr Johnson from someone at St Andrews, for Johnson's own account (cf. Penguin, 36–39) was not published until two years after Fergusson's death.

17. For a comprehensive treatment of Fergusson's and Burns's adaptations of the flyting tradition, see Kenneth G. Simpson, 'Burns and the Legacy of Flyting', in Carol McGuirk, ed., *Critical Essays on Robert Burns* (New York: Hall, 1998), 151–162.

18. References to ballooning also occur in the Postscript to Burns's 'To W***** S*****, Ochiltree', in which Burns solemnly informs his vernacular correspondent that the Auld Licht are planning a balloon flight to the moon (I, 98). For more on Vincenzo Lunardi's cameo appearance in 'To a Louse', see Carol McGuirk, ed. *Selected Poems of Robert Burns* (London: Penguin, 1993), 223.

19. This direction of social perspective further downward also characterises 'Love and Liberty''s echoes of Fergusson's 'The Daft Days'. Both poems stress the joys of feasting as a warm counterpoint to Scotland's dark winter, but Burns's characters are homeless beggars, not Edinburgh holiday-makers. Both poems also defend Scottish music by attacking the vogue for Italian melody. Fergusson enjoins his Edinburgh '*Fidlers*' to 'roset weel your fiddle-sticks/And banish vile Italian tricks/From out your quorum, / Nor *fortes* wi' *pianos* mix,/Gie's Tulloch Gorum' (II, 34). Burns uses mock-Italian to describe his beggar-fiddler's preparations for performance:

> Wi' hand on hainch, and upward e'e,
> He croon'd his gamut, ONE, TWO, THREE,
> Then in an ARIOSO key,

The wee Apollo
Set off wi' ALLEGRETTO glee
His GIGA SOLO– (I, 202)

20. Citations are from Walter Benjamin, *The Arcades Project*, transl. Howard Eiland and Kevin McLaughlin (Cambridge, Mass.: Harvard-Belknap, 1999).

21. The phrase 'the luckless rhyming trade' is from Burns's poem 'To R**** G***** of F*****, Esq'. [Robert Graham of Fintry, who was on the Board of Excise] (II, 585).

22. Hugh MacDiarmid, 'Robert Fergusson: Direct Poetry and the Scottish Genius,' in *Robert Fergusson, 1750–1774: Essays by Various Hands to Commemorate the Bicentenary of his Birth*, ed. Sydney Goodsir Smith (London: Nelson, 1952), 51–74.

23. For more on Burns's intertwined ideas of poetry and poverty, see Carol McGuirk, 'Poor Bodies: Burns and the Melancholy of Anatomy', in Carol McGuirk ed., *Critical Essays on Robert Burns* (New York: Hall, 1998), 32–48.

24. Burns, who uses the word 'banditti' several times, may have learned it from Fergusson.

25. Robert Crawford has discussed the 'Britishness' of Burns's song project; see *Devolving English Literature*, Second Edition (Edinburgh: Edinburgh University Press, 2000), 88–110.

DO RAIBEART MAC FHEARGHAIS

Sheas mi fo chraoibh ubhail sa mhadainn,
caithreamach àrd le srann nan seillean,
's iad air bhoil' a' deoghail gu domhainn
    às na cuachan geala,
is smaoinich mi orts', 'ic Fhearghais, ag obair
    le do sheillean sa challaid,

Agus ortsa gu dìomhain an doillearachd Bheadlaim,
an doillearachd inntinn cràidhtich caithte:
an tàinig aiteal tuigse a-steach ort
    mar a losgadh do chonnadh
ach mar nach milleadh an Tìm liath acrach
    do rannan sona?

Mura robh de neart agad a' chuach a thraoghadh
an robh thu air eòlas a chur air pòitear,
fear-lagha, lasgaire, meàrlach, siùrsach,
    tro ghèilean a' gheamhraidh,
no air blas fhaighinn air na h-eisirean sùghmhor
    no air fàilidhean Dhùn Eideann?

Cha robh feum agads' air maothalachd Raibidh,
air aibheiseachadh no seasamh eudmhor,
cha bu bhòidhche leat uchd na maighdinn na 'n lilidh,
    ach dh'òl thu a' chiall,
's rùsig thu cealgaireachd le faclan geura
    is taic bhon Diabh'l.

Nam b' e urra mhòr thu ann an dèise clò
a bhuilicheadh a bhriogais air an stàit,
fear air an robh cùram mu airgead is chliù
    ga fhiaradh o shaorsa,
am fosgladh dhut riamh uiread de shunnd
    no cheòl do-chasgadh?

                        Meg Bateman

TO ROBERT FERGUSSON

At morning I stood at an apple tree,
lofty and clamorous with the buzzing of bees,
returning intent on drinking deep
    from the shining cups,
and I thought of you, Fergusson, at work
    by your bee in the fence,

And of you broken in the gloom of the bedlam,
in the dark of an agonised, exhausted spirit;
did any glimmer of understanding reach you
    of how your fuel was spent
but how ravenous time would never wither
    your blithe verse?

Had you lacked the spunk to drain the cup,
would you have come to know the drunk,
the lawyer, dandy, thief and whore,
    while winter howled,
or savoured the caller oysters lush
    and Edinburgh smells?

You had no use for the sentiment of Rabbie,
for his protestations and zealous manners,
not fairer to you the maid's breast than the lily,
    for you drank sense,
exposed hypocrisy with wit laconic
    and Old Nick's help.

If you had been a worthy in good braid claith
who'd live to bestow his old breeks on the state,
a man concerned with wealth and fame
    to wile him from bliss,
would there have opened to you such joy
    or music without stint?   *trans.* Meg Bateman

162

Tonality and the Sense of Place in Fergusson's 'Elegy, on the Death of Scots Music'

MATTHEW WICKMAN

On the eve of Union in 1707, during the final meeting of the Scottish Parliament, Chancellor Seafield mourned Scottish independence as the 'end of ane auld sang'. Katie Trumpener remarks that this 'terse phrase announced the end of an autonomous Scotland as the end of an oral, vernacular world, yet it did so with pithy, "couthy" confidence in the survival of the Scots language as a necessary medium for articulating Scottish experience'.[1] Two generations later, in his 'Elegy, on the Death of Scots Music' (1772), the songwriter, singer, and friend of musicians Robert Fergusson echoed Seafield's speech by ringing the death knell of Scots music in an energetic Scots vernacular that seems in many ways to stand in for the music it describes. Scots vernacular and its perpetuation of local traditions are not the subjects of Fergusson's poem *per se*, but they provide the meaningful subtext of the 'Elegy', as they do for 'Caller Oysters', 'Auld Reikie', and virtually all of Fergusson's Scots poetry. Reacting against educational programmes and political agendas that seemed designed to ostracise the use of Scots, Fergusson's 'Elegy' deploys a vernacular that is as demotic as it is educated, modulating between an orotund pastoral and ironic counterpastoral. The poem opens with a Shakespearean epigraph, then shifts quickly into elegiac strains in a 'rudely' idealized Scots that is metrically encapsulated in the 'rudely' classical Standard Habbie (later dubbed the Burns stanza). The poem exhibits its verbal dexterity, moreover, while striking up an uneasy balance between lamentation and satire, and while performing the musical virtuosity whose death it announces, but thus defies.

One key to understanding and appreciating Fergusson's 'Elegy' and, through it, the tradition of Scots poetry in which it figures, lies in decoding and balancing the poem's divergent and beguiling tonal registers. These are of particular importance to Fergusson's poem because the 'Elegy' is not only articulated through them, but also seems to evoke tone itself as a thematic issue. Fergusson's engagement of tone is subtle, which seems fitting inasmuch as tone (generally signifying nuanced accents of voice, mood, and meaning) is an elusive, if palpable, quality of signification. Tone matters equally to poets and musicians.

Poetic tone finds an analogue in the 'Elegy' in the form of Scots music. Fergusson elicits this music as the subtle and elusive emblem of a culture that has come to exist primarily as an amalgam of memory and imagination, and to signify predominantly in modulations of mood. The poem opens by striking this note:

> On Scotia's plains, in days of yore,
> When lads and lasses *tartan* wore,
> Saft Music rang on ilka shore,
>   In hamely weid;
> But harmony is now no more,
>   And *music* dead.[2]

In effect, this opening stanza converts 'Saft Music' into its own epitaph. The lines that follow accordingly haunt their own expression: where the 'hamely weid' of the vernacular and its attendant culture irrupts, Fergusson seems to suggest, it now does so in the evanescent colour of accent rather than with the weight of cultural imprimatur.

In recent years numerous scholars have taken up the nationalist implications of vernacular language in works like Fergusson's. My aim in drawing explicit attention to the poem's tonality is to expand these discussions by displacing the focus from questions of nationhood *per se* to other implications of communal experience. In so doing I hope to show, first, how the 'Elegy's' divergent tonal registers implicitly convert tone into a key interpretive issue by making our understanding of the poem dependent on our perception of them. Second, I attend to eighteenth-century conceptions of tonality that underscore its associations of familiarity and common experience. Communal familiarity is what vernacular language implies, of course, but the theoretical dimensions of this issue seem to be achieving new currency in literary and cultural studies. Postcolonial theory in particular has explored the ramifications of familiarity in legitimating what Dipesh Chakrabarty, for one, calls 'affective history', "which finds thought intimately tied to places and to particular forms of life" (the "place" and culture of Scots music, for instance).[3] Fergusson's work merits reassessment in light of these recent discussions. However, in addition to locating Fergusson's poetry within the present climate of critical discourse, we might also ask what such discourse may owe historically and conceptually to work like Fergusson's. This leads me to the third and final aim of my essay, which is to reflect on the enduring and evolving significance of eighteenth-century Scottish culture to modern thought. There is a strong and well-documented critical trajectory that leads from eighteenth-century Scottish stagist conceptions of society through Marxian and post-Marxian assessments of Enlightened modernity. Given this tradition, my questions are, what do we make of Fergusson's seemingly counter-Enlightened, 'affective' evocation of Scots language and culture? And, how does his implicit rebuttal against stagist social history suggest an alternative critical legacy emerging from the Scottish Enlightenment?

While Fergusson, like Ramsay and Burns, wrote poems in English, most scholars believe his most significant poetic achievements are in Scots. This poetry seems above all else to have been a poetry of tone. Thomas Crawford asserts that '[t]he most distinctive . . . pleasure that can be derived from the poetry of the Scottish Vernacular Revival is got from verse whose language fits in with the ordinary meaning of the term "vernacular": that is, where the language reproduces the features of everyday speech'. Hence, Crawford claims, while we derive pleasure from the colourful characters portrayed in such verse, 'our pleasure comes also from the recognition of idiom and the rising and falling intonations of a speaking voice'.[4] Robert Crawford amplifies these observations by regarding tone not only as a feature of Fergusson's work, but also as its organising principle: 'Fergusson had inherited [the Standard Habbie] verse form and [its] tonal balance from Allan Ramsay, who, like its apparent inventor Robert Sempil, had used it to fuse high and low tones, mixing fun and solemnity. More than that, since as a young poet he enjoyed trying out the Standard Habbie, we may regard Fergusson as in part formed *by* the tonal mix, not simply as choosing to inhabit it'.[5]

In considering the 'high and low tones' of Fergusson's Scots poetry, we draw implicitly on the notion of tone that has been sketched most definitively in the past century by I. A. Richards. Richards defines tone as 'an attitude' held by a writer or speaker 'to his listener. He chooses or arranges his words differently as his audience varies, in automatic or deliberate recognition of his relation to them. The tone of his utterance reflects his awareness of this relation, his sense of how he stands towards those he is addressing'.[6] In Fergusson's 'Elegy' the protean 'relation' of the poet to his audience and subject matter passes through a series of fluctuating tonal registers, from the grave to the sarcastic, and from the ironic to the sincere. These fluctuations seem in turn to model the tenuous state of Scots music and, by implication, the authentic Scottish culture that is the poem's theme. For instance, Fergusson's poem echoes

Robert Sempil's 'The Life and Death of Habbie Simson, the Piper of Kilbarchan':

> Kilbarchan now may say alas!
> For she hath lost her game and grace,
> Both *Trixie* and *The Maiden Trace*,
>   But what remead?
> For no man can supply his place:
>   Hab Simson's dead.[7]

However, the poem also plays on the refrain of Fergusson's mock 'Elegy, on the Death of Mr. David Gregory, late Professor of Mathematics in the University of St. Andrews'. There, Fergusson drolly laments that

> He could, by *Euclid*, prove lang sine
> A ganging *point* compos'd a line;
> By numbers too he cou'd divine,
>   Whan he did read,
> That *three* times *three* just made up nine;
>   But now he's dead.[8]

In the 'Elegy, on the Death of Scots Music' Gregory's place is taken by William Macgibbon. Emerging from this poem of the 'hamely' and of 'hameil lays', Macgibbon apparently personifies Scottish vernacular culture:

> *Macgibbon*'s gane: Ah! waes my heart!
> The man in music maist expert,
> Wha cou'd sweet melody impart,
>   And tune the reed,
> Wi' sic a slee and pawky art;
>   But now he's dead. [37–42]

As Fergusson's editor Matthew P. McDiarmid points out, '[i]t is curious, considering the nature of Fergusson's praise, that when Macgibbon was leader of the Gentleman's concert at Edinburgh, he "was thought to play the music of Corelli, Geminiani, and Handel, with great execution and judgment"'.[9] In other words, Macgibbon excelled in performing exactly the kinds of 'foreign sonnets' that Fergusson condemns as 'A bastard breed!/ Unlike that saft-tongu'd melody/ Which now lies dead' (49, 52–54). Hence, if we determine Fergusson's tone, with Richards, as a function of attitude or relation to his readers, and if we observe that the poet's sorrow at Macgibbon's passing seems tinged with a touch of the sarcasm that laces the Gregory elegy, we might conclude that the poem's tone (at least, in these lines) lays coy claim to an emotional border that narrowly separates grief from mockery. The mildly ridiculous lines that conclude the following stanza underscore this ambiguity: 'The blythest sangster on the plain!/ Alake, he's dead!' (47–48).[10]

In his essay 'Mourning and Melancholia' (1917) Freud analyses this structure of emotion as a compound of melancholy and mania – states incurred by psychological wounds through which the ego comes either to be dominated by or temporarily frees itself from a consuming object-cathexis (e.g., the loss of a loved one). This state of mind is composed of 'three conditioning factors' – 'loss of the object, ambivalence, and regression of libido into the ego' – that ramify suggestively in Fergusson's 'Elegy'.[11] The purported loss that Fergusson laments, obviously, is that of Scots music, but the persistence of that music in his own verses complicates the poem's expressions of grief. For Freud, melancholy is distinct from mourning. This is because the subject in mourning gradually withdraws his or her affection from the departed object, whereas the melancholic subject experiences greater difficulty in admitting this loss, and thus introjects, or unconsciously incorporates, traits of the beloved into his or her own ego. The melancholic subject is then able to confront himself as the lost object of affection, and punish himself psychologically as a way of chastising the beloved for its departure. This dynamic refracts into Fergusson's 'Elegy' in that the 'occasions giving rise to melancholia . . . extend beyond the clear case of a loss by death, and include all those situations of being wounded, hurt, neglected, out of favour, or disappointed, which can import opposite feelings of love and hate into the relationship or reinforce an already existing ambivalence' (Freud, 161). In this way, death can inspire powerful and conflicted feelings, even if that death is only figurative.

The significance of Freud's theory of melancholy to Fergusson's 'Elegy' consists primarily in its enunciation of structures of grief that accentuate the complex tonal quality of the poem. For one thing, if we regard Scots music as metonymic of Scots poetry, then the poet occupies an oddly melancholic relation to his subject matter. Scots poetry was neither exactly 'dead' in 1772, nor does the poet seem fully to acknowledge the death he proclaims. Despite the longstanding existence of compulsory literacy programmes designed to refine the local citizenry into English speakers, there had actually been a modest resurgence of interest in Scots poetry throughout Britain during the long eighteenth century, starting with John Forbes's *Cantus, Songs and Fancies* (published in 1662, 1676, and 1682), and continuing through James Watson's *A Choice Collection* (1706) and Allan Ramsay's *Ever Green* and *Tea-Table Miscellany* collections in the 1720s. Ramsay also edited a collection of Scots *Proverbs* that ran through several editions after its initial publication in 1737. It is true, as A. M. Kinghorn points out, that the 'gulf between Fergusson and the Edinburgh *bon ton* towards modern literary Scots had widened since Ramsay's day, and the greater prosperity of "North Britain" in the second half of the century was accompanied by a leaning towards genteel culture as represented in London society'.[12] However, the community of readers Fergusson implicitly invokes testifies to a tradition of attenuated but enduring vitality. That tradition continues to echo even as Fergusson evokes images of social deterioration:

> At glomin now the bagpipe's dumb,
> Whan weary owsen hameward come;
> Sae sweetly as it wont to bum,
>   And *Pibrachs* skreed;
> *We* never hear its warlike hum;
>   For music's dead. [31–36, second emphasis mine]

We might also note that, like Freud's description of the subject suffering from melancholy, Fergusson has incorporated the alleged object of death into his own poetic voice. His concluding stanza underscores this point by sounding a virtual war cry in Scots: 'O SCOTLAND! that cou'd yence afford/ To bang the pith of Roman sword,/ Winna your sons, wi' joint accord,/ To battle speed?' (61–64) And yet, by reiterating the theme of death in its refrain, we perceive that the poem's alarum is riddled with an ambivalence that suspends it, Hamlet-like, between anticipation and futility: 'And fight till MUSIC be restor'd,/ Which now lies dead' (65–66).

This ambivalence manifests itself in numerous ways throughout the 'Elegy'. Partly it comes to define the poet's subjectivity. It also delineates the broader dimensions of tonality that extend beyond the relation of the speaker to his subject matter and audience. After pronouncing its own death in Latinate Scots (e.g., 'Scotia's' rather than 'Scotland's' plains) in the opening stanza, the poem veers into Scots pastoral:

Round her [Scots music] the feather'd choir would wing,
Sae bonnily she wont to sing,
And sleely wake the sleeping string,
    Their sang to lead,
Sweet as the zephyrs of the spring;
    But now she's dead.

Mourn ilka nymph and ilka swain,
Ilk sunny hill and dowie glen;
Let weeping streams and *Naiads* drain
    Their fountain head;
Let echo swell the dolefu' strain,
    Since music's dead. [7–18]

David Daiches argues that the use of pastoral lends Fergusson's elegy a 'stateliness' it might otherwise lack.[13] Perhaps; another, more ineluctable effect of pastoral, though, is to reduce the natural realm in which Scots music once resounded to a set of poetic conventions: 'the feather'd choir', 'the zephyrs of the spring', the nymphs and swains and 'sunny hill[s]', and so on. These conventions and later, counterpastoral stanzas (e.g., on Macgibbon's death) thus amplify the poem's ambivalence and complicate the alleged death of Scots music by according it a place within a poetic tradition – a 'sound . . . sprung frae [the] Italy' of Virgil's Eclogues, no less – that Fergusson seems in the 'Elegy' to want to resist. Furthermore, Fergusson himself had tried his hand at the pastoral forms associated with English writers from Spenser to Pope to Shenstone in his earlier poems, and his work in Scots seemed generally to mark a departure from that tradition.

So, there seems to be a contradiction between, on the one hand, the rousing Scots accents in the 'Elegy' and, on the other, the plangent residue of a pastoral tradition through which Fergusson figures the glorious past of Scots music, but against which his own music seems to rebel. In other words, the poem's language seems to be structured on a fault line that places it at odds with itself. Fergusson was far from the first writer in Scots to articulate this tension, of course. Ramsay, to cite only one example, had engaged pastoral conventions in Scots in numerous poems as well as his play *The Gentle Shepherd* (1725), seeking to dignify his work through these conventions even as he reworked them in ludic fashion. Fergusson's 'Elegy' strikes a similar chord. At the very least, the poem displays a fissure between the persuasive effects of rhetoric (e.g., the poet's vitriolic denunciation of 'foreign' influences) and the tropes that structure and potentially undermine those effects (e.g., the 'sunny hill[s]'' and 'weeping stream[s]'). Paul de Man, whose uneasy negotiations of 'cultural nationalism' resonate provocatively with the literary climate of eighteenth-century Scotland (as Robert Crawford has suggested), describes the rupture between persuasion and trope as an 'aporia . . . that both generates and paralyzes rhetoric and thus gives it the appearance of a history'.[14] The 'history' to which de Man refers consists of the difference between the writing of history and the facts of history that both legitimate and resist our efforts to express them. Rhetoric 'appear[s]' to be a history to the extent that it highlights this difference between the meanings we impose and those that impose themselves on us through the trails of alternative signification we leave in our use of language. Fergusson's 'Elegy' presents a particularly interesting history in this de Manian sense because in recounting the death of Scots music it seemingly promotes its own rhetorical excess (that is, its use of Scots *in* pastoral, and its reduction of Scots *to* pastoral) as a theme. But, if vernacular Scots and the Standard Habbie pose an implicit challenge to pastoral by revising the conventions they rehearse, then the death the poem announces may be that of traditional pastoral as much as Scots music. It may, moreover, be a death in which the poet exults as much as mourns. Using Freud's terminology, we might say here that the poem's melancholy tilts occasionally into mania.

So far I have focused on various traces of ambivalence in the 'Elegy' for the purpose of underlining the significance of our perception of tone to our understanding of the poem. At one level, we confront through tone the standard question of the relation of the poet to his subject matter – whether sombre, satirical or, in Freudian terms, manic. More significantly, however, the ambiguity of the 'Elegy' in shifting in and out of such registers also suggests a fuller cultural context in which to interpret these shifts. Our attention is directed to tone as a quality connoting a sense of tacit familiarity. For tone, in addition to associations of speakerly 'attitude', also carries with it an impression of voice that seemingly descants above the lexical units of a sentence; tone creates an atmosphere, we might say, that lends words their meaning.[15] This imputation of atmosphere potentially links tone in subtle ways with what modern critical discourse identifies as the phenomenology of 'place'. Place is distinct from space in that place implies familiarity and lived experience. More than a geographic sector or zone of abstract extension, place denotes the trace of the human on the external environment. This notion of place suggestively intersects with tone in reflecting on poems like Fergusson's 'Elegy' because for us place has come to signify the peculiar character – the *genius loci* – of specific locales and the endurance of certain kinds of cultural traditions.[16] And, however much vernacular poetry like Fergusson's may be implicated in the cosmopolitan nature of its composition and readership, it is this kind of locality and tradition that Fergusson's vernacular poetry seemed especially anxious to elicit.

In turning our attention to the tone of Fergusson's 'Elegy', we implicitly inquire into the specific place – the cultural parameters – of Scots music. In surveying one possible site of such music, F. W. Freeman has argued that since Fergusson was a 'romantic Jacobite, a Scots Tory . . . a Counter-Enlightenment apologist, and . . . an artist with Episcopal sympathies', his work nostalgically 'espouses the Tory ideal of a well-regulated rural society . . .'[17] In other words, Freeman suggests, Fergusson's poetry transports us to a place in the feudal past. However, if we consider the tonal place of the 'Elegy' in light of eighteenth-century theories of tonality, especially theories that conceptualised tone as more than a relation between speaker and audience, then a slightly more complex (though not necessarily a contradictory) picture emerges.

One thread that connects eighteenth-century theories of tonality with present-day discussions of place is the desire to consider extra-rational aspects of meaning. Thomas Sheridan's *Course of Lectures on Elocution* (1762), for example, elicited tone as a crucially liminal place in the mind. 'Tones,' Sheridan claims, 'are the types and language of the passions, and all internal emotions, in the same way that articulate sounds, are the types and language of ideas . . .'[18] In seeking subtly to revise Locke's empiricist model of the mind, Sheridan averred that tone mediates between the 'animal' and 'intellectual' faculties, between 'nature' as those feelings that are 'impressed . . . on the human frame' and custom as the contrivance of suitable expression for those feelings, and between the 'sense' signifying sensation and the 'sense' signifying meaning (121). Only a few months later, Sheridan would confide to James Boswell that he and his wife Frances had fixed the poems of the ancient Highland bard Ossian, whose *Fingal* had appeared in translation the previous year, 'as the standard of feeling', and had, Boswell said, 'made it like a thermometer by which they judge the warmth of everybody's heart; and that they calculated beforehand in what degrees all their acquaintances would feel [these feelings], which answered exactly'.[19] For Sheridan, *The Poems of Ossian* had become, in effect, the very emblem of tone, serving as a template by which to measure those passions that surpassed Locke's comparatively arid concept of human understanding.

Reiterating Sheridan's ideas concerning tonality in his own analysis of *Ossian*, Hugh Blair would concede that Homer excels Ossian in matters of variety and understanding; 'but if Ossian's ideas and objects be less diversified than those of Homer, they are all, however, of the kind fittest for poetry . . . In a rude age and country, though the events that happen be few, the undissipated mind broods over them more; they strike the imagination, and fire the passions in a higher degree . . .'[20] Blair would aphorise that Ossian's was 'the Poetry of the Heart'; more specifically, however, Blair would imply that Ossian's was the poetry of tone, in which a moody 'air of solemnity and seriousness is diffused over the whole. Ossian is perhaps the only poet who never relaxes . . . One key note is struck at the beginning, and supported to the end . . . [T]he mind is kept at such a stretch in accompanying the author; that an ordinary reader is at first apt to be dazzled and fatigued, rather than pleased. [Ossian's] poems require to be taken up at intervals . . .' (356–57).

These 'air[s]', 'note[s]', 'stretch[es]', and 'intervals' drew implicitly upon current theories of tone. Johnson's *Dictionary* invoked these qualities in defining tone not only as a 'note' or 'sound' (which he listed as the first of five definitions), or as a tactile 'elasticity' (the fifth of the five), but also as an 'accent' in the voice, as a 'particular or affected sound in speaking', and, perhaps most provocatively, as 'a mournful cry'.[21] Bearing in mind the associations we drew above between tone and place, we might note here that 'a mournful cry' almost reflexively calls attention for its auditors to the place and person whence it issues; and, significantly, this subtle implication of provenance inflects the very etymology of the word 'tone'. This connection becomes apparent if we consider first the more immediate connotations of the word, which derive from the Latin *tonus*, meaning 'tension' (with associations to the word *tonare*, or 'thunder'), and from the Greek *tonos*, meaning 'stretching', and implying the elasticity of a band or fibre. (We might recall here what Blair says about the mind being 'kept at a stretch' by Ossian's poetry.) The traditional association of tone with music issues, then, from the image of a string or chord being stretched and plucked, emitting sound. This image in turn refers implicitly to the etymology of the word 'chorus', which derives from the Greek word *choros*, designating the circumscribed ring in which the singers would participate in ancient Greek drama. The word is related to 'chord' – the chords which, when plucked, emit sound – but also to a similar word, *chòros*, meaning 'place', as in 'chorography'.

The concept of tone to which Sheridan, Blair, and Johnson refer thus appears to derive from a set of etymological and sensuous associations that, together, delimit an ethereal location of sound and impression. This location evokes an idea of place more than space in that the meaning that tone imparts (e.g., our sense of Fergusson's 'Elegy' as dirge or satire) implies a kind of familiarity – a basis for understanding that coheres in more than mere verbiage – that in turn suggests a shared basis in human experience. The demotic associations of vernacular poems like Fergusson's 'Elegy', and their air of local custom, exemplify such familiarity. The 'Elegy' amplifies these associations in that its rhetorical vacillation between pastoral formality and vernacular impishness lends the 'Saft [Scots] Music' a haunting quality that causes it to linger even after its purported death. In effect, Fergusson converts the residue of local culture into the fuel of nationalist sentiment. It seems particularly compelling to note here that Sheridan, Blair, and so many of the aesthetic and rhetorical theorists who drew upon a notion of tone during this period were writers who hailed from the peripheral regions of Britain – from Ireland and Scotland – where modern 'British' (as well as Irish and Scottish) identity may first have been cultivated. In addition to the work of Sheridan and Blair, images of tonality are evident in Francis Hutcheson's assertions of harmony in our judgments of beauty, in Adam Smith's claims of 'the harmonious and sonorous pronunciation peculiar to the English nation' and the 'certain ringing in [the English] manner of speaking which foreigners can never attain', and in Burke's theory of the sublime (whose key word for a state of sublime incapacity is 'astonishment', from the Latin *ex tonare*, meaning 'issuing from thunder', or 'of a powerful tone'), among others.[22]

As Sheridan and Blair both attested, the poet laureate of tonality, and of the evocative implications of place in language, may well have been James Macpherson, whose translations of *The Poems of Ossian* were monuments of sentimental resonance that elicited compelling images of a romantic and vital location in the Celtic past. Each of Macpherson's *Ossian* translations – the *Fragments of Ancient Poetry* (1760), *Fingal* (1761/62) and *Temora* (1763) – is extremely attentive to the moody dimensions of place in the misty past of the Scottish Northwest. The first of his *Fragments* begins 'My love is a son of the hill . . . Whether by the fount of the rock, or by the stream of the mountain thou liest; when the rushes are nodding with the wind, and the mist is flying over thee, let me approach my love unperceived, and see him from the rock'.[23] Katie Trumpener comments that 'Macpherson's *Ossian* . . . turned the Highlands into one enormous echo chamber, evoking an emphatically oral world' that resonated even in 'the landscape itself, which echoed with the remembered voices of the past'.[24] Even Macpherson's most virulent critics like Malcolm Laing recognised the powerful resonance and familiarity of the poems, only ascribing them to bowdlerised sources such as the King James Bible and *Paradise Lost.*

Scholars have reached a virtual consensus that in shaping his translations Macpherson drew from these texts as well as indigenous Gaelic poetic and oral traditions. This agreement has led in turn to provocative new work on the nationalist, generic, and epistemological implications of the poems' cultural syncretism.[25] Fergusson himself was educated in a milieu in which *Ossian* figured prominently. As the Introduction to the present book points out, he wrote approvingly of 'An *Ossian's* Fancy'. He also expressed enthusiasm regarding his friend Alexander Runciman's frescoes representing the Ossianic epics.[26] The 'Elegy' in its own right may be interpreted as an act of cultural translation similar to Macpherson's and Runciman's inasmuch as it too draws from multiple literary traditions, evokes nostalgia for a golden age, and disseminates a symbolic economy of nationalist icons and signifiers (e.g., Macgibbon in place of Ossian, Scots in place of Gaelic). To affirm a connection between Fergusson and Macpherson on the basis of *tonality*, however, is to elicit a slightly different set of implications from arguments geared toward an examination of tropes, cultural nostalgia, or a symbolic economy of nationalism. These other *topoi* imply communities bonded together through media such as language, desire, and ideology. Tonality, to be sure, does not exclude these constitutive facets of community. Yet it cultivates familiarity on slightly different grounds – specifically, by accentuating a common basis in experience that, though comparatively inarticulate, situates speech, and though relatively elusive, frames our interpretation of meaning.

In this light, it seems significant that both Macpherson and Fergusson attempt histories, or attempt, in effect, to account for the state of Gaelic legend and Scots music over time. The inclination in confronting these histories, of course, is to try to decipher their respective objects. Do *The Poems of Ossian* and the 'Dissertations' that Macpherson appended to them chronicle Highland Scotland's noble past, outline an earlier stage of social development, or document the defeatism that ensued from the vanquishing of Jacobite forces at Culloden? Is Fergusson's 'Elegy' the history of a vitiated cultural form, a satirical rendition of traditional pastoral, or an effort to mobilise nationalist sentiment? Our perception of the works' tone partly determines our response to these questions; once tone becomes an issue in itself, however, these particular questions begin to seem almost beside the point. Indeed, an understanding of tone as an indicator of common experience shifts the focus from the content of Macpherson's and Fergusson's histories to their modality. That is, a recognition that the nature of experience itself is at issue in these works turns attention from the matter on which they report to the manner in which they even conceive of it.

At this point, having shifted from a reading of Fergusson's 'Elegy' to a more theoretical discussion of its resonance in an eighteenth-century context, we might reflect briefly on the poem's significance to the complex critical legacy of eighteenth-century Scottish culture. A re-assessment of tone in terms of familiarity displaces the scholarly focus not only from the content of history but also from the cultural technology of nationalism, and hence from a scholarly subject in which analyses of Scottish culture have figured so prominently. As Benedict Anderson most notably has observed, nationalism depends on an ideology of historical progress, specifically on calculations of 'homogeneous, empty time' that enable conceptions of solidarity in the present (as a shared experience of time) and future (as a collective destiny) among people who otherwise bear little relation to each other.[27] Taking up a similar line of argument, Ernest Gellner, Tom Nairn, Katie Trumpener, and many others have analysed nationalism as a form of collectivity that arose in the later eighteenth century as a function of and reaction against the universalising logic of industrial capitalism. On this subject, Scotland has been portrayed variously as a nation whose early integration into 'Britain' prevented its cultivation of a strong national identity as well as a nation whose sense of marginality fostered an identity not only for itself, but also for Britain as a multi-national state.[28] Of less significance than the manifest differences between these perspectives, however, are the traits they seem to share. Common to all, for instance, is a fascination with Scotland's status as 'a stateless nation'.[29] Furthermore, and even more fundamentally, the antiphonal conclusions reached by these scholars reveal similar assumptions regarding historical change and the corresponding causality between material circumstances and cultural expression. For, whether perceived as imposed or conscientious (or, in effect, primitive or sophisticated), Scottish national identity reflects a historical moment of modernity that constitutes itself on its absolute and perpetual difference from the past. Eighteenth-century Scottish literati helped to identify such a difference by enunciating the stagist theories of historical progress that would underwrite Marxian dialectical materialism and a subsequent tradition of historical and sociological scholarship.[30]

All of which returns us, suggestively, to Fergusson's elusive 'Elegy', its resonant tonal modulations, and their attendant implications of place and experience. History in this poem underlines, in de Man's language, the problem of its own 'appearance' through a brooding sense of melancholy that encompasses the present as well as the past, and that inflects the poet's subjectivity as well as his linguistic medium. This mood in turn elicits an experience of culture that is irreducible to the modern (i.e., 'homogeneous, empty') concept of nationalism. Indeed, despite the poem's seemingly spirited defence of local traditions in language and song, and despite its invocation of a golden age in Scots music, its emphasis on tonality accentuates a less mediated relation to cultural artifacts that are neither relegated to an earlier stage of development nor projected through 'empty' time onto the image of a collective future. Ultimately, then, 'history' in Fergusson's 'Elegy' seems to chronicle an experience of the present. It documents an idiosyncratic, affective relation to the social climate of Edinburgh in the early 1770s, and to the multivalent cultural traces (e.g., Scots and English, Enlightened and sentimental) that hung in the air. In fact, if only by association, the 'Elegy' casts Enlightenment into a play with its own shadows. It suggests ways in which we might reconsider the affective dimension of stagist histories enunciated by figures like William Robertson and John Millar (or for that matter, Karl Marx and Fredric Jameson), whose expressed aims are to articulate a different, more systematic portrait of modern society. In this light, Fergusson's 'Elegy' may not only exemplify, but also integrally participate in, a 'provincialising' critique that resituates objectivist and universalising paradigms within the specific localities – the familiar or once-familiar places – of their production.[31] To the extent, then, that the 'Elegy' turns our attention toward tonality, and hence toward impressions of place and experience, it would seem to underscore not only its own complexity, but also the complexity of an eighteenth-century Scottish culture that contributed to the formation of modernity as well as the accompanying and ongoing project of its critique.

Notes

1. *Bardic Nationalism: The Romantic Novel and the British Empire* (Princeton: Princeton Univ. Press, 1997), 73.
2. *The Poems of Robert Fergusson*, ed. Matthew P. McDiarmid, 2 vols. (Edinburgh and London: William Blackwood, 1954), II, 37, ll. 1–6, Fergusson's emphasis. Subsequent references to this edition will be cited in the text.
3. *Provincializing Europe: Postcolonial Thought and Historical Difference* (Princeton: Princeton Univ. Press, 2000), 18.
4. 'The Vernacular Revival and the Poetic Thrill: A Hedonist Approach', in *Scotland and the Lowland Tongue: Studies in the Language and Literature of Lowland Scotland*, ed. J. Derrick McClure (Aberdeen: Aberdeen Univ. Press, 1983: 79–99), 80, 81.
5. 'Robert Fergusson's Robert Burns', in *Robert Burns and Cultural Authority*, ed. Robert Crawford (Iowa City: Univ. of Iowa Press, 1997: 1–22), 4, Crawford's emphasis.
6. *Practical Criticism: A Study of Literary Judgment* (New York: Harcourt, Brace and Company, 1930), 182, Richards's emphases deleted.
7. See Roderick Watson, ed., *The Poetry of Scotland* (Edinburgh: Edinburgh University Press, 1995), 208.
8. *The Poems of Robert Fergusson*, ed. McDiarmid, II, 1, ll. 13–18, Fergusson's emphasis.
9. *The Poems of Robert Fergusson*, II, 257.
10. F. W. Freeman apprehends these lines as a 'mock elegy form for reductive effect'. *Robert Fergusson and the Scots Humanist Compromise* (Edinburgh: Edinburgh Univ. Press, 1984), 172.
11. 'Mourning and Melancholia', in *Collected Papers*, trans. supervised by Joan Riviere, 5 vols. (London: Hogarth Press, 1950), IV, 169. Subsequent references will be cited in the text.
12. 'Watson's Choice, Ramsay's Voice, and a Flash of Fergusson', *Scottish Literary Journal* 19:2 (1992, 5–23), 16.
13. *Robert Fergusson* (Edinburgh: Scottish Academic Press, 1982), 46.
14. *Allegories of Reading: Figural Language in Rousseau, Nietzsche, Rilke, and Proust* (New Haven: Yale Univ. Press, 1979), 131. For Crawford's discussion of de Man, see *Devolving English Literature*, Second Edition (Edinburgh: Edinburgh Univ. Press, 2000), 3–4.
15. See Roland Barthes on song in *A Lover's Discourse: Fragments*, trans. Richard Howard (New York: Hill and Wang, 1978), 77; Peter Fenves, *Raising the Tone of Philosophy: Late Essays by Immanuel Kant, Transformative Critique by Jacques Derrida* (Baltimore: The Johns Hopkins Univ. Press, 1993), 3.

16. For an overview of these issues, see Robert Eric Livingston, 'Global Knowledges: Agency and Place in Literary Studies', *PMLA* 116:1 (2001), 145–57.

17. 'Robert Fergusson: Pastoral and Politics at Mid Century', in *The History of Scottish Literature, Volume 2: 1660–1800*, ed. Andrew Hook (Aberdeen: Aberdeen Univ. Press, 1987: 141–156), 141, 142.

18. *A Course of Lectures on Elocution* (London: W. Strahan; reprinted Menston, Yorkshire: Scolar Press, 1968), 129. Subsequent references will be cited in the text.

19. *Boswell's London Journal*, ed. Frederick A. Pottle (New York: McGraw-Hill, 1950), 182.

20. *A Critical Dissertation on the Poems of Ossian*, in *The Poems of Ossian and Related Works*, ed. Howard Gaskill (Edinburgh: Edinbugh Univ. Press, 1996, 343–408), 357. Subsequent references will be cited in the text.

21. *A Dictionary of the English Language*, 3rd ed. (London: A. Millar, 1766).

22. See Hutcheson, *An Inquiry into the Original of our Ideas of Beauty and Virtue*; Smith, *Lectures on Rhetoric and Belles Lettres*, ed. J. C. Bryce (Oxford: Oxford Univ. Press, 1983; reprinted Indianapolis: Liberty Fund, 1985), 16; and Burke, *A Philosophical Enquiry into the Origin of our Ideas of the Sublime and Beautiful*, ed. Adam Phillips (Oxford: Oxford Univ. Press, 1990), 53.

23. *The Poems of Ossian and Related Works*, ed. Howard Gaskill (Edinburgh: Edinburgh Univ. Press, 1996), 7.

24. *Bardic Nationalism*, 70–71.

25. See, for example, Leith Davis, *Acts of Union: Scotland and the Literary Negotiation of the British Nation, 1707–1830* (Stanford: Stanford Univ. Press, 1998), esp. Ch. 3; Trumpener, *Bardic Nationalism*, esp. ch. 2; and Colin Kidd, *Subverting Scotland's Past: Scottish Whig Historians and the Creation of an Anglo-British Identity, 1689–c. 1830* (Cambridge: Cambridge Univ. Press, 1993).

26. See McDiarmid, *The Poems of Robert Fergusson*, I, 57, 59.

27. See *Imagined Communities: Reflections on the Origin and Spread of Nationalism* (New York: Verso, 1991), 24.

28. These positions are sketched by Tom Nairn in *The Break-Up of Britain: Crisis and Neo-Nationalism* (London: New Left, 1977) and Trumpener, *Bardic Nationalism*. Nairn reverses his position somewhat in *Faces of Nationalism: Janus Revisited* (New York: Verso, 1997).

29. The phrase is used by David McCrone. See *Understanding Scotland: The Sociology of a Stateless Nation* (London: Routledge, 1992).

30. Ronald Meek is the authority on this issue. But for a more recent discussion, see James Chandler, *England in 1819: The Politics of Literary Culture and the Case of Romantic Historicism* (Chicago: Univ. of Chicago Press, 1998), 127–35.

31. I borrow the term 'provincialising' from Chakrabarty's *Provincializing Europe*.

AND THE MUSIC PLAYED ON

Fragile, lost soul, *beautiful friend,*
dark hair loose over a white shift:
Kristen, musician, self-taught, departed

this *demented, ugly world* sometime late evening
on the sixteenth of June, the heroin
pure as a note cleanly sung, then

the needle on vinyl swinging
out into silence. Her bass guitar
is propped against a wall, still

to be laid in its open case. Her long,
slender fingers are magnified
by the bath water: outside early summer

tightens its throat. The night constricts.
The curtains are drawn. Only a little
light shines on her skin. The window

is open, the sounds of Seattle float through.
But she didn't much like it here. She was going
home, back to *her* music, back to old friends.

We are deeply anguished, the press release read
at the loss of a talented musician, a beautiful soul.
Her father has come to the city up north,

by plane to take his girl back home. *Someone
could have missed a bus,* he said, believing
that her new friends hadn't even noticed she'd gone.

                                        Tracey Herd

Robert Garioch and Robert Fergusson: Under the Influence?

ANDREW MACINTOSH

> My ain toun's makar, monie an airt
> formed us in common, faur apairt
> in time, but fell alike in hert . . .[1]

In his poem 'To Robert Fergusson', Robert Garioch (1909–1981) reveals
in the most explicit fashion his debt to a poet whom he appeared to
regard as his spiritual predecessor. Fergusson is a presence so tangible
that, in the opening lines of the poem, his long-dead image 'is mair
clear/ nor monie things that nou appear'. Yet Garioch and Fergusson,
two Edinburgh men two centuries apart, were utterly unlike each other.
Aside from the biographical fact that Fergusson died as a young man on
the brink of fame and Garioch lived, less well known than most of his
literary contemporaries, into old age, there are more fundamental
differences. Unlike Fergusson's stream of publication, Garioch's writing
occurred in fits and spurts and was never prolific; it seems to have been
affected by the malaise of his unhappy existence as a schoolteacher. It
may be slightly clichéd to suggest that Fergusson lived fast and died
young, but those are the bare facts of his life; Garioch was a shy,
reclusive and (financially) rather mean soul, happy to share his flat with
a pigeon called Doody and to buzz around the New Town on a motor
scooter picking up bargains.[2] The juxtaposition of these bald facts
makes it inconceivable that the two should ever have been linked.

However, the similarities are just as striking. Both are identifiably
poets of Edinburgh, seen to have produced their best work in Scots.
Each has been overshadowed to some extent by contemporaries who
were willing to write in English. Both have suffered from publishing
neglect of some degree. It is true to say that Garioch often exploited this
undoubted kinship, in his poetry and in his other writings. However, it
is equally true that Garioch often felt uneasy about the comparison
being taken too far. In a letter to his close friend, the poet Sydney
Tremayne, in 1974 Garioch hints at this flippantly, referring to 'this
Fergusson industry, in which I have become an essential cog or even
gaffer',[3] although in a letter written a month previously Garioch

provides a perceptive reading of the dangers of becoming associated too intimately with Fergusson's reputation:

> There is a tendency now hereabouts to think of my poems as somewhat akin to Robert Fergusson's, and indeed I have studied his poetry with a hope of learning from him, but I don't want to have too much of this sort of thing, even though I look like getting more money from events associated with the bicentenary of his death than he ever got in his day . . . Anyhow, there is a sort of pious tendency to make me a sort of vicariously rewarded Fergusson: this could easily make me foolish, apart from looking foolish.[4]

Garioch's involvement in the bicentenary included selecting the poems of Fergusson's in *Fergusson: A Bi-Centenary Handsel*,[5] and taking part in a farcically chaotic conference for senior school pupils,[6] but that could hardly be regarded as overkill. However, it is tempting to conclude that, by making this kind of pronouncement, Garioch is guilty of trying to do two separate and incompatible things: to be regarded as Fergusson's successor, with all the potential praise by association, and to be regarded as his own man. Although we should be wary of any poet's assessment of his own work and influences, this was a private letter to a friend who, more than anyone else, recognised Garioch's abilities and knew the man and his poetry. Douglas Dunn, however, has written of his suspicion of Garioch's viewpoint in this particular letter. He suggests that

> Two decades after 'To Robert Fergusson', then, we find Garioch trying to give the slip to the critical temptation of overstating the extent to which he depended on Fergusson's example. Should we believe him? On the evidence, the answer must be 'Mibbe' . . .[7]

Dunn's use of that gloriously inexact Scots word 'mibbe' – which, depending on the speaker, can mean anything; he suggests 'only up to a point' – shows that there is still plenty of doubt which needs to be clarified. This essay aims to separate the myth and the supposition from the reality by showing that, certainly, there are occasional uncanny moments in Garioch's poetry where the presence of Fergusson is very strong, but that to portray Garioch as a latter-day Fergusson is simplistic and misleading in the extreme. Rather, it seeks to suggest that Garioch's trademark is his confident and easy distillation of the Scottish poetic tradition, in its widest sense, into his own work. There is no room here to discuss the all-but-ignored cross-currents between Garioch and his contemporaries (Edwin Morgan being the most profitable example), but it should still be clear that tradition has misrepresented both Garioch and Fergusson.

The obvious starting point is Garioch's magnificent poem 'To Robert Fergusson', one of the few post-Burns poems in Standard Habbie which does not sound like mere pastiche (Garioch's achievement in sustaining this successfully for 46 verses should not be underestimated). The opening stanzas of the poem describe Fergusson's Edinburgh in terms which, by implication, deprecate the twentieth-century city. These were

> . . .times when Embro was a quean
>   sae weill worth seein
> that life wi her still had a wheen
>   guid things worth preein. [*CPW*, p. 18]

This difference is made more explicit later on:

> But truth it is, our couthie city
> has cruddit in twa pairts a bittie
> and speaks twa tongues, ane coorse and grittie,
>   heard in the Cougait,
> the tither copied, mair's the pitie,
>   frae West of Newgate.
>
> Whilk is the crudd and whilk the whey
> I wad be kinna sweirt to say,
> but this I ken, that of the twae
>   the corrupt twang
> of Cougait is the nearer tae
>   the leid ye sang. [*CPW*, p. 21]

Here Garioch underlines the *volte face* in attitudes to Scots writing that had taken place since Fergusson's death: while he and his contemporaries wrote in a language that seemed to be dying and felt the need to author significant quantities of verse in English, twentieth-century poets such as Garioch have been able to write largely in Scots. However, Garioch seems quite content to gloss over this one improvement and contrast it with the consequences of progress elsewhere, such as pollution–

> Our fulyie's pusionit the Firth
> and caused, I dout, an unco dearth
> of thae Pandores of muckle girth
>   ye thocht sae fair [*CPW*, p. 21]

–and nuclear warfare:

> Ye didnae hae to fash your thoombs
> wi hydrogen or atom boombs [*CPW*, p. 23]

But Garioch is concerned mainly with Fergusson's city, a place brimming with life and characters, people who – invoking the titles of some of Fergusson's Scots poems – 'kick owre the traces/ in the Daft Days or at Leith Races' [*CPW*, p. 19]. Later the poem becomes more personal, as Garioch mentions first that both he and Fergusson were educated at the (Royal) High School; he then imagines a dream-vision in which the two poets tour the streets of Edinburgh:

> But aye we'd rise wi little hairm
> and cleik ilk ither by the airm,
> singan in unison to chairm
>   awa the skaith,
> syne seek some cantraip, harum-skarum
>   and naething laith. [*CPW*, p. 24]

Garioch realises that, in his Edinburgh, this dream-vision is something that would elicit disapproval from 'the nippie-tongue of morn' which 'pits aa sic glaumerie to scorn'. The image of the poet spending time with Fergusson is an interesting one, because one of Fergusson's contemporaries uses much the same technique in a poem of the same name. Like Garioch, this writer pays tribute to Fergusson by mentioning his poetry, and imagines that

> When I again *Auld Reikie* see,
> And can forgether, lad, with thee,
> Then we wi' muckle mirth and glee
>   Shall tak a gill,
> And of your *caller oysters* we
>   Shall eat our fill . . .[8]

The writer (identified only as J.S.) has not produced a poem worth lingering over, but the interest lies in Fergusson's reply, which seems to swither between modest refusal of J.S.'s compliments and uneasy insults:

Awa', ye wylie fleetchin *fallow*,
The rose shall grow like gowan yallow,
Before I turn sae toom and shallow,
      And void of fusion,
As a' your butter'd words to swallow
      In vain delusion. [*F*, II, p. 71]

Fergusson goes on to claim that 'Ye mak my Muse a dautit pett', but by the end of the poem he seems quite keen to have a drink with him, and in the final stanza hopes that 'Lang may ye thrive,/ Weel happit in a cozy hive'.

Fergusson's reply to a poem of the same title by Andrew Gray is similarly awkward, and betrays irritation as much as modesty:

Can you nae ither theme divine
To blaw upon, but *my* engyne?[9]

Obviously there is little to be gained from speculating over what Fergusson's reply might have been to Garioch's poem – one hopes rather more positive, although it seems odd that there should be an echo here of these two less than illustrious predecessors. The poem makes clear Garioch's admiration not simply for Fergusson but for Fergusson's era and an older Edinburgh. In fact, though Garioch's respect for Fergusson is clear, it is the attractions of Fergusson's Edinburgh (or, at least, a very romanticised vision of it) which are the main theme of the poem, which concludes with Garioch wandering off to 'some suburb new and bare'.

The other poem of Garioch's which is directly about Fergusson is the sonnet 'At Robert Fergusson's Grave', which describes a ceremony at the poet's graveside. The poem is one of the Edinburgh Sonnets, about two dozen in number, most of which are sarcastic, amusing, subversive and rebellious. But this is completely the opposite; it is subdued and respectful – attributes conspicuously absent from all the other sonnets. It describes what is, by all accounts, a sombre affair:

Canongait kirkyaird in the failing year
is auld and grey, the wee roseirs are bare,
five gulls leam white agin the dirty air:
why are they here? There's naething for them here. [*CPW*, p. 86]

The poem concentrates on the tragedy of Fergusson and has rather a gloomy air. Only in the final words are we told why Fergusson is so important, why all these people are standing in the gloom looking at a headstone:

> . . . Lichtlie this gin ye daur:
> here Robert Burns knelt and kissed the mool. [*CPW*, p. 86]

Although the meaning of the poem only really becomes clear in the final couple of lines, the whole piece is effectively an allegory of Fergusson's place in the Scottish literary tradition: the faithful few supporters turn out in an inhospitable atmosphere to show their support and continuing appreciation. There is no doubt that Garioch was one of Fergusson's most passionate supporters and a great admirer of his poetry, but that does not necessarily mean that his own poetry is influenced by Fergusson to a similar level. In both these poems, Garioch makes plain his respect for Fergusson. However, neither poem can really be simplified to the extent that it proves Fergusson to be a major influence. In any case, as Sydney Tremayne recognised in an unpublished letter, there are plenty of other candidates who have tended to be ignored:

> It's Hugh Mac-You-Know-Who's mantle you will inherit, not Fergusson's. Don't you realise that you are the only Scots language poet there is and Scottish literature would die without you . . . Incidentally, you are a far better poet than Fergusson. From what I've seen of him he was crude and you never are, and he didn't have your sense of timing. But it's typical of Scotland: everything has to be secondhand somehow.[10]

Tremayne's assertion that Garioch will inherit the mantle of Mac-Diarmid seems rather a strange one; Garioch's own opinion of Mac-Diarmid is now unhelpfully smothered in innuendo, but Tremayne's letters hint that Garioch's friend had little time for Grieve (a detailed examination of the personal papers of both poets suggests that their relationship was not as simplistically confrontational as is often assumed). That is not to suggest that Tremayne's comment is intended as an insult – far from it – but it underlines the fact that to cite Fergusson as Garioch's principal precursor is to forget the possibility of other influences existing and to ignore the distinctly cosmopolitan nature of Garioch's writing. To judge from the fact that one wall of Garioch's study 'was dominated by a large portrait of George Buchanan',[11] the sixteenth-century Scottish Humanist would appear to have been an equally important figure. Garioch produced translations into Scots of two of Buchanan's plays, *Jephthes* and *Baptistes*, of which he was immensely proud.[12] He had a great deal of affection for this, his favourite work, and put a great deal of energy into his struggle to have it published;[13] his affection for Buchanan is so clear that Buchanan as much as Fergusson might seem Garioch's poetic ancestor. There are two major poems concerning Buchanan. One of these, 'The Humanist's Trauchles in Paris', is a translation into Scots of Buchanan's 'Quam misera sit conditio docentium literas humaniores Lutetiae', and 'Garioch's Repone til George Buchanan' is Garioch's reply to this poem. Buchanan's original poem describes his lot as a teacher in Paris, which was not a happy one, as his biographer, I.D. McFarlane, makes clear:

> The seamy side of boarding life, the loudmouthed janitor, the raw recruits to learning, the excessive use of the cane, all this seems to have jarred badly; but the curriculum had its antiquated aspects too.[14]

This sense of incompatibility is evident in the unpublished introduction to the poem, cited by Robin Fulton, which suggests that Paris is a place

> whaur men o pairts were nocht respeckit,
> but ilka day begowkt and geckit
> by dozent, impiddent or glaikit
>   colleginaris [*CPW*, p. 296]

It seems from the poem itself that 'men o pairts' were respected least of all by their scholars. Garioch's choice of language paints a particularly bleak picture of Buchanan's existence: while the dominie 'taks a text/ apairt, examines and dissects/its moniplies', his Neanderthal charges

> . . .snore like grumphies
> or wauken wi the thochts of tumphies
> or nane ava, puir donnart sumphies,
>   as wyce as cuddies. [*CPW*, p. 31]

This is a poem entirely devoid of optimism. Later we hear that

> In short, if poetry's your lot,
> there's unco little to be got
> frae scrievin or frae teachin o't
>   for bread and butter. [*CPW*, p. 33]

The poem concludes with the plea

> Fusionless muses, haud awa!
> Seek out some ither Johnnie-raw
> to sair ye. As for me, I'll caa
> anither jig. [*CPW*, p. 34]

The reason for Garioch's insistently depressing tone becomes clear in the 'Repone', where he points out that 'I've felt the same mysel'. In a manner not dissimilar to his technique in 'To Robert Fergusson', Garioch points out the similarities between their situations and shows that he sympathises with the older poet. He does this initially by mentioning Buchanan's indirect rôle in Garioch's university education:

> I've scrievit monie a sang and sonnet
> sin owre my heid they waved thon bonnet
>   made out of your auld breeks,
> and see me nou, a makar beld
> wi bleerit een and feet unstell'd,
>   no worth a cog of leeks. [*CPW*, p. 35]

As Mario Relich points out, Garioch's use of the phrase 'auld breeks' brings to mind the poem of Fergusson, 'To my Auld Breeks', which also deals with poverty, and inevitably suggests that 'Garioch, in short, implies that he is modernising Buchanan by way of Fergusson'.[15] Here, however, Fergusson is a tangent: the poem is about Garioch and Buchanan. All the way through the poem is a feeling of the helplessness of the teacher's situation, expressed with weary humour:

> A kep and goun – what dae they maitter?
> a kep and bells wad suit him better. [*CPW*, p. 36]

However, the final line shows anything but humour, and is a resigned plea to anyone considering following in the footsteps of Garioch and Buchanan:

> MORAL
> Lat onie young poetic chiel
> that reads thae lines tak tent richt weill:
>   THINK TWICE, OR IT'S OWRE LATE! [*CPW*, p. 37]

It is easy to understand why Garioch felt this way. He retired from schoolteaching at the earliest opportunity, despite the financial consequences, and his letters make clear not only that teaching was a struggle but that the stress he encountered affected his writing as well:

But it is an awful strain, this Deacon Brodie sort of life, Sutherland by day and Garioch by night, schoolmastering and making poetry being such different things, and yet both tiring you out in the same way, that's the damn thing about it. So for the last fortnight I've had a kind of revulsion or scunner and can't bear to read or write or do anything serious in the evenings. Usually I'm half-gyte with the thought of so much to do and only the evenings to do it in, so that the day seems an irrelevant and maddening interruption . . . What a life.[16]

Alexander Scott underlines this, and suggests that

there is nothing more savage, in the whole of contemporary Scots verse, than the 'Repone's' picture of the awful fate of the Edinburgh arts graduate condemned to a life sentence of schoolteaching, without the option. At the end of his appalling illustration of treadmill tomfoolery, Garioch rubs in the moral . . . not only once but – adding insult to injury – twice times over, as if forced by habit to employ the methods of the schoolmaster even when he functions as a poet.[17]

Though these poems are riven with bleak personal experience, it is notable that Garioch finds it necessary once again to emphasise his similarities to his predecessors, when the poem would work just as well without such an approach. It is almost as if he is too modest – or uncertain – to allow his work to stand up and be regarded on its own, and he feels the need to justify himself by pointing out his similarity to the great figures who came before, hindering any attempt to view Garioch in his own right.

Instead of just looking for similarities between work by Garioch and by earlier poets, we should be at least as alert to differences. Robin Fulton attempts to relate the Garioch's poem 'Embro to the Ploy' back to Fergusson by suggesting that it has 'several notable ancestors – e.g. Fergusson's "Leith Races" '. [*CPW*, p. 293] There are indeed many convenient similarities between the two poems, but they are not striking enough to suggest that Fergusson's poem is simply a progenitor of Garioch's. For example, the rhyme schemes are *almost* identical, but part of the distinctive appeal of Garioch's poem is his use of the bob and wheel at the end of each verse to emphasise a cutting aside before finishing with a comparatively innocent-sounding refrain. There are also obvious differences in the way the poets treat their subject matter –

Fergusson starts his poem with an attempt at a neo-Classical conceit that he is being shown the sights by a 'braw buskit laughing lass' who is Mirth, but she evaporates almost as soon as she is described; Garioch uses no such method. As well as this, the Leith Races in Fergusson's poem are a peripheral background to the poet's description of typical Edinburgh characters, including his favourite target, the City Guard (Sir Walter Scott commented that Fergusson 'mentions them so often that he may be termed their poet laureate').[18] By contrast, the 'Ploy' – i.e. the Edinburgh Festival – is the subject of Garioch's satire, and although he satirises other specific things – journalists, wealthy Americans, 'furthgangan Embro folk' – they are all part of the main target. In short, although this comparison with a poem of Fergusson's seems convenient, it is also a little pointless: there are similarities, but the differences reveal Garioch's special signature.

Indeed, if one is to insist on finding a poem which is an obvious predecessor of 'Embro to the Ploy', then one should look beyond Fergusson to the anonymous mediæval poem, 'Peblis to the Play'. Comparing opening verses, we can see an astonishing similarity of form and structure between the two, suggesting that 'Embro to the Ploy' is not simply an update of one of Fergusson's poems; rather, it shows Garioch's awareness of the 'Christis Kirk' tradition which is represented not only by Fergusson but by Dunbar, Lindsay, Drummond of Hawthornden, Ramsay and Burns among others. The way in which 'Embro to the Ploy' feeds into this tradition has been mentioned briefly by Allan H. MacLaine but generally ignored elsewhere.[19] That is unfortunate, since Garioch's poem is a splendid example of the genre, with a keen sense of its traditions. Some of these are summarised by MacLaine in the introduction to his anthology:

> [T]here is a satiric description of working-class folk (usually peasants or town tradesmen) shown on some festive occasion such as a wedding or a fair. The people are engaged in all kinds of revelry, wooing, drunkenness, horseplay, ribaldry, brawling, and bungling. This descriptive method gives a panoramic impression of the whole crowded and colourful scene by highlighting carefully chosen details. (MacLaine. *The Christis Kirk Tradition*, p. v.)

In effect, 'Embro to the Ploy' is a sophisticated literary joke, taking a recognised traditional form (and, specifically, its earliest known poem) and turning the convention on its head – for the subject of the satire is not 'working-class folk' but the elite. This satirical method is a favourite of Garioch's, and this underlines that any attempt to map this poem straightforwardly on to the work of Fergusson is rather crude.

In fact, 'Embro to the Ploy' is a *tour de force* which shows Garioch at his best: rhythmic dexterity which belies the secondhand structure, apposite choice of Scots vocabulary, deadly accurate satire, *faux* Philistine narrator and a consciously contemporary voice. We hear how

> Americans wi routh of dollars,
> wha drink our whisky neat,
> wi Sasunachs and Oxford Scholars
> are eydent for the treat
> of music sedulously high-tie
> at thirty-bob a seat;
> Wop opera performed in Eytie
> to them's richt up their street,
>   they say,
> in Embro to the ploy. [*CPW*, p. 14]

But the attraction of the poem lies not so much in this kind of general carping but in the more specific engagement with the reality of the Festival. The tenth verse tells how

> A happening, incident, or splore
> affrontit them that saw
> a thing they'd never seen afore–
> in the McEwan Haa:
> a lassie in a wheelie-chair
> wi naething on at aa,
> jist my luck! I wasna there,
> it's no the thing ava,
>   tut-tut,
> in Embro to the ploy. [*CPW*, p. 16]

This verse seems to combine an acid observation of the typical Edinburgh reaction to any slightly shocking Festival production with a small dose of eccentric fantasy; however, this newspaper report shows that the incident did occur and is actually reported without exaggeration:

> In the midst of the International Drama Conference of 1963 a naked model on a trolley was pushed across the organ gallery of the McEwan Hall. This was one of a number of 'happenings'

organised by the American director Kenneth Dewey. A publicity storm erupted. The conference organiser, John Calder, and the model, Anna Kesselaar, were charged with indecency (Kesselaar was acquitted). It remains a landmark in post-modern performance.[20]

For all its qualities, this poem reveals Garioch's occasionally odd approach to his own work. It should be obvious from both the basis and the content of this poem that it is a significant work into which a great deal of thought has gone; it is also one which was revised and added to on several occasions.[21] Like much of Fergusson's poetry it contains that strong element of 'performability' which is often strong in Scottish verse and which make 'Embro to the Ploy' perfect for poetry readings. Yet it appears that Garioch neglected the poem almost entirely when reading in public. The National Library of Scotland possesses the notes Garioch made for his poetry readings between 1964 and 1981.[22] These show that, while certain poems were repeated over and over again, he used 'Embro to the Ploy' on only six occasions, and even here he did not always read the complete poem.

Digressions aside, the genesis of 'Embro to the Ploy' makes it clear that Garioch's influences were much wider-ranging than the connection to Fergusson implies, and his empathy with the makars of the fifteenth and sixteenth centuries is stronger than might be obvious. In an early article entitled 'The Makars' the apprentice poet identifies himself with the difficulties which they faced:

> As a journeyman makar, I wonder how the makars set about their job. Each had a huge vocabulary; where did they mine the golden words to form their aureat diction: Did they compose by dint of hard work, putting together a jigsaw puzzle without a reference pattern, composed of pieces few of which would fit? Had they lists of words and especially of rhymes?[23]

Evidently, at this stage of his career, Garioch was giving a great deal of thought to the way these writers worked – he produced his own list of rhyming words[24] – and was in awe of their abilities.

Even in some of the later, longer poems, such as 'The Big Music', 'The Bog', 'The Wire' and 'The Muir', where Garioch is at his most successful and original, there are occasional echoes of this fascination. These poems are particularly interesting, partly because it is not their rhythmical structure which marks them out; rather it is the ambitious nature of their engagement with primarily twentieth-century issues: warfare, in the case of 'The Bog' and 'The Wire', atomic theory in the case of 'The Muir' ('The Big Music' deals with piping, a more traditional subject, but in an explicitly twentieth-century setting). These topics are apart from the mainstream anyway, but Garioch is brave for attempting to deal with them in quite broad Scots without making it feel hackneyed or deliberately synthetic.

Garioch's most ambitious poem, 'The Muir', brings us back to the question of Fergusson, that poet who could write of surd roots and geometry. 'The Muir' is an astonishing piece, which attempts to present atomic theory not only in an accessible manner, but in Scots. Such an enterprise might sound unwise, but the poem is a masterly discussion of Heaven and Hell, reality and existence. The poem opens with a discussion of Dante's Hell, which in this case sounds suspiciously like Morningside:

> Monie a time in Hell was Dante faced
> wi glowres frae weill-kent neibors, nou disgraced,
> aa ettlan for a crack, even amang
> the busie dool of Hell, tho aye in haste . . . [*CPW*, p. 54]

After introducing his vision of Heaven–'Badenoch in simmer, wi nae clegs about' – Garioch begins his exposition of atomic theory:

> What maks the solid substance of this muir
> I walk on, that wad seem to be a dour
> vault for the cryptic damned, a flair for us
> meantime? Electrons in ellipse attour
> the atomy's wee massive nucleus,
> balanced in void atween their impetus
> to flee awa frae central government
> and minus chairge that ettles for the plus. [*CPW*, p. 57]

The beauty of the use of Scots in this context is that, aside from the humour of descriptions such as 'the atomy's wee massive nucleus', it removes any formal or explicitly scientific vocabulary that would put off the general reader. This effect is heightened by Garioch's willingness to compare the important parts of his description to recognisable things: the sun's rays are scattered like 'the tracer-bullets splairgin frae a gun'; he asks if people 'sit/ and watch the atom dance an echtsom reel/ in whilk the figures never seem to fit'.

This is not to suggest that the poem is simple or straightforward. The tolling chorus of 'And Fergusson gyte, gyte in Darien', which appears twice following Garioch's initial discussion of the nature of matter, seems at first glance to be an unnecessary and irrelevant intrusion, which smacks of an obsession with the eighteenth-century poet. However, it gradually becomes clear that the image of Fergusson, alone in Edinburgh's madhouse,[25] is an opportunity for Garioch to discuss the nature of reality. He returns constantly to the nature of Fergusson's madness, asking

> Hou can we say that Fergusson was wud
> to skar at an eternity of Hell,
> whan our conception of the Yird itsel
> is like a tree kept growan wi nae root,
> nae less absurd nor fire that winna quell
> even in a vacuum of time? [*CPW*, p. 60]

Later, he casts doubts upon whether Fergusson's melancholia was itself reason enough for him to be regarded as mad: he cannot see

> that folk are gyte, semply becaise they gie
> the trauchle up of fechtin wi this thing
> and faa at last intill melancholy [*CPW*, p. 61]

Fergusson here is a useful and effective image, but one that is slightly peripheral to the real meaning of the poem, which is emphatically not 'about Fergusson'. Rather, the poem represents a reassuring continuity – Robin Fulton suggests that 'the one constant is our inescapable human dimensions, the only scale which gives any meaning to ideas of hell'[26] – and a scepticism about the nature of scientific knowledge:

> The best of scientists, for aa their skill,
> hae never seen an atom, never will,
> for aa their instruments of utmaist pouer;
> the benmaist evidence wi whilk they deal
> is no the atom, but the atom's spoor,
> readings or cathode-blips. [*CPW*, p. 63]

The tone is questioning without being narrow-minded, and it is a neat portent of the conclusion to the poem, which blames 'the dour/ pedal-note, in fremmit key' of an unpreached faith, a 'soun [that] is man-made' for obscuring our view of the big picture, and concludes by suggesting, in a rare moment of Christian comment, that 'Jehovah by the hairt maun aye be socht' [*CPW*, pp. 66–7].

With no slight intended, Garioch has reached a philosophical level never attained by Fergusson, and worthy of an even older makar, Dunbar, whose presence is equally tangible here, not just in the obvious reference to 'the samyn sup Kinde Kittock wycelie walit/ thon time that, quod Dunbar, God leuk't and lauch't . . .' [*CPW*, p. 56], but in the elevated nature of the subject matter and the grandness of the language–

> God's ire maun gorroch and amidthwart thraw
> intill the sempiternal buller, doun. [*CPW*, p. 54]

> God the Force supern
> may kyth Himsel til us in an equation
> in finite terms . . . [*CPW*, pp. 56–7]

It is fitting that it is Garioch himself who is able to underline the quality of his verse craftmanship, equal to that of his distinguished predecessor. This poem underlines the fact that Garioch could be a champion of Fergusson while finding his own voice: the poems about Fergusson show that the inflence is strong, but his other work shows that he found other things important too. Some of what is by common consent Garioch's best work – 'The Wire', 'The Muir', the Belli sonnets, the Buchanan translations – has little or nothing to do with Fergusson, and instead shows off the distinctiveness of Garioch's voice, one that could draw on a variety of other voices while developing its own distinctiveness. While acknowledging that Garioch was in *some* ways Fergusson's heir, it is with that distinctiveness that we need to engage if Garioch and, indeed, Fergusson are to be regarded with the respect they deserve.

Notes

1 Robert Garioch. *Complete Poetical Works*, ed. Robin Fulton. Edinburgh: Macdonald, 1983, p.23. Hereafter *CPW*.
2 James Caird, 'Robert Garioch–a Personal Appreciation', *SLJ* vol. 10 no. 2 (December 1983), p. 73.
3 Letter to Sydney Tremayne, 30 Oct. 1974. National Library of Scotland, MS26673, fol. 54. Of all Garioch's correspondence, that with Tremayne offers most insight into his personality. Manuscript quotations are reproduced here with kind permission of the Trustees of the National Library of Scotland.
4 Letter to Sydney Tremayne, 24 September 1974. NLS, MS26673, fol. 52.
5 Edinburgh: Reprographia, 1974.

6 NLS, MS26673, fols. 54–8. The final plenary session descended into an atmosphere of such ill-feeling that Garioch walked out.

7 Douglas Dunn. 'Cantraips and Trauchles – Robert Garioch and Scottish Poetry', *Cencrastus* 43 (Autumn 1992), p. 40.

8 *The Poems of Robert Fergusson*, ed. Matthew P. MacDiarmid, 2 vols. Edinburgh: Blackwood, 1954 and 1956, vol. II, p. 69. Hereafter *F*.

9 *The Poems of Robert Fergusson*, ed. Matthew MacDiarmid, vol. II, p. 153.

10 Letter from Sydney Tremayne, 28 September 1974. NLS MS26569, fols 40–41.

11 James Caird, 'A Personal Appreciation', p. 72.

12 Robert Garioch, *George Buchanan's Jephthah and* The Baptist *translatit in Scots*. Edinburgh: Oliver & Boyd, 1959.

13 Among those who rejected it was T.S. Eliot at Faber & Faber. Though he was impressed, he found the Scots difficult and doubted that any London publisher would be interested. See letter from T.S. Eliot, 13 November 1957. NLS, MS26561, fol. 131.

14 I.D. McFarlane, *Buchanan*. London: Duckworth, 1981.

15 Mario Relich, 'Scottish Tradition and Robert Garioch's Individual Talent', *Lines Review* 136 (March 1996), p. 10.

16 Letter to J.K. Annand, 1 October 1955. Robin Fulton (ed.), *A Garioch Miscellany*. Edinburgh: Macdonald, 1986, p. 32. Hereafter *GM*.

17 Alexander Scott, 'Robert Garioch: The Makar and the Mask', *Scottish Review Arts and Environment* 23 (August 1981), p. 14.

18 Cited by David Daiches in *Robert Fergusson*. Edinburgh: Scottish Academic Press, 1982, p. 5.

19 Allan H. MacLaine (ed.), *The Christis Kirk Tradition: Scots Poems of Folk Festivity*. Glasgow: Association for Scottish Literary Studies, 1996, p. vi.

20 Andy Lavender, 'It's weird, it's wonderful – it must be Edinburgh'. *The Times*, 2 August 1999, p. 44.

21 There exist at least three additional verses to this poem. As well as the verse quoted by Robin Fulton [*CPW*, p. 293], NLS, MS26595 contains, at fol. 61:

They say that, in the George Hotel
(George Street, first on the richt)
the maist-respeckit clientèle
hae haggis ilka nicht.
Whatever gaes intill't . . . aha!
it grees wi them aa richt,
for when the piper gies a blaw
they dance wi aa their micht,
    hoots toots
[in Embro to the ploy] (this last line is missing)

Meanwhile, another exists in a letter to Sydney Tremayne of 3 August 1967:

I truly hope we'll try and please
our guid Lord Provost Brechin,
and burn yon film of 'Ulysses'
(I've read the book, a dreich ane)
wi miles of bleizan celluloid,
a hunder pipers screichan,
and effigies of Dr Freud,
and fountains of free skeechan
    (jist a copy)
at Embro to the ploy.

Garioch goes on to explain: 'You may not have heard the exciting news that our City Fathers . . . have decided not to allow the showing of the film of *Ulysses*. (I nearly went to see it in London, but the seats were aafie dear.) Anyhow, Lord Provost Brechin . . . said in a speech that this film should be burnt in public . . .' [*GM*, p. 41].

22 NLS, MS26616.
23 NLS, MS26581, fol. 80. In the MS the words 'a reference pattern' are unclear; this is my reading.
24 NLS, MS26583.
25 Which was located, as Garioch's note to the poem points out, in the former headquarters of the Darien Company [*CPW*, p. 298].
26 Robin Fulton, *Contemporary Scottish Poetry: Individuals and Contexts*. Edinburgh: Macdonald, 1974, p. 172.

TO ROBERT FERGUSSON

The daftest o deys atween a heap
o festivals is when Eh keep
meh wurd tae skell ye frae yir sleep
        and yell in yir skull,
'Here comes yir tribute frae a creep –
        ut's lang and dull!'

Atween meh duck-bunged Yule and that
dank Hogmillennium o tat,
thi shampers and fireworks equally flat:
        oor kulchur's treh
at haein fun – lyk spaein thi cat
        or a turd in a peh.

Atween thi nicht that Scots forgot
(St Andrew's) and thir loss o plot
that mairks thi birth o Mister Sot
        (that's Rab, yir namesake),
Eh blaa oot lines lyk a neb blaas snot
        jist fur yir fame's sake.

Atween a thoosan years o gore,
and, wi a glisk at Grozny, a thoosan more,
atween a parliament o whores
        and independence,
Eh scrunt and chap at yir coffin's door
        lyk a mim defendant.

Insteid o aa thae legal drones
fur you tae copy, here's a poem
that micht elicit ghaistly groans
        and gar ye shift
yir young man's under-usit bones:
        meh gab's your gift.

199

But lyk thi gant atween thae times –
thi fairs, thi races – in your rhymes,
and oor homogeny o mimes
        and thon Dumbo dome,
ye'll find meh crambo bad as crimes
        against garden gnomes.

Compared tae Garioch's canny habbie
meh stanzas drehv lyk a weel-tipped cabbie:
whaur Boab turns terse is whaur Eh'm blabby –
        Ach, Eh'm aa effect –
whit Eh mak tolter he kept slabby,
        he showed respect.

But Eh shair nae britherhood wi you
at laist o thi kind Boab Garioch knew
o vennel, brae and brat-time view
        o thi Seat and Forth –
tho Dundee High and St Andrews drew
        you further north.

Yet that's lyk Wallace: wha can find
a whiff o hum doon Dundee's wynds,
thi saviour o aa Scottishkind
        wha geed Selby paiks?
Noo aa that Wallace brings tae mind's
        thi Land o Cakes

– and Gibson gibbering like an ape
oan Freedom and pair Scoatlan's rape
while Pat McGooghan peels a grape
        and skites a midge,
Mel's prick is proven Oscar-shaped
        at Stirlin Bridge.

Tho there's yir learnin at thi Uni,
thae years that left yir leths sae puny
and mebbe helped yir harns turn loony
        at thi thocht o Hell,
thi leir that sticks lyk hair wi chewnie –
        Eh ken that well.

Not whit a college crehs success
nor recognised noo by oor Press
as Scots – atween them nanethiless
        nor heich nor hard,
Horace and Leith shares your address,
        oor double bard.

And that's whaur Eh wauk up: tae feel
thi caller splash o verse congeal
thi current notion naethin's real
        but prose schemes whaur
McDivots rant and writhe lyk eels
        in grit and glaur.

You brocht tae *Luckie Middlemist's*,
whaur poetry lay panned and pished,
lyk pandour eysters, lines sae kissed
        wi that dose o saut
crehd "history" – we cam alist,
        stood up, and wrote

fur Mnemosyne, that usefu muse,
wha minds us tae pit oan wir trews
afore we laive thi publishin hoose:
        there have been books
in which oor ancients sang thi blues
        while we squeezed plooks.

Although wir journos cannae read
and Jockstar belters lost in greed
think punters shid furget thi leid
        o Henryson,
Dunbar and Douglas haud a gleid
        that burns thi tongue.

Oor nation's literature extends
thru dialects and dowie pends
tae depths whaur divots get thi bends
        while readin Hogg,
and heichts whaur Hugh MacDiarmid tends
        tae pop thir lugs.

Sae Fergusson, oor double bard,
you kent tae pley thi joker's card
when Reekie's ghaists – they micht hae jarred –
        talked politics;
and hung auld Hector's tag oan a scarred
        drunk bein sick.

Frae Musselbrugh tae Tuscany,
frae Tiber til thi Tay, ye'd pree
thi prospect syne tak aff thi gree –
        nor gowdspink nor
thi catwalk-flichty butterflee
        wad you ignore.

And keepied up thi wurds sae well
fae Robin Gibb tae pair Jock Bell,
wha passed tae Sawney, fa aa could tell
        wiz Aiberdeenie:
he sliced leid at thi auld Tron Bell
        lyk Paolo Maldini.

Frae Buchan boadies, browster wives,
frae tinkler billies, shairpenin knives,
frae tonguey weemen, drinkin dives
        tae Marion on
thi cuttie stool – you plucked oor lives
        frae Acheron.

Ye mairried Pluto's dreary toun
tae Reekie in hur broukit goun
o wurds lyk snortirs hingin doon
        or Watson's shrood
fur ainly wurds when ye're in thi groond
        are ony good.

There's thirty-odd that Burns hiz borraed
that you and Allan Ramsay quarried
frae lodes and seams fur whilk auld Murray'd
        near OEDed:
a hundred, Pound said, 's aa thi hurried
        warld poet'll need.

You kept thi door stapped open atween
thi antique and thi eident scene
of Embro's prime, sae baith can glean
    frae thi ither's hairst,
sae we can free whit still can mean
    noo thi doorframe's burst.

And sae thi strain o stentin past
thi een o ithers telt at last:
thi gardyloo o hellfire waasht
    yir mind til thru it
drows and jowes, wanwordy, thrasht
    a clamihewit.

Lyk Burns' bairns' births, maist daith's unplanned:
yours fell atween oblivion and
oor grubbin need tae understand,
    and wha's tae say
hoo late sall lowe thi dim's demand –
    biography?

Young Fergusson under a drumly mune's
heard John Broon o Haddington denoonce
aa ribaldry and's felt thi poonce
    o thi Bible's wecht:
uts black knock is thi worst o stounds
    whaur his wits are steghed.

Young Fergusson wan nicht is fleggit
by a ghaist baith fell and fower-leggit
wha claas a speug and trehs tae dreg ut
    oot frae uts cage
thi burd's skreiks tear his wits near nekkit
    wi haly rage.

Young Fergusson faas doon thi sterrs
and cracks his harns ayont repairs,
and Darien hears his final prayers
    devoid o suss –
and Hugh MacD, tae muss his hairs,
    fell aff a bus.

Thi Clapham omnibus, nae doot:
he landit oan his lyric snoot
and banged, fowk sey, his rhythms oot –
    they dwyned tae prose
as gyte as you or goons that toot
        shite up thir nose

But Eh wad airgue Mister Grieve
could wipe mair verse aff oan his sleeve
than them wha waant us tae believe
    that he turned sad
not in thir nelly puff could scrieve –
        ut's them that's mad.

And sae wi you, yir granes and greets,
ye nearies til a Northern Keats,
ye poet o the clartit streets
    and ragman's cart,
oor Jimmy Dean o thi canty beats
        oor ain Kit Smart.

Lyk Cowper, Clare or Thomas Gray
yir sanity wiz wede away
by trehin tae turn whit people say
    tae somethin rare,
hud you recovered, we wad hae
        a rivin quair.

Tho literary Scots are prone tae yearn,
thi wey that paper's prone tae burn:
we tint thi pleys o Wedderburn
    and thi myths o thi Picts,
you drank Leith's waaters at yir turn
        and crossed thi Styx.

Yet fur twa years ye swyved thi city
ejaculatin verse sae glitty
ut faithered mony an urban ditty
    lyk this wan noo;
ye dodged thi blackest o banditti –
        ahent yir broo.

Ye geed us aa a double gift:
a language able aye tae shift
frae causey stane tae streamery lift,
    sae, Fergusson,
Eh hail ye in that speerit drift –
    and sae ye're gone.

Skell – spill, rouse; neb – nose; glisk – glimpse; scrunt – scratch; chap – knock; mim – restrained, affected; gar – make; gant – yawn, gap; crambo – rhymes, doggerel; tolter – unbalanced; vennel – narrow lane; brae – hill; paiks – blows (William Wallace stabbed Selby, the son of the English captain of Dundee Castle, to death in a street brawl around 1290); skites – smacks; leths – limbs; harns – brains; chewnie – chewing gum; caller – fresh, invigorating; glaur – mud; pandour eysters – large succulent oysters caught near Prestonpans at the doors of the salt pans; saut – salt; cam alist – were revived; trews – trousers; leid – language; gleid – glowing coal; dowie pends – dismal alleys; pree – taste, test; syne – then; tak aff the gree – extract the best; browster wives – women who brewed and sold ale; cutty stool – the place in a church where those guilty of misconduct were obliged to sit; broukit – dirty, streaked; snortirs – beads of phlegm dangling from the nose; stapped – forced; eident – bright, living; hairst – harvest; stenting – stretching, straining; een – eyes; gardyloo – warning that waste water, etc., was about to be poured into the street from an upper storey, here transferred to the substance itself; drows – spasms of anxiety; jowes – judders; wanwordy – unworthy, inappropriate; clamihewit – drubbing or hubbub; lowe – flame; drumly – gloomy, troubled; stounds – blows; steghed – stuffed; fleggit – scared; speug – sparrow; skreiks – screams; haily – holy; dwyned – shrivelled up, fell away; gyte – mad; in their nelly puff – in their lifetime; granes – groans; greets – crying fits; clartit – muddied; canty – lively; wede away – withered; rivin – full or bursting; quair – book; tint – lost; swyved – copulated with; glitty – fertile; ahent – behind; broo – brow; causey stane – cobblestone; streamery lift – sky filled with the Aurora Borealis; speerit – spirit.

W. N. Herbert

Fergusson and the Bycultural Canon

W.N. HERBERT

Writing this essay places me in a position somewhat analogous to that of Fergusson in his address, 'To the Principal and Professors' of St Andrews. When he referred to them as 'my winsome billy boys', he was, as poets often are, simultaneously of the academic world and not of it.[1] Fergusson borrowed aspects of the discourse of his old university for a critique of those professors' adulatory welcome to 'Samy' Johnson – and I am borrowing something of the descendant of that discourse to offer some suggestions about the present role of literary Scots. May our different results equally distort their borrowed accents.

I too am obliged to retain my iambic foot in the world beyond the academy, that land over the Wall where both our methods and our subject are strangers. Because when I stand up to read my poems in Scots or English to any audience, Scots or English, I face people who are not particularly informed as to the language or the forms I use, or the predecessors who I believe give me the ground from which to proceed. Therefore I plan to be more alert than usual to what might be described as Fergusson's interface with his reader, since it is in that subtle invitation to hooly that I believe most of the issues I wish to raise here reside. I am also conscious that Fergusson shares with many Scots writers the dubious distinction of not yet having been done (or done over) by that academy, and in this respect he is still the responsibility of the poets he inspires and the readers he entertains.

Fergusson's work in Scots and English appeared in a newspaper of sorts, *Ruddiman's Weekly Magazine* (also, tellingly, known as the *Edinburgh Amusement*); more, he was asked to perform it, as well as sing songs, at parties, in public houses and as part of the Cape Club where he was known as Sir Precentor, because of his fine voice. The editor of my 1879 edition of Fergusson's poems, Alexander Grosart, comments on the Cape: 'This club sustained a respectable and sober character: but the "Convivalia" in Mr Chambers' admirable "Traditions of Edinburgh," opens to us the crapulent habits of the whole society of Edinburgh at this period'.[2] Which is as circumspect a way of saying 'pissheads' as you could hope to hear. So Fergusson was addressing an intimate audience who were familiar, thanks partly to the efforts of

Allan Ramsay, with his sphere of reference and the strategies he deployed within it. The regularity and conviviality of these appearances both in print and in person bear some comparison with the special intimacy enjoyed (and sometimes endured) today by the poet in performance.

Only in Fergusson's case we have a poetry of performance that draws on a broader and more assured frame of reference than it now usually commands. When he mock-celebrates the 'King's Birth-Day in Edinburgh', he takes his epigraph from William Drummond's scatological macaronic poem the 'Polemo-Middinia', itself a kind of oblique take on the genre of Christis Kirk, the depiction of country life that presents rural fairs and the brawls within them in mock-heroic terms. Fergusson, who worked with the Christis Kirk stanza and subject elsewhere, is here indicating an extension of the genre to cover urban burlesque, and, after rejecting Helicon as 'That heath'nish spring', requesting instead that 'Highland whisky scour our hawses', goes on to produce a mock-lament for the cannon, Mons Meg:

> Oh willawins, MONS MEG, for you,
> 'Twas firin' crack'd thy muckle mou;
> What black mishanter gart ye spew
>   Baith gut and ga'?
> I fear they bang'd thy belly fu'
>   Against the law.
>
> Right seldom am I gi'en to bannin,
> But, by my saul, ye was a cannon,
> Cou'd hit a man, had he be staunin
>   In shire o' Fife,
> Sax long Scots miles ayont *Clackmannan*,
>   And tak his life.[3]

In these two swift stanzas he hints at elegy in the cry 'willawins', slips in hyperbole, sending his allusive cannon-ball soaring over the scene of dispute in Drummond's poem, and manages an extremely vulgar reference to the impregnation of Mons Meg, which is of course mentioned in the 'Polemo-Middinia' in terms which are just as vulgar, when the 'mistress of Scotstarvit' (how shall I phrase this?) lets one slip: 'Elatisque hippis magno cum murmure fartum/Barytonum emisit, veluti Monsmegga cracasset . . .'[4]

And his audience understood all this, but in that partly engaged, partly glancing way that we bring to performance, where it is not necessary to understand every word because the next word, the next phrase, is already among us. In *Ruddiman's*, too, the next article, the next issue, would tend to crowd out what was not fully understood. The particular relevance of this to Scots, a language we have long been more accustomed to hearing than to reading, will, I hope, be apparent. The lug, as long as it is being entertained, is more forgiving than the ee when it comes to obscurities of reference or vocabulary. And even in print, the critical eye may be cajoled by a humorous context into lightly acknowledging a complex subtext.

But in the cold clear light of two hundred odd years later, the reading experience is somewhat different. The local reference begs for a footnote, the no longer colloquial requires the dictionary, the milieu as a whole is tantalising but estranged from us. And, if we are outwith the academy, and our livelihood does not depend on enabling understanding or gamefully attempting to enable understanding, there is always another performance nearby, in which at the click of a switch or a mouse, or the drumbeat of hype, we can immerse ourselves – perhaps even one which offers a simpler solution to the kind of questions raised by Fergusson's work, which I would frame as follows: how complex can a Scottish poet be when writing in Scots before he or she loses an already marginal audience? And what does this tell us about the role of literary Scots itself within our society? What possible function can this kind of aggrandised, allusive, obscure language have? This is where I wish to locate my sense of Fergusson as a living but under-realised influence; indeed, as one of the most flexible models *in potentia* for a modern poet writing in Scots, the most generous in his complexity. And a poet who posits the limitations of that language and its readership in a more pertinent manner than Burns, due to his skills and sphere of reference.

Those skills and that sphere may be set forth briefly: he is an urban poet in a country convinced that its verse is a pastoral affair; he is a poet animated by the transformation of tradition in a culture waterlogged by its past; and he is a poet unaffected by the moral niceties that afflicted the likes of Mackenzie – 'The Sow of Feeling,' indeed. In his little Scotlandism, however, Fergusson could also seem the narrowest model. His attacks on French food ('*snails* and *puddocks*') and Italian music ('crabbit queer variety') have to be seen in the specific context of his cultural stance.[5] Rather than xenophobia, they are tokens in the construction of a self-sufficient Scotland, independent in mind if not in actuality. This was a point overlooked by his nineteenth-century admirer, Robert Louis Stevenson. In 'A Lowden Sabbath Morn', a tame satire on kirk-going, we catch the echo right down to a sly reference to 'Sir Precentor' himself, but the nationalistic sentiment has simplified to attack:

> The tunes are up – *French* to be sure,
> The faithfu' *French*, an' twa-three mair;
> The auld prezentor, hoastin' sair,
>   Wales out the portions,
> An' yirks the tune into the air
>   Wi' queer contortions.[6]

The cognoscenti of Enlightenment Edinburgh were so keen, as Roderick Watson tells us, to produce works of home-grown genius, that they hailed the author of *The Epigoniad* as a significant figure.[7] Fergusson, William Wilkie's student, confined his search for approval to those more reliable cultural signifiers: the haggis and the fiddle. And he confined his considerable energies during those brief years of brilliance to a similar act of metonymic faith, relying on a series of traditional forms to communicate his nationalist beliefs.

This essay oscillates between two remarks on form made by two of our finest poets in Robert Crawford's edited collection of essays on Robert Burns. The first is by Douglas Dunn in his excellent essay on Burns's metric:

> The more Burns made these Scottish verse-forms his own, then the more he became their servant . . . They guided him, and they refused to let him go. Whatever their origins, those Scottish stanzas were, or were made to be, and maybe they still are (but by now I think the matter is historical) as aboriginal as native melodies.[8]

He returns to that troubling parenthesis (troubling, that is, for those of us who are still in fee to these metrical masters) later: 'It was left to Robert Garioch, through his attachment to Fergusson more than to Burns, to try to revive them significantly. It is difficult to see how these stanzas . . . can inform contemporary and future Scottish poetry'.[9]

The second is by Seamus Heaney in his essay on 'Burns's Art Speech': 'I think . . . that we can prefigure a future by reimagining our pasts. In poetry, however, this prefiguring is venturesome and suggestive, more like a melodic promise than a social programme'.[10] I believe both poets are right: to look at Fergusson's influence, we have to enter this difficult but melodious zone. What does it mean to use the Scots stanzas – the Habbie, the Christis Kirk, the Cherrie and the Slae, the ballad and the tetrameter couplet? What does it mean to use them today?

The first thing to observe is a tension between the deliberateness of this gesture in Ramsay, Fergusson and in Burns – their conscious decision to inhabit these forms – and the more irrational compulsion Douglas Dunn describes such forms as placing their users under. In the eighteenth century there was perhaps less sense of an unconscious demand in these terms, but you certainly could explore the resonance of a 'folk' form. That is in part what Allan Ramsay's addition of two further 'cantos' to 'Christ's Kirk on the Green' was intended to signify.[11] Their decision can be described as having elements of faux-folk, but it could have had few connotations of being unlearned. And yet Douglas Dunn uses the distinctly ancient and, I think, accurate analogy of master and servant. If these writers served an apprenticeship, then the masters from whom they received instruction were not so much previous writers as the various examples of previous writers gathered into an idea, almost an identity, based on the forms themselves.

Here I'd like to expand on that metaphor with a 'venturesome and suggestive' reference to the debatable but intriguing argument put forward by Julian Jaynes in *The Origin of Consciousness in the Breakdown of the Bicameral Mind*. My purpose is to come at this idea of the Scots stanzas as culturally resonant containers from a different enough angle to make some suggestions about their continued viability. Put extremely briefly, Jaynes argues that consciousness as we perceive it, with its analogies of the self, of morality, of will-power, is a result of language and specifically the capacity of language to generate metaphor, including such metaphors as an interior space which this self can inhabit. Which puts a different spin on W.S. Graham's line, 'What is the language using us for?'

Before this piece of social evolution, Jaynes argues, we were as the heroes of Homer, unreflecting automata reliant on Athena or Apollo or Zeus; on socially constant hallucinatory voices, as religions based on possession, such as voodoo or Candomble, still are. These voices, although interpreted as those of the gods, were the instructions received from the now largely silent speech centres of the right hemisphere of the brain, a more intuitive region capable of handling a wider series of possibilities than the stick-em-with-a-spear reasoning of the left hemisphere. In other words, before consciousness, there was inspiration.[12] This is Jaynes's take on Helicon, the spring abjured by Fergusson in favour of whisky:

Let it be stressed . . . that the Muses were not figments of anyone's imagination. I would ask the reader to peruse the first pages of Hesiod's *Theogony* and realise that all of it was probably seen and heard in hallucination, just as can happen today in schizophrenia or under certain drugs. Bicameral men did not imagine; they experienced. The beautiful Muses with their unison "lily-like" voice, dancing out of the thick mists of evening, thumping on soft and vigorous feet about the lonely enraptured shepherd, these arrogances of delicacy were the hallucinatory sources of memory in late bicameral men, men who did not live in a frame of past happening, who did not have 'lifetimes' in our sense, and who could not reminisce because they were not fully conscious.[13]

It sounds uncannily like the heroes of the Ossianic *Fragments*, doesn't it? Or, rather, it sounds related to the common ascription by poets of intent to the poem, eloquently put by Michael Donaghy:

Thales teaches that all things are full of gods. Anaximenes teaches that every stone on the beach has a soul. I'd certainly credit a page of poetry with a mind of its own. In our desire to locate the presence of the poet behind the frame of the words, we tend to animate the poem – the organic analogy – so it seems to be *returning* our attention, or we breathe life into its inanimate imagery – a marble torso of Apollo, London's mighty heart, a wafer lifted and consecrated.[14]

I would like to suggest that Scottish poetry, if it can hardly be described as bicameral (though many of its practitioners, imbibing freely of Fergusson's tincture, could be thought of as 'not fully conscious'), might be depicted as bycultural. By this I mean that the literature of a small country yoked so closely in political, cultural and linguistic terms to the affairs of a large country, will often be seen as a by-product of that larger country's literature. So we have the Scottish Chaucerians; so we have the troubled role within the English canon of James Thomson's *Seasons* (not to mention his 'Rule Britannia'); so we have the interesting puzzle of Lord Byron. To be constantly in the shadow inspires two main courses of action: to become one with those who cast the shadow; or to get out of the shadow, and attempt to be seen in your own light. Versions of these choices have taken place down the centuries: on one side we might place Thomson, along with Drummond of Hawthornden, Boswell, and the other Thomson who toiled in the City of Dreadful

Night. On the other we would certainly rank Ramsay, Fergusson and Burns. In this arena the choice of language becomes equally polarised, and the choice of a stanza form almost totemic.

Notice that it is not easy to be assimilated by the Borg-like library cube of the English literary canon, and that the reasons for exclusion have a similar ring to them. Drummond is accused of using an antiquated English that is not only a pastiche of Elizabethan sonneteering, but steals from English and continental practitioners. Macpherson, despite initially satisfying the sensibilities of an English and European audience, is then dismissed as a forger. Alexander Smith, first fêted as the promising young author of *A Life-Drama*, is then charged with Spasmodical plagiarism. To be Scottish and to write in English was to court the charge, not of being untrue to your origins (which were hardly relevant), but of textual unoriginality. Their verse was rejected by the body literary as though they were foreign organs attempting self-transplantation.

To write in Scots, on the other hand, has traditionally been to place yourself beyond the pale of readability, in the Land of the Constantly-Dying Out. In Enlightenment Edinburgh, which put Burns so precisely in his pastoral place, it was to associate yourself increasingly with the lower orders and was evidence of the unlearning of proper culture. With our Lesmahago-like genius for taking on both sides of any good-going argument, we even divided ourselves neatly into warring twins: Christopher North and the Ettrick Shepherd; Edwin Muir and Hugh MacDiarmid. To relate this self-division to the dominant left hemisphere and irrational, muted right hemisphere of post-bicameral man, is to restate Muir's fury-provoking remark about Scots and English being the languages of the heart and the head in a Scottish psyche that supposedly embodies Eliot's theory of the dissociation of sensibility. Except I am talking about the poets' attitudes towards the languages and forms at their disposal, rather than making any judgement about the actual natures of Scots and English, or their verse forms. Instead I would like to apply Jaynes's narrative of consciousness to Fergusson's perspective on Scottish literature. Jaynes depicts the gradual recession of bicameral certainties in the Greek poets in an almost elegiac mode:

> Why as the gods retreated even further into their silent heavens or, in another linguistic mode, as auditory hallucinations shrank back from access from left hemisphere monitoring mechanisms, why did not the dialect of the gods simply disappear? Why did not

poets simply cease their rhapsodic practices as did the priests and priestesses of the great oracles? The answer is very clear. The continuance of poetry, its change from a divine given to a human craft is part of that nostalgia for the absolute . . . And hence the frequency even today with which poems are apostrophes to often unbelieved-in entities, prayers to unknown imaginings . . . The forms are still there, to be worked now by the analog 'I' of a conscious poet. His task now is an imitation or mimesis of the former type of poetic utterance and the reality which it expressed. Mimesis in the bicameral sense of mimicking what was heard in hallucination has moved through the mimesis of Plato as representation of reality to mimesis as imitation with invention in its sullen service.[15]

When Jaynes mentions 'that nostalgia for the absolute', I have a very Scottish twinge of recognition. Why, given the linguistic prejudices of many Enlightenment thinkers, did poets persist in writing in Scots? I would argue that Fergusson, witnessing the overthrow of Scots by proper English (and English standards), took refuge in the conscious revival of what were seen as folk elements in Scottish culture, that for him too, the 'forms are still there, to be worked now by the analog "I" of a conscious poet . . .'

Jaynes's identification of poetry with an original divine language echoes James Thomson in his 1726 Preface to 'Winter', where he states that poetry constitutes 'The sublimest passages of the inspired writings themselves and what seems to be the peculiar language of heaven'. And of course by the 1780s Hugh Blair was to discuss such poetry in terms that prefigure Wordsworth, defining it as 'the language of passion, enlivened imagination'.[16] Though Blair's position on Scots and his failure to mention Fergusson in his *Lectures* are well known, the implication of his definition had already been explicitly stated by Burke: '. . . very polished languages, and such as are praised for their superior clearness and perspicuity, are generally deficient in strength . . . whereas the languages of most unpolished people, have a great force and energy of expression . . .'[17] It is hardly surprising that nationalist Scots should have applied a nostalgia for such absolutes to the past splendours of their own downgraded language; or that such sentiments led Thomas Ruddiman, in reprinting Gavin Douglas's *Aeneis*, to argue that Scots possessed both the merits of the unpolished *and* those of the perspicuous; as F.W. Freeman points out, he thought

Middle Scots literature is classic; on a par with that of Chaucer and Gower; and, as a language, equal to Greek and Latin. With Mackenzie of Rosehaugh and the early primitivists, he distinguishes between the 'full Force and genuine Meaning' of Scots and the weak, diffuse quality of English . . . He is among the first to suggest that the living speech of 'the Vulgar' is in great part Old Scots. This was a necessary ingredient for the literary status of the colloquial Scots used by Ramsay and his successors.[18]

This misprision strikingly prefigures the twentieth-century Greek poet George Seferis when he comments: 'Our folk song can, in the sensitivity of one and the same person, throw fresh light on Homer and fill in the meaning of Aeschylus'.[19] Strikingly, because Fergusson, with his grasp of classical models, appears to have thought something similar: that the use of Scots in its traditional stanza forms is sufficient for the recovery of the lost unity of the learned and the aboriginal, the classically fluent and the folk as inspired. In 'Hame Content' he drops a Virgilian reference to 'the Dog-day heats' before comparing the delights of riverine Scotland with those of Italy:

> The ARNO and the TIBUR lang
> Hae run fell clear in Roman sang;
> But, save the reverence of schools!
> They're baith but lifeless dowy pools.
> Dought they compare wi' bonny Tweed,
> As clear as ony lammer-bead?
> Or are their shores mair sweet and gay
> Than Fortha's haughs or banks o' Tay?[20]

That dismissive reference to 'the reverence of schools' would seem to hold the key to Fergusson's recurrent Italophobia: it is the Enlightenment's over-veneration of the classics that inhibits the appreciation of native poetry; or, as he continues, 'ARCADIAN herds wad tyne their lays,/To hear the mair melodious sounds/That live on our POETIC grounds'. The melodic resonance of Scots, for Fergusson, surpasses that of literature filtered through and approved of by the academy.

That this is a recurrent sentiment is evident from MacDiarmid's comments on that ultimate right hemisphere of the Scots, Jamieson's (as opposed to Johnson's) dictionary: 'There are words and phrases in the Vernacular which thrill me with a sense of having been produced as a result of mental processes entirely different from my own and much more powerful'.[21] MacDiarmid's utilisation of the dictionary (and of plagiarism) in an effort to jumpstart those Muses is well-documented. Equally noteworthy is his eschewal of the stanza forms he felt had been corrupted by writers following Burns, in favour of the more overtly folk resonances of the ballad. Yet Stevenson had asserted the survival of the learned Fergussonian Habbie: in 'Ille Terrarum' he emphasised that acquaintance with classical literature, and not just rehashed Burnsisms, was still possible:

> Here aft, weel neukit by my lane
> Wi' Horace, or perhaps Montaigne,
> The mornin' hours hae come an' gane
>   Abune my heid –
> I wadnae gi'en a chucky-stane
>   For a' I'd read.[22]

I think that the Habbie and its sibling stanzas held, for the eighteenth-century poets, a very specific cultural resonance. That it was simultaneously a kind of ikon and a sort of machine: that it enshrined aspects of Scottish identity they valued, and enabled them to manufacture new variations on that identity. In this the Habbie and the other stanzas resemble an aspect of bicamerality explored by Julian Jaynes: the idol that speaks.

Jaynes notes the widespread appearance of carved figures not just in the temples, but in domestic dwellings, graves, and even in the foundations of buildings, whether in Mediterranean, Mesopotamian or Central American cultures. His conjecture is this was not merely evidence of our delight in creating gods in our own image, but the construction of exterior versions of the driving admonitory voices of the right hemisphere – amplifiers, if you like, or portable temples. Pointing to the large hypnotic eyes of many of these idols and the elaborate mouth-cleaning rituals that feature in Sumerian accounts, he suggests that we take literally evidence in cuneiform literature, and in the Bible, that the worshippers of such idols experienced them as talking gods, as in the accounts of the Spaniards who conquered the Incas: 'The very first report back to Europe said, "in the temple [of Pachacamac] was a Devil who used to speak to the Indians in a very dark room which was as dirty as he himself'.[23] Some cousin, presumably, of the 'Auld Nick' overheard by Fergusson in 'To The Tron-Kirk Bell':

216

I dreamt ae nicht I saw Auld Nick;
Quo he, 'this bell o' mine's a trick,
'A wylie piece o' politic,
    'A cunnin snare
'To trap fock in a cloven stick,
    'Ere they're aware.'[24]

The trick being, again, metonymy: the people will associate the 'Wan-wordy, crazy, dinsome thing' with the preacher within, and avoid the Tron.

The Scots poets of the revival used their stanza forms as more positive containers, resonant symbols of continuity in a culture where the voice of poetry in Scots was becoming increasingly difficult to validate. So Fergusson's devil relates to Burns's 'Auld Hornie, Satan, Nick, or Clootie'; just as when that devil sneaks into 'Eden's bonie yard', he's revisiting the ground of Fergusson's 'Caller Water', where 'father Adie first pat spade in/The bonny yeard of antient Eden . . .'[25]

The Scots stanzas are used as repositories of authenticity, and as a means of establishing their credentials in relation to each other and their anonymous or less exalted predecessors. Fergusson's address 'To the Principals and Professors' doesn't just tilt at academic jargon, it borrows from Allan Ramsay's own playful use of Latin in his 'Epistle to James Arbuckle of Belfast', which he too divides into increasingly daft sub-points: 'Now, Jamie, in neist place, *Secundo,*/To give you what's your due in *mundo*;' is followed by '*Imprimis* then, for Tallness I/Am five Foot and four Inches high . . .' and capped by 'Second of thirdly, – pray take heed/Ye's get a short Swatch of my Creed'.[26] Of course, Fergusson's satire, on a cultural hegemony which excludes his literary heritage in favour of Johnson's, has more bite than Ramsay's epistle, just as Burns's 'Address to the Deil' is a more profound development of a minor theme in 'Caller Water'.

There is another sense in which the major Scots stanzas, in Fergusson's hands, yield up voices. When we look at the models for Ramsay and Fergusson's Christis Kirk poems, for instance, it is immediately apparent that, like the ballads, they are full of speeches. The audience is placed in the position of overhearing snatches of dialogue from these previous centuries: in the second stanza of 'Peblis to the Play' we hear 'the wenchis of the west' wondering what they're going to wear: 'Ane said, "My curches ar nocht prest!"/Than answerit Meg full blew,/"To get a hude I hald it best."' The poem is full of exchanges, not between primary characters in the manner of a play, but from within the community:

> Than thai to the taverne hous
>   With meikle oly prance;
> Ane spak with wourdis wonder crouss,
>   'Adone with ane mischance!
> Braid up the burde,' he bydis tyt,
>   'We ar all in ane trance.
> Se that our napre be quhyt,
>   For we will dyn and daunce
>   Thair out,
>   Of Peblis to the play.'[27]

In 'Christis Kirk on the Grene' there is a litany of aggressive exchanges: '"Lat be," quod Jok; and cawd him javell'; 'The toder said "Dirdum Dardum" . . .'; and Ramsay's continuation is similarly spiky, like Kate's repelling of Claud Peky: ' "Had aff," quoth she, "ye filthy slate,/Ye stink o' leeks, O figh!" '[28] But Fergusson's 'Leith Races' and 'Hallow-Fair' extend this convention to present a range of voices. The Doric of the hosier and the fishwives (familiar to him from his uncle's farm), and the Gaelic English of the City Guard, stand out in both poems:

> The Buchan bodies thro' the beech
>   Their bunch of Findrums cry,
> An' skirl out baul', in Norland speech,
>   'Gueed speldings, fa will buy.'

While poor Jock Bell falls foul of the Guard:

> He peching on the cawsey lay,
>   O' kicks and cuffs weel sair'd;
> A *Highland* aith the serjeant gae
>   'She maun pe see our guard.'[29]

The effect is reminiscent of Boswell's *Journal* in the early 1760s, excitedly recording verbatim exchanges between strangers in the inns of London.[30] The result, however, is very different. Fergusson has adapted this element of the Christis Kirk stanza to put an implicit case: that Scots is not only a lively language with its own dialects, but that his own poetic voice, buttressed by the stanza form, can contain all this variety. He indicates this by switching, between two stanzas of *Hallow-Fair*, from a Biblical reference to linguistic chaos, to a serene classical image:

> . . . there's sic yellowchin and din,
>   Wi' wives and wee-anes gablin,
> That ane might true they were a-kin
>   To a' the tongues at Babylon,
>   Confus'd that day.

But:

> Whan *Phoebus* ligs in *Thetis* lap,
>   Auld Reikie gie's them shelter . . .[31]

Jaynes has described the breakdown of the bicameral mind as just such a torrent of conflicting inner voices, as the simple pantheons were broken apart by invasion and trade, and the redeeming metaphor of the self straddled the breach.[32] Fergusson's image hankers back to the certainty of Homeric values at the same time as it prepares the way for his long poem, 'Auld Reikie', by equating the city as refuge, with the stanza which is able to shelter such diversity.

Why Fergusson placed his faith in the Scots stanza forms can best be explained, I believe, in terms of the anxiety of the eighteenth-century Scot in the face of England's cultural dominance. William Wilkie's *Epigoniad* was an attempt at a proper Augustan epic in heroic couplets, but, bar the nod to Gavin Douglas, it had little organic link with the culture that produced it: what's Wilkie to Thebes, or Thebes to Wilkie, for all Hume's support? Home's *Douglas*, Beattie's *Minstrel*, and above all Macpherson's *Ossian*, each present Scottish themes according to the dominant taste of the day. Each experiences a vogue of approval and passes into neglect or, in Macpherson's case, controversy and neglect. Within a decade of Blair's *Dissertation* praising Ossian, it is salutary to think that two genuine examples of the native genius he was proclaiming must have had some form of probably unproductive encounter: Robert Fergusson who wrote of 'that black banditti,/The City-Guard . . .' in 1772; and the Gaelic poet Duncan Ban Macintyre, who from 1768 had been a member of that less than august body.[33]

We now know that Burns surveyed the scene and realised that he must present himself as 'the Scotch Bard' in order to meet with Blair's approval (as long as he didn't print the *Jolly Beggars*), and thus appear to confirm for subsequent centuries Scots as a fading rural voice.[34] And it is this aspect of Burns's reputation which led MacDiarmid to throw out the bardic forms with the bathwater of Bardolatry. But how stultifying that scene must have appeared to Fergusson, who, as Edwin Morgan says, 'is not to be taken only as a John the Baptist for Burns'. The significant detail being that Fergusson didn't know that Burns was coming. What he did know was that his own university had hailed the arrival of Dictionary Johnson in 1773, as a kind of vindicator of the process of assimilation. What he did know was that the previous century, racked by Covenanter, Cromwellian and Claverhouse, had cast up few examples of Scottish poetry, and beyond Ramsay and the anonymous ballads there seemed only to be the Sempills, father and son. Robert contributed 'Habbie Simson' to the canon, hardly a masterpiece except for its stanza; and Francis probably wrote 'The Blythsome Wedding', which, although it confines itself to a list of the guests and the food, is nonetheless in the Christis Kirk tradition.[35] Fergusson can hardly be blamed for placing greater faith in the forms than in the practitioners.

In the address 'To the Principal and Professors', Fergusson makes another reference to Drummond of Hawthornden. I am reminded of the two heads that formed the emblem for Allan Ramsay's bookshop: one head being Drummond and the other Ben Jonson.[36] The first Jonson had made the trip to Hawthornden as Drummond's friend, someone with whom dialogue is possible, even if Jonson did say his work 'smelled too much of the Schools'.[37] But Drummond is cited here half as host, half as opponent to the second Johnson, and the poem has recourse to the strategies of the food fight:

> Drummond, lang syne, o' Hawthornden,
> The wiliest an' best o' men,
> Has gi'en you dishes ane or mae,
> That wad ha' gard his grinders play,
> Not to *roast beef*, old England's life,
> But to the auld *east nook of Fife*,
> Whare Creilian crafts cou'd weel ha'e gi'en
> Scate-rumples to ha'e clear'd his een:
> Than neist, whan SAMY'S heart was faintin,
> He'd lang'd for scate to mak him wanton.[38]

Johnson as symbol of hegemony has more layers than his treatment of the Scots in his Dictionary. There is also his canonisation of Shakespeare in the famous *Preface* of 1765 as the English genius incarnate. In this, Johnson not only places Shakespeare 'above all writers, at least above all modern writers' as 'the poet that holds up to his readers a faithful mirror of manners and of life', but he goes on to displace the likes of Ben

Jonson or Drummond, to argue in a sense that Shakespeare is the only writer, that his mimesis is absolute:

> It was observed of the ancient schools of declamation that, the more diligently they were frequented, the more was the student disqualified for the world, because he found nothing there which he should ever meet in any other place. The same remark may be applied to every stage but that of Shakespeare. The theatre, when it is under any other direction, is peopled by such characters as were never seen, conversing in a language which was never heard, upon topics which will never arise in the commerce of humanity. But the dialogue of this author is often so evidently determined by the incident which produces it, and is pursued with so much ease and simplicity, that it seems scarcely to claim the merit of fiction, but to have been gleaned by diligent selection out of common conversation and common occurrences.[39]

We can only wonder at the reception by Scots of this kind of pronouncement, which removes the possibility of cultural dialogue because it removes the possibility of equality. English literature, in the hands of its greatest exponent, has become a transparent mode of access to reality in much the way that the Bible was claimed to be a transparent mode of access to truth. Johnson's assertion is a clear prefiguration of what Harold Bloom claims to be Shakespeare's 'invention of the human':

> For Johnson, the essence of poetry was invention, and only Homer could be Shakespeare's rival in originality. Invention, in Johnson's sense as in ours, is a process of finding, or of finding out. We owe Shakespeare everything, Johnson says, and means that Shakespeare has taught us to understand human nature. Johnson does not go as far as to say that Shakespeare invented us, but he does intimate the true tenor of Shakespearean mimesis: 'Imitations produce pain or pleasure, not because they are mistaken for realities, but because they bring realities to mind.'[40]

You shall have no god but Shakespeare, Johnson argued, and the men of Edinburgh, just as they had when presented by Knox with a Bible in English, smashed many of their idolatrous icons of locality. As Carlyle comments, when Knox was presented with an image of the Virgin he denounced it as ' "a pented bredd" . . . and flung the thing into the river.'[41] And it was Carlyle who, in the same volume, *On Heroes and Hero-Worship*, helped to establish Burns as a Caledonian counter to the cult of

221

William.[42] But Fergusson, who we remember Freeman groups with the 'Episcopal subculture', had to look elsewhere for his native mimesis, and it is in this context that the phrase 'Standard Habbie' takes on special resonance.[43] The stanza has a name, as though it is an individual, and it is 'standard', both a means of taking measurement, and something to rally round. Further proof, if proof were needed, of the causes of MacDiarmid's aversion to the Habbie, might be found in the new name it acquired as Carlyle's heroic standard came in: the Burns stanza.

There was an alternative notion of mimesis still current in Scottish literature which may have given Fergusson the confidence with which he renovated these stanzas, rendering them suitable for urban subjects and learned reference. Scottish writers, byculturally challenged, had long been in the business of borrowing their subjects, forms and methods from a wide variety of sources, usually bringing a new emphasis to the acquired material. Thus Henryson's *Testament of Cresseid* continues where Chaucer leaves off; and thus *The Complaynt of Scotland* takes its structure, if not its bizarre prologue, from Alain Chartier's *Quadrilogue Invectif.* But this borrowing went still closer to the bone, as is exemplified by the practice of the Wedderburn brothers in the *Gude and Godlie Ballates.* Here popular folk songs were emptied, as it were, of their more jovial content, and a proper Lutheran message was inserted instead:

> The Paip, that Pagane full of pryde,
> He hes vs blindit lang,
> For quhair the blind the blind dois gyde,
> Na wounder baith ga wrang;
> Lyke Prince and King, he led the Regne,
> Of all Iniquitie:
> > Hay trix, tyme go trix,
> > Vnder the grene wod tre.[44]

Drummond of Hawthornden had a similar approach to the models he is accused of plagiarising, securing many of his most characteristic effects at this level of redirecting existing meaning within set forms. As Edwin Morgan suggests, he, like the Wedderburns, has a most particular approach to the doctrine of Imitation:

> Drummond relished these European blueprints . . . because the doctrine suited the subtle and delicate movement of his own mind: the making of small distinctions, the slight renewal or slewing

round of established metaphors or comparisons, the infusion of a personality drop by drop into a tradition . . .[45]

The freedom with which Scots poets approached their sources may have had as much to do with the ballad tradition, with its variants of equal standing, as the Renaissance technique of *imitatio.* But this practice has an ancient antecedent in that most subtle and delicate of poetries, Chinese, which is perhaps relevant here. There are several forms in Chinese which are based on folk songs, in which the task of the poet is either to match the syllable counts but fill the frame with a new message, as in *ci* poetry; or to produce wilder variations based on looser stress-based metres, as in *sanqu.*

And there are several Chinese poets whose contributions to these genres have a familiar ring to them: the Northern Song poet Liu Yong, for example, who, as Greg Gao explains, '. . . wrote lyrics of urban prosperity, grievance of the frustrated literati scholars, the miserable life and misfortunes of the ordinary people . . .' One poem, called 'In the tune of "Welcome in the New Spring"',

> . . . celebrates the joy and laughter of life, youthful flirtation and opportunities for romantic encounter. It presents a vivid picture of a traditional festival with all its happy excitements which had never entered the realm of ci poems before. This evolvement of poetic leitmotifs in a sense was a reflection of the urban development during the Song Dynasty.

And the poem ends:

> On the fragrant paths,
> Countless hat-strings are broken and fruits thrown.
> As the night wears on, in the candles' shades and flowers' shadows,
> A young man often
> Has an unexpected adventure,
> In this times of peace.
> The court and the country are full of joys; the people, happy and
> > prosperous,
> Gather together in contentment.
> Facing such a scene,
> How could I bear to go home sober alone?[46]

My point here is that practitioners of literature from Scotland have, as I mentioned earlier, sometimes laboured under the accusation of plagiarism. What I believe Fergusson's faith in the Scots stanzas indicates is that there was perhaps a different attitude to text in the two countries; that the Scots, like the Chinese, had access to a concept very like variation. Whilst Augustan standards placed great stock in fine models, they did not regard such models as quite so literally sources for quarrying. Instead Dryden upgraded Chaucer, and Pope corrected Donne: the variations on themes and within forms that the Scots performed, imply a sociable equivalence between original and variation, between past and present, and not the inevitable superiority that such poets believed themselves to have arrived at. Whereas, as Freeman puts it, 'The humanist believes that traditions and traditional wisdom aid his understanding, thereby helping him to over-come barbarity; he does not believe that man and his institutions evolve to a state of perfection'.[47] And Fergusson, in the forms and the language of his country, explored just such an alternative paradigm.

At this point I must step back into the performative space familiar to the modern reader. Because the first thing that occurs to such a reader confronting Fergusson relates directly to the above: it is that he is not Burns. This fortuitously points us towards the same target he set himself in relation to the English tradition: it indicates that variation is possible, and variation of a particular sort. His verse is, as I said at the beginning, learned without loss of vitality, urban without losing sight of the pastoral, ironic without losing faith in the traditional. I'd like to move toward a conclusion by returning to this performative aspect of Fergusson, and to relate that to contemporary practice. In 'Caller Water' he returns to the primal scene depicted by Jaynes, the apparition of the muses to Hesiod, and replaces Helicon with Arthur's Seat:

> What makes Auld Reikie's dames sae fair,
> It canna be the halesom air,
> But *caller burn* beyond compare,
>   The best of ony,
> That gars them a' sic graces skair,
>   And blink sae bonny.

> In *May-day* in a fairy ring,
> We've seen them round St Anthon's spring,
> Frae grass the caller *dew draps* wring,
>   To weet their ein,
> And water clear as chrystal spring,
>   To synd them clean.[48]

These stanzas seem to tug us as Scots in two contrary directions: one is the intense half-recognised pull of the words we are less familiar with, the cry from the past; the other is the vigorous forward push of the metre, the gallusness of spoken Scots, the crack of the present. An audience might conclude this form is well suited to Scots because the little lines give you space to tolerate the peculiar effect of hearing something that is not English, but is so close.

But then we have to admit that, on the page, this kind of work is still difficult for contemporary readers – and that this difficulty extends to reading contemporary writers who work in literary Scots. People frequently come up to me after readings to say that they found my Scots more comprehensible when I read it, than they had when they'd read it silently. Part of that is to do with the low standard of my verse; but much of it must relate to the continued barrier of the appearance of Scots on the page. It is a curious thought that this most literary of languages should be augmented by performance. It points again to the continued proximity of such Scots to the folk idiom. And it is almost paradoxical how performable Fergusson's Scots is; how performable literary Scots can be. Much of this is due to our increased awareness of sound textures and relates directly to the unfamiliarity of his lexicon as opposed to our over-familiarity with Burns. But some of it is just the sturdiness of those stanzas.

Fergusson's poetry projects you into paradox: the melodious diffi-culty as well as the difficult melody. It directs you away from Burns, yes, but also away from the Johnson-derived analogy of poetry with reality, and its Blair/Wordsworth-derived corollary, the analogy of poetry with plain speech. Here is a language at once baroque and rauchle, both folk and learned. And in the descendents of his endeavours, the new work in old stanzas, we are able to display this, as a straightforward case, ignorable perhaps, but a thorn in the side of simplicity. A necessary thorn, because without the issue of literary Scots, it is possible to simplify and mistake the purpose of a literary Scot.

Fergusson, like Burns, was engaged in an act of complexification, of declaring Scots and Scotland to be more resourceful than the theore-ticians of his day gave credit for. It's hard to build on complexity because each generation needs to be taught anew the subtleties of its predecessors, but subtleties survive like dormant viruses, within the stanzas, whereas simplification cannot last. It is based on a flawed metonymy, the critical substitution of the part for the whole: a single poem or a single poet stands in for an entire oeuvre or movement, or, in the case of Ossian, for an entire culture. It permits an English critic like Ruth Padel to thumbnail Don Paterson in *The Independent on Sunday* as being 'a contemporary Burns'.[49] Don is a poet of massive accomplishment who is engaged among other things in the development and partial translation of the themes and techniques of Northern Irish figures such as Muldoon and Longley. He might very interestingly be described as a contemporary Drummond. But he doesn't use the stanzas, or more than a smattering of Scots. To equate him with Burns is surely a profound misreading of both Don and Rabbie. And it is only possible if the complexity of the language question, foregrounded by Fergusson's example, is overlooked or ignored.

One of the functions of modern poetry in Scots, therefore, smacks unashamedly of eighteenth-century Edinburgh: it is to edify. In this respect it also reaches back to the belief of Ramsay and Fergusson, that there was something to preserve and promulgate in the older forms. Contemporary poets share with these predecessors the desire to enable a wider unit of the population to contemplate why they should read their older poets. This is where the role of form reinforces that of language: if I employ the Habbie I am expressing an anxiety in relation to Burns and Fergusson: my anxiety is that my precursors should be read.

But post-MacDiarmid, post-Garioch, these forms are also sources of pleasure. It is as though they have been scoured clean by the one's scorn and the other's scrutiny, and delivered fresh as caller oysters. It is no longer required that you believe in the aboriginal, it seems to be enough that we can reapply their resonances and their raciness to a country in a parallel but opposite state of flux to the eighteenth century's recently United Kingdom.

In poems like 'The Graduates', Kathleen Jamie rehearses in a Scottish context the argument put forcefully by Tony Harrison: that to be educated is to travel away from your roots, your Scottishness, which is therefore defined not just as working or lower middle class, but as unlearned.[50] She is working forcefully towards a more complex notion of nationhood, one that Fergusson's example would imply is possible and desirable. That Scotland is a country which contains an educated middle class hardly sounds like the central tenet of a revolutionary manifesto, but it is not how we are perceived in literary terms and, to some extent, it is not how we perceive ourselves. I would suggest that Fergusson's work positions this issue – like that of Burns and Hogg and even the Wilson of *Noctes Ambrosianae* – as the central trope of Scottish literature: we are constantly making ourselves strange to ourselves, and estranging ourselves by the act of making.

Contingent upon this definition is a reassertion of the standard implied by the Habbie, a renewal of the space within the stanza as a negotiation with tradition: an opened ground in which more complex notions can be stored to be enacted in the small confrontations of page and performance. In this sense each poem is a virtual Scotland in which the issues of our culture as it becomes or fails to become defined are broached. By our Habbies you shall know us, and Fergusson's depict a habitable zone:

> *Auld Reikie!* thou'rt the canty hole,
> A bield for mony a caldrife soul,
> Wha snugly at thine ingle loll,
>   Baith warm and couth;
> While round they gar the bicker roll
>   To weet their mouth.[51]

Notes

1. Robert Fergusson, 'To the Principal & Professors of the University of St Andrews', in *The Poems of Robert Fergusson*, ed. Matthew McDiarmid (Edinburgh: Blackwood for the Scottish Text Society, 1954–6), 2 vols, II, p.183. All future references Fergusson's poetry are from volume II of this edition, and are referred to as *F*.
2. *The Works of Robert Fergusson*, ed. Alexander B.Grosart (London, Edinburgh and Dublin: Fullerton, 1879), p.lxxxiii; see also pp. lxxviii – lxxix.
3. *F*, pp. 52–3.
4. *The Christis Kirk Tradition: Scots Poems of Folk Festivity*, ed. Allan H. MacLaine (Glasgow: Association for Scottish Literary Studies, 1996), p. 46.
5. *F*, pp.130–32 ; p. 183; p. 39.
6. Robert Louis Stevenson, *Poems* (London: Chatto & Windus, 1914), pp.53–8.
7. Roderick Watson, *The Literature of Scotland* (London: Macmillan, 1984), p.180.
8. Douglas Dunn, 'Burns's Native Metric', in *Robert Burns and Cultural Authority*, ed. Robert Crawford (Edinburgh: EUP, 1996), p.76
9. Dunn, p.83.
10. Seamus Heaney, 'Burns's Art Speech', in *Robert Burns and Cultural Authority*, p.221.
11. *The Christis Kirk Tradition*, pp. 54–68.
12. Julian Jaynes, *The Origin of Consciousness in the Breakdown of the Bicameral Mind* (Harmondsworth: Penguin, 1990), pp. 67–83.

13. Jaynes, p. 371.
14. Michael Donaghy, 'My Report Card', in *Strong Words: Modern Poets on Modern Poetry*, ed. W.N. Herbert and Matthew Hollis (Tarset: Bloodaxe, 2000), p.243.
15. Jaynes, p.375.
16. See Stephen Prickett, *Words and The Word: Language, Poetics and Biblical Interpretation* (Cambridge: CUP, 1986), pp.41–3.
17. Prickett, p. 59.
18. F.W. Freeman, *Robert Fergusson and the Scots Humanist Compromise* (Edinburgh: EUP, 1984), p.4.
19. George Seferis, 'Theophilos', in *On the Greek Style* (Limni: Denise Harvey, 2000), p.8.
20. *F*, p. 159.
21. C.M. Grieve (Hugh MacDiarmid), from 'A Theory of Scots Letters', in *Strong Words*, p.78.
22. Stevenson, p.50.
23. Jaynes, pp.165–175.
24. *F*, p. 98.
25. Robert Burns, 'Address to the Deil', *Poems and Songs*, ed. James Kinsley (Oxford: OUP, 1969), pp. 135–139; *F*, p. 106.
26. Allan Ramsay, *Poems*, ed. H. Harvey Wood (Edinburgh: Oliver & Boyd, 1946), pp.25–30.
27. *The Christis Kirk Tradition*, pp.1–9.
28. *The Christis Kirk Tradition*, pp. 10–17; p.56.
29. *F*, p. 165; p. 92.
30. James Boswell, *Boswell's London Journal, 1762–3*, ed. Frederick A. Pottle (London: Harborough, 1958), pp. 68–9; pp.83–4.
31. *F*, p. 91.
32. Jaynes, pp. 204–222.
33. *F*, p.34.
34. Watson, pp. 220–21.
35. Watson, pp.147–9; *The Christis Kirk Tradition*, pp.50–3.
36. Watson, p.172.
37. Edwin Morgan, 'Gavin Douglas and William Drummond as Translators', in *Crossing the Border: Essays on Scottish Literature* (Manchester: Carcanet, 1990), p.71; see also 'How Good a Poet is Drummond?' in the same volume.
38. *F*, p. 184.
39. Samuel Johnson, 'Preface to the edition of Shakespeare', in *Selected Writings*, ed. R.T. Davies (London: Faber & Faber, 1965), pp. 264–5.
40. Harold Bloom, *Shakespeare: The Invention of the Human* (London: Fourth Estate, 1999), p.2.
41. Thomas Carlyle, 'The Hero as Priest', in *On Heroes, Hero-Worship and the Heroic in History* (Lincoln/London: University of Nebraska Press, 1966), pp. 147–8.

42. Carlyle, 'The Hero as Man of Letters', *On Heroes*, pp. 188–195.
43. Freeman, p.20.
44. See Douglas Dunn, 'Dundee Law Considered as Mount Parnassus', in *Gairfish*, vol.1, no. 4, pp.17–28.
45. Morgan, p. 72.
46. Greg Gao, 'Hao Fang: An Expansion of Thematic Scopes', Term Paper Submitted to the Department of Asian Studies, University of British Columbia, April, 1992 (downloaded from the Internet).
47. Freeman, p.26.
48. *F*, p.108.
49. Ruth Padel in *The Independent on Sunday*, March, 1998.
50. Kathleen Jamie, 'The Graduates', in *Jizzen* (London: Picador, 1999), p.3.
51. *F*, p. 33.

HORSEMAN

efter Rilke, i.m. Rab Fergusson

Look up at the skeh: whar's the constellation
crehd 'The Horseman'? Gi'en this is wir sang –
a baist's wull, and some heh'r distillation
that ca's and brakes it, and wham it kerts alang.

Is this no' jist wir sinneny existence,
gaddin wirsels on, reinin wirsels back in?
Road an sheddin; then ae tip – a new distance
fa's awa, and the twa are yin again.

But this is a' wrang, surely? Dinna they signifeh
jist the rake wih tak thegither? As it is,
thir sindered beh the table and the trough.

Even thir starnie union is a leh;
a' wih can dae is doorly insist
wih merk it up there. Mibbe thon's enough.

crehd - called; *ca* - drive; *kert* - carry; *sinneny* - sinewy; *gaddin* - goading;
sheddin - fork, parting; *tip* - touch; *rake* - wander; *starnie* - starry

Don Paterson

Index